Reweaving the Tapestry of Tenure

Also from TERRA NOSTRA PRESS

Community Matters: Conversations with Reflective Practitioners
about the Value & Variety of Resident Engagement
in Community Land Trusts

Common Ground: International Perspectives
on the Community Land Trust

En Terreno Común: Perspectivas Internacionales
sobre los Fedeicomisos Comunitarios de Tierras

REWEAVING
THE TAPESTRY OF
TENURE

Eight Elders of the CLT Movement
Who Championed Community Ownership of Land

Edited by John Emmeus Davis

TERRA NOSTRA PRESS

TERRA NOSTRA PRESS

Center for Community Land Trust Innovation
3146 Buena Vista Street
Madison, Wisconsin, USA 53704

Illustrations: Bonnie Acker
Book design: Sara DeHaan

Publisher's Cataloging-in-Publication data

Names: Davis, John Emmeus, 1949–, editor.
Title: Reweaving the tapestry of tenure : eight elders of the CLT movement who
championed community ownership of land / edited by John Emmeus Davis.
Description: Includes bibliographical references and index. |
Madison, WI: Terra Nostra Press, 2023.
Identifiers: Library of Congress Control Number: 2023918103
ISBN: 979-8-9861776-2-5 (paperback) | 979-8-9861776-3-2 (ebook)
Subjects: LCSH: Social reformers—Biography. | Social justice—Biography. | Land
trusts. | Land use. | Community development. | Housing development. | BISAC:
BIOGRAPHY & AUTOBIOGRAPHY / Social Activists | SOCIAL SCIENCE / Activism
and Social Justice | | BUSINESS & ECONOMICS / Development / Sustainable
Development | POLITICAL SCIENCE / Public Policy / City Planning &
Urban Development | SOCIAL SCIENCE / Sociology / Urban
Classification: LCC HD257 .R49 2023 | DDC 333.2—dc23

Dedicated to the memory of
Gus Newport *(1935–2023)*
gregarious maker of good trouble
in the fight for freedom, justice &
community ownership of land

The community land trust is about people caring for people.
It is also about caring for the land and introducing practices
that make us better and more participative citizens.

—María E. Hernández Torrales

The feeling of people living on community-owned land is that
they are stronger together in front of market forces or in front of
public evictions. . . . Many are more politicized or more conscious
of what community land trusts and other forms of cooperative and
communal forms of land tenure can do to generate not only a new
model of urban development or a new model of affordable housing,
but a pathway to building an alternative society.

—Yves Cabannes

One of the things that I would often say during my community
development days, when I was speaking to groups, is that you have to
control the dirt. If you don't control the dirt, you don't control anything.

—Mtamanika Youngblood

CONTENTS

Championing Community Landownership: An Introduction

John Emmeus Davis

A larger-than-life hero of my childhood was Johnny Appleseed. Like many kids, I was introduced to that familiar figure of American folklore through a Disney cartoon. I knew him only as a fictional animation, rendered in technicolor and surrounded by singing birds. He loped merrily across the landscape with a cookpot on his head, planting seeds that magically sprouted into blossoming trees.

I didn't realize until much later that he had actually been a real person. John Chapman was a rather eccentric fellow who had earned his nurseryman nickname while trudging barefooted through Pennsylvania, Ohio, and Indiana in the 1800s. As he wandered hither and yon, he gratuitously sowed the seeds of many varieties of apples in fields he didn't own.

My daughter had a similar encounter with a fictional character. In her case, the heroine who captured her imagination was Miss Rumphius. As portrayed in a charming children's book by that title, published in 1982, Alice Rumphius is known to her neighbors as the "Lupine Lady." It is a nickname bestowed on her because of her endearing practice of quietly scattering lupine seeds along seaside roads and meadows in Maine.[1]

It was a story that I read to my young daughter many times. Only later did I learn that Miss Rumphius, like Johnny Appleseed, was based on a real person. Hilda Edwards Hamlin immigrated to coastal Maine in 1904. In her 60s, she began planting lupine seeds imported from her native England. She would carry a handful of seeds in her pocket whenever she walked to the post office or general store and secretly scatter them along the roadside. She couldn't drive a car. When friends would give her a ride, they'd catch her throwing lupine seeds out the window.

What do two stories for children have to do with the eight conversations collected in the chapters that follow? Quite simply, the individuals featured here are cut from the same bolt of cloth as Chapman and Hamlin. Each has played a different role in supporting the global growth of community land trusts; each has brought a different set of sensibilities and skills to that endeavor. But the most consequential role played by all of them has been the sowing of seeds in multiple places. They have taken seminal ideas imported from elsewhere and scattered them across an ever-widening geography. Without their efforts, the hundreds of CLTs now springing up in a dozen different countries might not have happened. Without their advocacy for community ownership of land, moreover, championed by them as a core commitment of the CLT, the model now spreading across the world might have looked very different.

By the early 1980s, the disparate strands of organization (community), ownership (land), and operation (trust) had been woven together into a coherent strategy of affordable housing and community development known as the "classic CLT."[2] Within a very short time, however, that model of tenure began to be modified in countless ways—often for better, sometimes for worse.

Most practitioners who adopted the model left intact the basic fabric of the CLT, even as they added textures and colors of their own. They made only those changes that allowed the CLT to be a more compatible fit with local preferences, circumstances, customs, or laws. There were others, however, across a broad spectrum of nonprofit practitioners, public officials, and private developers, who disliked the CLT from the very beginning. They picked at the multi-hued strands that held the model together, threatening to pull them apart.

Some disliked the idea of opening the process of development to the scrutiny and direction of residents who lived in or around what was being built. They picked at the "C" in CLT, insisting that development would be faster and cheaper without a CLT's commitment to giving voice to members of its chosen community.

Some disliked the idea of imposing controls on the use and resale of homes and enterprises entrusted into a CLT's care, which happened to be a rather radical idea in the 1980s and 1990s.[3] They picked at the "T" in CLT, insisting that the model's commitment to permanent affordability was contrary to the "America Dream."

What many critics liked least of all, however, was the "L" in CLT. They bristled at the CLT's commitment to removing land from the stream of commerce, taking a valuable commodity normally used for private gain and converting it into a nonmarket resource for the common good. They were quick to challenge the CLT's form of tenure, insisting it was better to put land into private hands, better to sell land than to lease it, better to combine land and buildings into a single real estate package instead of separating community ownership of the land and individual ownership of the structural improvements. Even public officials and nonprofit practitioners who were supportive of the CLT's other features were sometimes skeptical of community-owned land and long-term ground leasing, believing them to be too difficult to explain, too cumbersome to implement, or too difficult to finance.

Rather than repeat arguments I've previously made in response to critics and skeptics like these,[4] I shall yield the stage to eight individuals whose words and deeds offer a more eloquent rebuttal. During their storied careers, they have made a compelling case for retaining and combining *community*, *land*, and *trust*, although community-owned land has been given pride of place. To be sure, they

have supported the participation of residents in the CLT's affairs and
the lasting affordability of housing (and other buildings) for which
a CLT is responsible. But listen closely to the interviews that follow.
Tenure is the melodic refrain running through them all. These eight
elders of the CLT movement remind us that "land" is not only the
model's middle name; it is the model's organizational and operational imperative. The distinctive manner in which a CLT's land is
owned and used is the foundation for everything else that a CLT is
and does.

A number of years ago, I had a colleague who was visiting a
community land trust in New England which has a dual mission
of promoting affordable housing *and* urban agriculture. An elderly member of the CLT's board volunteered to show my colleague
around. As they toured the CLT's holdings, the old lady paused for a
moment. She looked around to make sure they were alone and then
confided in a conspiratorial whisper, "You know, dear, what we are
really about is land reform. But we hide behind the tomatoes."

The individuals who take us on a tour of their lives and labors in
the present book tell a similar tale, although *their* agenda is hardly
hidden. They may point with pride to CLT projects involving affordably-priced homes, community gardens, neighborhood shops, cultural spaces, forests, and farms, but of paramount importance is
what lies beneath. What CLTs are "really about" in the eyes of these
long-time veterans of the CLT movement is reforming the way that
land is owned, enabling a place-based community to determine the
trajectory of its own development. As Mtamanika Youngblood used
to say, when talking to groups hoping to revitalize their neighborhoods, "You have to control the dirt. If you don't control the dirt, you
don't control anything."

I have referred to these eight individuals as "elders" of the CLT
movement. To call them such is not to overlook the creativity, courage, and conviction of the previous generation of thinkers and activists on whose shoulders they stand.[5] Nor is it to belittle the

accomplishments of the present generation of reflective practitioners who are expanding the portfolio of resale-restricted homes on community-owned land and extending the reach of CLTs into new countries and new applications. Years from now, some of them will be venerated as "elders" in their own right, having enabled the movement's vigorous, variegated growth in the 21st Century.[6]

The people featured in the present book occupy a special place in the movement's history, however, a result of both the longevity of their commitment and the pivotal contributions made by each of them in pioneering, refining, or promoting this unusual model of tenure. Significantly, they are also a bridge between the trailblazers who assembled the raw materials of the "classic" CLT and today's practitioners who are turning that homespun model into a global movement.

That gives our elders a unique vantage point from which to trace the CLT's early development and from which to anticipate opportunities for the movement's continued growth. There is a lot we can learn from them. Historical details and future projections are definitely a part of it, but so are larger lessons of resilience and mission. They teach those who would build on their legacy how to keep going and how to stay grounded.

CLTs go against the grain. They remove valuable real estate from the speculative market. They prevent the displacement of vulnerable people and essential jobs, shops, and services from areas buffeted by successive waves of disinvestment and gentrification. They attempt to improve the lives of people who have been marginalized because of their race, class, religion, or immigration, legal or otherwise.

None of that happens easily. Or quickly. Or without mistakes. Martin Luther King Jr. would often remind audiences of his day that "change does not roll in on the wheels of inevitability, but comes through continuous struggle."[7] A similar message is to be found in the stories told by the people featured in the chapters that follow. During their long careers, they have preached an unpopular message that challenges the dominant ideology of property. They have struggled to sustain organizations in the face of active opposition or passive resistance. They have experienced setbacks. They have made mistakes. But they have persevered and, little by little, they have moved the needle and made a difference.

Just knowing that people like these, some of whom we may have put on a pedestal, have frailties like our own and have surmounted losses often greater than ours can help us to accept our personal limitations and inevitable setbacks—and to push on despite them. It can help us to learn the fine art of resiliency.

We are taught by these same people not to put the CLT itself on a pedestal, which might seem a somewhat ironic message coming from individuals whom I've dubbed "elders of the CLT movement." As much as they may individually value this unconventional form of tenure, however, and as much as they may have collectively done to scatter its seeds and to enable its growth, their eyes have been fixed on a larger prize. They each regard the CLT—and the lands entrusted to it—as a means to an end. For all of them, the CLT is less an object of veneration than a tool of transformation in pursuit of loftier goals, whether securing power and dignity for a racially oppressed people (Shirley Sherrod), revitalizing neighborhoods without removing low-income and moderate-income families (Mtamanika Youngblood), addressing deep-seated problems of dispossession and poverty (Kirby White), crafting a "human-scaled economic system" (Susan Witt), creating "workable communities" (Gus Newport), gaining agency for people and communities in the development of affordable housing (Stephen Hill), achieving security of tenure for the residents of informal settlements (María Hernández Torrales), or building a pathway to an alternative society (Yves Cabannes).

Even as they have defended and promoted the CLT's core commitment to community-owned land, therefore, they have not forgotten *for whom* this land is being held, developed, and stewarded. A long-departed CLT colleague of ours, Chuck Matthei, was fond of chiding his peers to ask themselves constantly, "Who sits at your table? Whose faces do you see when you're doing your work?" What we discover in the words of the elders interviewed here is a daily mindfulness of the people being served in the present, while keeping in mind those for whom homes and enterprises are being kept affordable in the future. They remind us of values of equity and sustainability and inclusion that attracted us to this work in the first place. They keep us grounded.

Like John Chapman and Hilda Hamlin, each of these elders has spent a lifetime quietly, generously making small improvements in whatever landscape they traversed, plantings which have prospered and proliferated in their wake. Johnny Appleseed made his world more bountiful. The Lupine Lady made her world more beautiful. The heroes and heroines of the present publication, by ensuring access to spaces and places from which people of modest means are regularly excluded, have made the world a bit more just.

Notes

1. Barbara Cooney, *Miss Rumphius* (New York NY: Viking Press, 1982).

2. For a detailed description of the three components of the "classic CLT," see: John Emmeus Davis, "In Land We Trust: Key Features and Common Variations of Community Land Trusts in the USA," Chapter One, *On Common Ground: International Perspectives on the Community Land Trust*, J.E. Davis, L. Algoed, M.E. Hernandez-Torrales, eds. (Madison WI: Terra Nostra Press, 2020).

3. In the first two or three decades of the CLT's appearance in American cities, the CLT's commitment to the lasting affordability of publicly subsidized, privately owned housing could be described as a "hard sell." The CLT's insistence on imposing limited-equity resale controls on *owner-occupied* housing, in particular, was met with indignant resistance by many public officials and nonprofit housing providers. The interviews with Kirby White and Gus Newport in the present

volume speak to the initial unpopularity of this idea, which today has become a widely accepted goal of public policy.

4. See, for example: "Ground Leasing Without Tears," *Shelterforce* (January 29, 2014); "Common Ground: Community-Owned Land as a Platform for Equitable and Sustainable Development," *University of San Francisco Law Journal* 51 (1), 2017; and "Better Together: The Challenging, Transformative Complexity of Community, Land, and Trust." Chapter Twenty-six, *On Common Ground*, op cit., 2020.

5. This "previous generation of thinkers and activists" who laid the foundation for the modern-day CLT includes Henry George, Ebenezer Howard, Vinoba Bhave, Ralph Borsodi, Mildred Loomis, Arthur Morgan, Slater King, Fay Bennett, Albert J. McKnight, Bob Swann, Charles Sherrod, Lucy Poulin, Marie Cirillo, and Chuck Matthei, among others. See: John Emmeus Davis, "Origins and Evolution of the Community Land Trust in the United States," *The Community Land Trust Reader*, J.E. Davis, ed. (Cambridge MA: Lincoln Institute of Land Policy, 2010). More information on the "Roots of the CLT," including a timeline of CLT development, can be found on the website of the Center for CLT Innovation (*https://cltweb.org*).

6. A number of today's leading CLT practitioners were interviewed in *Community Matters: Conversations with Reflective Practitioners about the Value & Variety of Resident Engagement in Community Land Trusts* (Madison WI: Terra Nostra Press, 2022).

7. The first reported use of this phrase, which Martin Luther King Jr. later repeated a number of times, appeared in a sermon he delivered at the Cathedral of St. John the Divine in New York City, 1956.

1.

Shirley Sherrod

The Civil Rights Activist
Who Bent the Arc of Landownership
Toward Justice

Interviewed by Helen Cohen
May 2, 2012

*Shirley Sherrod was one of the found-
ers of New Communities, Inc. in 1969,
widely considered to be the first community land trust. Earlier, she and her husband, Charles Sherrod, also started the
Southwest Georgia Project to continue
the civil rights activism begun by him as
an organizer for the Student Nonviolent
Coordinating Committee (SNCC). When
New Communities lost its land to fore-
closure in 1985, Shirley joined the staff of the Federation of Southern Cooperatives, helping farmers to avoid land losses of their own. Since 2011,
she has helped to lead the rebirth of New Communities at Cypress Pond
Plantation, now named* **Resora***. Shirley serves today as Executive Director of the Southwest Georgia Project for Community Education.*

HELEN COHEN: I'd like to start with your childhood in Baker County and to ask what led you to become active in the Civil Rights Movement.

SHIRLEY SHERROD: Well, I grew up on a farm about twenty-five miles from Albany, Georgia. I was the oldest of five girls, so I had to do a lot of work helping on the farm from when I was very young. Initially, we were using mules to plant the crops. During those days, you used a distributor with the mule pulling it to put the fertilizer out and then a planter to put the seeds down. I would actually hold a planter in the row to get from end to end. My father would turn me around, so that I could take the mule back to the other end. I grew up doing that on the farm, very early. Then we finally got a tractor and he would have to get the truck and the tractor to the field we were planting. So I learned to drive a tractor; that was the first thing I drove.

I grew up in a place called Hawkinstown. That name is my grandmother's family name. I don't know when they arrived in Baker County or whether they arrived as slaves, but I've been able to find my great-grandfather's name listed on the rolls where he registered to vote in 1867. So I know they were there in Baker County at least that early.

They started as sharecroppers and worked together to help family members buy land. The area where my family started buying land is called Hawkinstown today, because they were all Hawkins and because of the amount of land they bought. The goal they achieved was to buy land for each family unit. My grandmother had twelve sisters and brothers and her father had at least seven sisters and brothers.

All the farmers in the area were Black and there was lots of Black-owned farmland. Now, did that make me want to stay on the farm? No. It was hard work.

I also grew up in a place where the sheriff was the ruler. The sheriff before my time, Claude Screws, actually beat to death a relative of mine by the name of Bobby Hall and displayed his body at the court-house steps in Newton. That case became known because the sheriff was convicted by an all-White federal jury, not of murder, but of depriving Bobby Hall of his civil rights. It was appealed all the way to the US Supreme court where the conviction was overturned. The Justices said you had to prove that, as he was murdering Bobby Hall, he was *thinking* of depriving him of his civil rights. The whole issue of proving intent came from that case of *Screws v. United States*. I'm told that all lawyers have to study that case.

During my years of growing up, L. Warren Johnson was the sheriff. He was known as the "Gator," as in alligator. It was a really, really tough place to grow up, with a sheriff who murdered Black people and who ruined everyone.

HELEN COHEN: Did you ever think of leaving?

SHIRLEY SHERROD: Yes. I had two reasons for wanting to leave Baker County. One, I didn't want to ever have anything to do with agriculture or farming beyond high school. My goal was to go to college and go as far North as I could [laughter]. I thought all people were free in the North, during those years.

The other reason was the conditions we had to live under, where White people ruled. I wanted to get out of that. That was my dream. I was not even applying to schools in the South. I wanted to go to college in the North. Back then, when women married, they found their husbands in college [laughter]. I didn't want to take a chance on marrying someone from the South, so I wouldn't even think of going to school in the South. But, as I say to young people now, you can never say what you'll never do.

My father was murdered during March of my senior year. He was murdered by a White man who was never prosecuted. I made a commitment on the night of my father's death that I would not leave the South, that I would stay and devote my life to working for change. I was actually seventeen years old. I was not involved in the Civil Rights Movement at that time and didn't know how I would carry out that commitment. But it didn't take long. March of 1965 is when he was murdered. By June of Sixty-five, we had started the Baker County Movement, with the help of Charles Sherrod and others from SNCC. I saw that as the way to begin fighting back and to begin living true to the commitment I made.

Baker County has not been the same since. By the end of the summer, we had an injunction against the Gator and a lot of things he was doing. He had to stop. Within eleven years, my mother became the first Black elected official in the county. She's still serving, thirty-five years later [laughter]. I guess within fifteen to eighteen years, we had a Black sheriff in Baker County. We had fought back against that hold they had on us. It was finally enough to take their hands away.

Charles Sherrod & the Student Nonviolent Coordinating Committee (SNCC)

HELEN COHEN: Could you talk about meeting Charles Sherrod?

SHIRLEY SHERROD: He and others from SNCC had been talking to people in Baker County, which probably included my father. Once my father was murdered, it seems that it gave everyone the courage and the strength to really fight back. The SNCC organizers returned in June, right at the time when my aunt had insisted that I needed to be in this pilot program for Upward Bound that was being held at Clark College in Atlanta, so I had to leave. I was there for six weeks and was not here for the first mass meeting.

My sisters were writing to me about things that were happening in Baker County. Bloody Saturday had happened. That was the first march where Sherrod and a couple of other people were beaten bloody by White policemen and White men who just came out of stores in the little town of Newton.

I came home for the Fourth of July. I'd been hearing about this person, Charles Sherrod. I'd been hearing about this person who wanted to meet me. He'd already met all of my sisters. He later tells the story that they showed him a picture of me and he said, "I'm going to marry her." I met him, but wasn't overly impressed when I first met him [laughter].

Then I went to my first mass meeting and I saw how he had led people there in Baker County to stand up. They were saying all these great things in the mass meeting and planning for more demonstrations and other things to be done. And singing, oh the singing was just great. And I remember being in that meeting and just crying.

That's when I thought, "My goodness, this is a great person." All of a sudden, he looked different to me, and I knew then that this was a way that I could live true to the commitment that I made. I would work in Baker County and I would work wherever else that work would take me.

I couldn't wait to get back home. At the end of that course in Atlanta, I came home and immediately got involved. In fact, the night of the first day that I arrived back home, there was a hearing being held at the courthouse. I had three sisters in jail in Newton. I had an aunt and lots of other friends also being held in jail. So we went to the hearing that night at the courthouse. CB King was the only lawyer we had in this area, the only Black lawyer. CB was there for the hearing. I remember that the judge decided to allow the juveniles to be released. That meant, I think, two of my sisters got out of jail that night.

But the thing that happened at the end of that hearing, we were upstairs in the courthouse. As we were about to leave, the sheriff just kicked the door shut and said, "Sit your goddamn asses down." Then he just cursed and said all of these things he wanted to say to us that night. When he had enough, he opened the door and said, "Get your goddamn asses out."

We knew that we had to travel in groups. There were about four cars, so we left the courthouse that night and started driving back to Hawkinstown. About three miles out of town, there was this flashlight. It was one of these deputies, actually his son, stopping us. He's shining the light at us and saying we didn't stop at a stop sign back in the city.

They did many other things like that and worse to intimidate us. But I was firmly committed. The next week, I was attempting to register to vote and the sheriff pushed me and two others who were with me down on the ground. Sherrod was with us. The sheriff pushed him down on the ground too. So I couldn't register to vote.

By the end of the summer, we had arranged for some hearings in DC. We raised money and five carloads of us left the mass meeting one Sunday night, driving to Washington. We knew we couldn't go north up Highway 91 toward Albany, which was the route we needed to take. We went east into Camilla, the next county over, and then drove north. When the sheriff later heard we were talking about the conditions we had to live under here in Baker County and the things he was doing, he was quoted as saying that if he had known we were going to DC, we would never have made it. We knew that, which is why we didn't go up Highway 91.

Two weeks later, one of my sisters was sitting up in the dining room studying, and she saw all of these cars coming around the curb far away, just a lot of lights. She got up and told my mother there were lots of cars. They looked out and there was this big cross being burned in front of our house.

Now, in that house was my mother, four of my sisters, and my young brother, who had just been born in June. (My mother was seven months pregnant when my father was murdered.) My mother actually went out on the porch with a gun [laughter] and she recognized some of the men and called them out. The sheriff and the GBI

[Georgia Bureau of Investigation] came later, but of course nothing was ever done.

When I graduated from high school, I didn't know whether I'd get to go to college because my father had been the main support when we had farmed. But we couldn't farm anymore. I just didn't know what would happen. But I managed to get a student loan to go to Fort Valley State, which was a hundred miles away.

I left to go to school, but I came back and jumped right back into the work with SNCC. Part of that work was in Albany. We were now working not just in Baker County, but in Worth County and in Sumter and Lee and other counties.

By the end of the year, I knew that Sherrod was a winner [laughter] and we were getting married. I went back to school, but later transferred to Albany State so I could be closer.

HELEN COHEN: Where was Sherrod?

SHIRLEY SHERROD: He was based in Albany and working in all of these counties. You can give Sherrod the credit for really organizing the movement in Albany and all these other movements around southwest Georgia.

HELEN COHEN: What struck you about his leadership?

SHIRLEY SHERROD: You know, he could really motivate people and give them the courage and the strength to stand up. He could have been a different kind of leader, but he would simply say, "I'm Sherrod." I think his style of leadership did more to pull people into the work and into the movement and did more to give them the strength to fight. That was different from some others who were involved in the movement at the time—some big-name folks I won't mention, who usually get all the credit for what was done.

Sherrod was quietly bringing change to a large area here in

southwest Georgia. He's continued to do that. Where so many other SNCC projects faded after a period of time, his work has continued here, fifty-one, fifty-two years later.

HELEN COHEN: Could you tell me the dates again, just so I'm clear?

SHIRLEY SHERROD: My father was murdered on March 25, 1965. I graduated from high school on June 6, and my brother was born on June 6, 1965. Then I went away to college at Fort Valley. It was the next September of 1966 that I actually married Charles Sherrod.

HELEN COHEN: Did you move to Albany then?

SHIRLEY SHERROD: I moved to Albany in September of 1966, but I went back to school at Fort Valley that year and then transferred to Albany State for my third and fourth years of college.

HELEN COHEN: Your relationship with SNCC eventually changed. Could you talk about that?

SHIRLEY SHERROD: Well, you know, by the end of the Sixties we had sort of gone out on our own. The leadership of SNCC had changed. Stokely Carmichael was the leader and said that all Whites had to leave SNCC. Of course, we had lots of Whites working with us here in southwest Georgia. We didn't agree with the new direction at SNCC. That's when we knew we had to incorporate the Southwest Georgia Project, an organization that we have that's still surviving today.

There were other issues within the leadership of SNCC that Sherrod didn't always agree with. If you know anything about him, he's quite stubborn; he's determined. He will spend years working to make something work. None of us had a problem with following *his* leadership. He had proven himself to us here in southwest Georgia over and over again. He had been beaten so many times and taken so much abuse, but he always jumped right back up.

HELEN COHEN: Why was it important to Sherrod and you to keep people together, keeping an integrated movement?

SHIRLEY SHERROD: Well, the work can be much more effective when you have Black and White working together on it. As I've said to people here recently with our racial healing work, "How can there be racial healing when you don't deal with White people in this area?" If you want to bring change, what better way than to have White and Black working together for change. I think we hit the target much more often, when there's an effort in that way.

We were willing to stand up too. We had lots of White students working with us. Sherrod had gone back to seminary to get another degree from Union Theological Seminary in New York. He was in bed with a lot of White people who wanted to do good, so he brought them here [laughter]. We had many, many students from Union who came and stayed. Some of them stayed in the area for years, working with us here. I don't think we would have made as much progress without many of them.

Land Is Power:
The Creation of New Communities, Inc.

HELEN COHEN: Your activism in the Civil Rights Movement evolved to include a focus on economic rights and access to land. Would you talk about how that happened?

SHIRLEY SHERROD: When you look at my grandmother's family, the Hawkins, they were clearly focused on landownership. They knew that meant a better life. They worked hard to make that happen.

Education and landownership were two things that were big for them, so I knew what it was to be a landowner. I know how we felt as a landowner. Yeah, we were living in a county where Sheriff Gator ruled, but we still had our own land.

You can help people fight for their rights, but when they don't have a base, when they don't have something that they own and they get kicked off the property, that's a really, really, really tough position to be in. You go to enroll your children in the White school, and you get home and find that you don't have a place to stay.

What do we do? We led you there, but we didn't have an answer to what happened. So we knew that part of bringing change to this area was to deal with that issue. You have to try to bring a revolution economically as well. You can fight for your rights, but if you don't have anything, what does it mean?

HELEN COHEN: Could you talk about the origins of the community land trust? Who was involved in starting New Communities?

SHIRLEY SHERROD: When the group went to Israel, there were seven people in addition to Sherrod. That was June of 1968. We started having meetings when they returned in July and decided to create this organization that would be called New Communities.

Slater King was very much involved, he was the brother of CB King, who was the only Black lawyer. Slater was the only Black real estate agent and insurance person. He had lots of contacts outside of the area. I think that's how Bob Swann and others became involved, because Slater knew them.

Just as we started pulling this organization together, land became available. Slater was in real estate and that's how we knew that the Featherfield Farm in Lee County was available. Some money was put together from church groups, from the National Sharecroppers Fund, and from other contacts that Slater had. There was also a rich guy out of Texas, I think, who put up some money. All of this was supposed to be for one year, just to hold the land until other money could kick in.

HELEN COHEN: Before you could purchase the land, I know that you had a major setback.

SHIRLEY SHERROD: Yes. Slater had played a key role in finding the land and he had all of these contacts with people from outside the area who knew him. They had lots of confidence in Slater. I remember it was 1969, I believe, when he was killed in a car wreck coming from Columbus. It was so devastating to what we were trying to do – which meant that Sherrod had to step up even more if we were going to hold onto this land and try to make this happen.

I'm sure there were some who didn't believe in his leadership as much, but many of them didn't have the commitment we had, the commitment to the area. Maybe they had a commitment to the ideas, but not to the area. And they didn't have a full understanding of what having that much land meant to us.

HELEN COHEN: How much land were you able to buy?

SHIRLEY SHERROD: Six thousand acres. It was actually five thousand seven hundred and thirty-five acres, I think, more or less, but it was always seen as 6000 acres of land, even at the tax office. It was about the size of the State of Rhode Island. That's how we compared it back then.

HELEN COHEN: What was your personal reaction to acquiring that land?

SHIRLEY SHERROD: This was so exciting to me. I grew up in Hawkinstown, like I said, where we were landowners. I knew what that meant. I knew right away what having that much land would mean, even if you don't think about all that we were planning to build. Having land, having a base, this was very powerful.

It was like having a plantation. We grew up around plantations. There were plantations all around me when I was growing up: Ichauway Plantation that was owned by Robert Woodruff; the Pineland Plantation that was owned by the Mellon family. These were big plantations, twenty-five thousand, thirty-thousand-acre plantations. And here we were, Black people having a plantation of our own.

I had an uncle who didn't totally understand all that we were trying to do. He was from Baker County. They called me "Ann" down there. He would say to me, "So, you are no longer Ann. You are **Miss** Ann now [laughter]." He teased me about that until he died. But he knew what it meant to have access to that much land, and what it could mean not just to those of us who were working at New Communities on a daily basis, but to all of us.

I think that Black people, even if they were not involved with New Communities, felt proud that we could actually get our hands on that much land. Land meant power. Land established you as somebody.

Planning for the Land's Use & Development

HELEN COHEN: You were a major force behind the master planning that went on, pulling people into the process, organizing them.

SHIRLEY SHERROD: Yeah, well, we actually had many other people helping with the organizing, pulling people together from the various counties.

HELEN COHEN: Could you describe the process that you went through, early on?

SHIRLEY SHERROD: Initially, New Communities received a federal grant of nearly $100,000 from the Office of Economic Opportunity to do the planning. We had this firm out of DC that had the major contract with us to lead us through that planning process. We organized charettes in an old equipment shed. We put sawdust on the ground and hung strong plastic all around. That was our meeting place, so we could actually bring people in.

HELEN COHEN: What were some of the things that you hoped to do on the land?

SHIRLEY SHERROD: We were able to talk about the kind of educational system you might want. The kind of health system. We had some land where there was a railroad going through it, there was a spur onto it, so we actually had an area that could be set aside for industry, for business.

You had land that could be farmed. I grew up on a farm. I had said I didn't want to have anything to do with a farm ever again [laughter]. But here I was, involved in one of the largest farms in the area. But that was exciting too.

We had picked three sites for villages and we were planning the

Planning charette at New Communities, circa 1970.

kind of houses that could be built in those villages. We had a health committee. We had a committee dealing with industry. We had a farm committee. We had an education committee. Oh my goodness, if we had only been able to put some of those plans in place, I think that education for children in this area would be so different.

HELEN COHEN: How many people were you hoping might live on the land?

SHIRLEY SHERROD: We actually had five hundred families that had signed up, saying that they wanted to move onto the property. So we had the people who would live in those villages.

It was some exciting times, you know. You're planning villages, you're planning education, you're planning all of these things. You basically have a chance to plan a life and lives and plan ways to help our people. So we've gone from fighting for our rights to now having rights and trying to do something with them.

A Dark Tide of White Opposition

HELEN COHEN: What was the reaction to New Communities from the White leaders in Albany and from White people in general?

SHIRLEY SHERROD: You know, I was young and new to this work. I just didn't think people would fight you when you were trying to simply help yourself and others. You're not asking them for anything. I was really shocked at the opposition, the shooting at our buildings. I mean, they just came at us in every way to try to stop us, to block us, to do anything to get that land away from us.

There was so much bad press. I can remember that each time they talked about us in the local paper they would refer to my husband's hair as "the Brillo patch." He was fighting to hold onto the land in Lee County, but he was still having to wage these other fights and lead people to fight other things that were happening. Kids were still being put out of school for various reasons. I can remember a lady washed a young Black child's mouth out with soap. Because of the role that Sherrod had played in the Civil Rights Movement, people came to him and asked for his help. I remember the mayor in Albany saying in the press that Charles Sherrod should seek gainful employment. You know, they did just anything they could do to hurt him.

It was dangerous because White people didn't take this lying down. They actually shot at buildings with some of our people in them. I think about the many nights that we drove to New Communities up and down on this road from where we lived in Albany to the farm, which was twenty-five miles north of Albany. I think about how dangerous it could be. But we did it, because it was work that had to be done. We were having the opportunity to build something that would be good for our people.

HELEN COHEN: What was the reaction among members of the Black community? Were they affected by the hostility you were facing? Was there skepticism about what you were doing or the unusual way you were planning to handle the land issue at New Communities, leasing it rather than selling it?

SHIRLEY SHERROD: We had these traveling insurance people who were White. They would come around to collect money on a weekly basis from people and would invariably try to have these conversations with Black folks. They would say, "Why would you want to be a part of that? How are you going to own a house and not own the land?" You know, just trying to put a lot of doubt into our people.

Then, when the Governor blocked the money coming into Georgia for New Communities, after that initial planning grant, there were so many who said, "It just can't be done. You can't do it without that money. You can't do it."

But we still had a large group of people who believed in it. And *we* believed. With Sherrod leading all of us, we believed that we could do it. We said, "We've never had our hands on this much land. We just cannot walk away. We have to fight to keep it." And that's what we did.

HELEN COHEN: Say more, if you would, about the opposition from the Governor.

SHIRLEY SHERROD: Lester Maddox was Governor of the State of Georgia when the money was officially vetoed, when those funds were blocked. He referred to us as "Sharecroppers City." The Congressmen from our area had entered it into the Congressional Record that we were communists.

HELEN COHEN: There were supposed to be additional grants?

SHIRLEY SHERROD: There was supposed to be a major grant at the end of the planning process to begin implementing the plan. The Office of Economic Opportunity, at the time, was making grants to organizations like New Communities. That planning grant was a direct grant from Washington. OEO didn't go through the local officials to get that money to us.

Washington had assured us that we would get the major grant to implement a lot of these plans that we had worked so hard to develop. But that didn't happen because of the opposition that started immediately after the word was out that we had the land and we had the planning grant. The opposition started immediately to block any more funds coming to us.

Back in those days, you really had to look outside of the area for help. That's why we had to look to the federal government. We didn't go to anyone locally for money or for anything to make this happen. We had been assured by OEO that they would give us the implementation money directly. But things started happening politically, so they would not do it. They sent us back through the process that required local officials to approve it and then the state, which effectively killed it.

Today, when I hear these people talking about "state's rights," it's scary, because we could *never* depend on local or state officials to try to move things forward.

The Pivot to Farming to Retain the Land

HELEN COHEN: Even though you had told yourself that you didn't want to have anything to do with a farm ever again, you were back to being a farmer. Talk about the farm operation at New Communities and some of the people who worked there.

SHIRLEY SHERROD: Once the funds were blocked, we couldn't build homes, we couldn't implement the many plans we had put in place, but we could hold onto the land by farming, and that's what we were doing.

We ended up with a person at New Communities who was actually my uncle, who had been one of those Black extension agents in Harris County, Georgia, when they had a Black one to deal with Black farmers and a White one to deal with White farmers, all under the University of Georgia system. He was like a walking textbook, so we got him involved at New Communities.

We diversified and had vegetables. We planted eight acres of muscadine grapes. No one else was doing that. We raised hogs. I think back then we had something like a seventy-five brood sow operation. Instead of just selling all of those hogs at the market, we would take them to be slaughtered, so that they could be USDA inspected. Then we would bring them back to the farm, where we had the farmer's market with a cooling system and all. We had these trays with salts, so we cured hams and bacon and turned some of them into whole hog sausage.

We had a smokehouse. We actually built an old-fashioned smoke-house right on the road, US Highway 19. We were known for our smoked meats, for sausage. Young kids and others could come and see an old-fashioned smokehouse with meat actually being smoked.

We raised sugar cane and we had syrup making. We had a green-house, where we were rooting azaleas and starting other plants from seed. That was years before many others were doing that. We were doing many innovative things on the farm during those years.

We sold watermelons to Safeway back then. I think some of the White students that came, you'd see them tossing watermelons. Someone later wrote a book about that called *Watermelon Summer* [laughter].

Helen Cohen: How did you meet Mtamanika Youngblood?

Shirley Sherrod: Mtamanika came one summer as a student. I think it was the summer of 1970. We would get students during the summers. She was from New York. She came here and had to go back for a year, her last year of school. But she made a commitment that she would come back to work with us after graduating, and she did. This young lady from New York City decided to come to work on the farm.

It was really, really good back then to see someone who didn't have to be involved in this grueling work here in the South and on the farm, with the land. She had other choices, you know. She had graduated from a well-known school in New York and was very smart. She didn't have to come here and give the years that she gave to this work for little money. I don't know how much she was get-ting, but I was getting like sixty-five dollars a week for my family. Maybe it wasn't even sixty-five dollars when she initially came. I think she was getting less than that. But we were all willing to do that. Any money we made, we put it into the common treasury so that we would have money to work with. It was exciting for me to have someone of her ability being willing to come into this work and give all that she had to it.

HELEN COHEN: Have you remained friends?

SHIRLEY SHERROD: Yeah. Things were kind of bad for New Communities when she made the decision to go Atlanta to get an MBA. We didn't have much money at the time, so she and I had taken on the work that initially, I guess, five or six of us had done. Then she made the decision to go to school. I was so hurt. Because, you know, there was no one else. She and I were the lone females at that time who were there every day, attending all of the farm committee meetings and making sure that all of the office work was being done. Now she was leaving me.

You know, we had farm committee meetings every Monday night. After she left, I'm the only female there with all of these men and, of course, my husband as the leader. It made it very difficult, but I stood up [laughter]. There would be these conversations aimed

Meeting of the NCI farm committee. Pictured (l to right): Shirley Sherrod, Monroe Gaines, and Stanley Harden.

at me. The farm committee consisted of three board members and everybody working at the farm. Two other board members worked at the Marine Corps base. They would drive out every Monday evening and they'd go around and look at things. Then we'd all get back to the office to sit down and meet, but before the meeting would start, they would start talking about the role of women. I knew the message they were trying to send to me, but did it get to me? No [laughter].

Pushed Into Foreclosure

HELEN COHEN: Throughout the 1970s, as you focused on farming and farm-related enterprises like the smokehouse, greenhouse, and store, were you able to pursue any of the other parts of the master plan that you'd developed for the land?

SHIRLEY SHERROD: The farm was the only thing we could keep going. We couldn't keep the education committee, the health committee, and all of those things. When you don't have money to make things happen, it's hard to keep people interested in meeting. But the farm was going on. We could keep that going.

HELEN COHEN: Talk about the experience of dealing with the Farmers Home Administration. How did New Communities get mixed up with that federal agency?

SHIRLEY SHERROD: We were doing quite well after a while. We could make enough money to pay the land notes and expand the farm operation. We didn't have to go to the Farmers Home Administration to borrow money. So we didn't.

But then we had a drought, followed by a second year of drought. So we decided, just like all farmers were doing, to go to Farmers

Home to borrow money. The farm manager and my husband went over to the office in Dawson, Georgia. And the guy said, "You'll get a loan here over my dead body," and he meant it.

So we complained. Eventually they sent three people from Washington to meet at our office on the farm. The district director from this area, who was White, also met us there. They had one Black person working in the state office of Farmers Home, who also came down.

Then a delegation that included those individuals went to the local office in Dawson to get the application. Now, you know, that was powerful for that day, but they didn't stay around to make sure things would go smoothly. It still took, I think, about three years for us to eventually get a loan. Every stumbling block that could be put there to stop us was used. Eventually we got a loan, but three years is a long time to go without money, production money, for operating the size operation we had.

Because the droughts were continuing to happen, we were also trying to get them to finance irrigation. But they denied it every time.

HELEN COHEN: When you were finally able to borrow money from them, what happened?

SHIRLEY SHERROD: What Farmers Home would do is you would have to give them all available assets as collateral—and that's how they got us.

Now, initially, they didn't have all our assets. There were two parts to our farm. We bought one farm from one landowner, and another farm from another. The second farm was like nine hundred and thirty-five acres. They were there together, so Farmers Home didn't know about the nine hundred and thirty-five acres.

Farmers Home would make things go really, really slow. We

eventually had to make the decision to cut some timber on the nine hundred and thirty-five acres. Being honest people, Sherrod and the farm manager, during a visit to Farmers Home said, "You know, we had to cut some timber just to survive." They were trying to tell the guy how hard they were making things, because this process was so slow and they wouldn't finance irrigation.

The guy's like, "What?! You cut timber!? You can't . . ." Sherrod said, "Well, we didn't cut it on land you have a lien on." The guy said, "That doesn't matter. You have to bring that money in."

We had gotten like $50,000 from the sale of that timber. They made us bring all that money to them before they would consider making the loan for that year. They then put a lien on that nine hundred and thirty-five acres, and wouldn't give us a loan after all.

HELEN COHEN: What happened next?

SHIRLEY SHERROD: Once the Farmers Home Administration had a lien on all available assets, they could now engineer the foreclosure of the property. When they started moving in that direction, we didn't have any way to maneuver. Farmers Home would not allow us to pay the first lienholder, which was Prudential Insurance Company, and that led to Prudential foreclosing on us, which was what Farmers Home was trying to make happen from the very beginning.

That was such a tough time to endure. June 1985 was supposed to be when the land would be sold at the courthouse steps. I can remember thinking, "I can't be here when the land is sold." I actually entered a Master's degree program, which meant I had to be at UC Davis in Davis, California for a month. But it didn't happen in the month of June; it happened in September of 1985.

We were basically kicked off the land and what they did was, they dug holes and pushed all of our buildings over in them. Every building but that main house and the shed that was on the property, they dug a hole and pushed them in there. So we were gone.

A Slow Recovery & Sudden Shot at Reparation

HELEN COHEN: Did you see your buildings being bulldozed?

SHIRLEY SHERROD: I heard what had happened. I didn't go and see it. I couldn't even drive north on US Highway 19 for about ten years. I just couldn't ride by there and see it.

When we lost the land, it was a really, really, really rough time for many reasons. I had made a commitment in 1965 to stay in the South and work for change. Here was something that we had worked so hard on, and now it was gone. What do I do now? How do I continue to work on this commitment?

I had children. Our daughter was graduating from high school that year and going on to college. We didn't have much money, but I had to make sure she could go to school. What do we do? I was involved in an effort to start an adult day rehab program. It's named the Slater King Center. I started helping out with that part-time to have a little money.

And, of course, I started in a Master's program at UC Davis, which meant I had to be away for a month. I would then come back to try to begin implementing part of that Master's. It was an individualized Master's program with Antioch University, which meant you had to have a project.

My project then was to develop a system for assisting farmers in this area. I was able to get the Federation of Southern Cooperatives to sponsor me. Then they made the decision to bring me onto the staff. It gave me the opportunity to continue with the commitment. I was able to use so much of what I had learned growing up on the farm and working in the movement and being involved with New Communities to help others. I had an opportunity to pour myself into work to keep other farmers from experiencing the losses we had gone through.

Now, it deeply affected my husband. It took a long, long time for him to recover. Nine years later, we were still dealing with the fact that he just couldn't pick himself up and move on. We would have to push him and keep pushing him to get involved and to do something else, especially because we had two children in college. Financially, I needed help with trying to keep things going.

HELEN COHEN: Talk about your time at the Federation of Southern Cooperatives.

SHIRLEY SHERROD: Pouring myself into the work with the Federation, I had this golden opportunity to develop programs to assist Black farmers in this area. I was able to get some Vista volunteers. Because I had worked in the movement in this area, I decided that rather than trying to have seven volunteers right here under me, I could choose one from each county and really start rebuilding the movement in seven counties to assist Black farmers. That group of Vista volunteers increased from seven to ten to seventeen. I had volunteers in fifteen different counties in southwest Georgia and two retired vocational ag teachers that I used as my extension staff.

I'm on a roll now. I'm organizing cooperatives and really helping farmers to get better farming systems and operations. But the main problem was still the struggle to try to get loans for our farmers, so I decided to learn the regulations of Farmers Home Administration.

That made me really go face-to-face with county supervisors. I remember one in particular who I thought we would actually get into a physical fight. He was threatening to foreclose on a farmer. Because I knew the regulation and knew he wasn't saying the right thing, I tried to be nice to let him talk, but he wouldn't stop. I stopped him and said, "Will you put that in writing?" He actually sat there, pushed his chair back from the desk, and started staring at the floor in front of him. He finally turned the chair all the way around, looking at the floor, and said, "I ain't putting nothing in writing." We actually went at it. I complained so much about him, and was on him so much, that he left the agency. And that farmer still has his land. They were threatening to foreclose on him.

I did that for so many others, so many others. Through the years, I developed a reputation for assisting farmers. That's why White farmers also came to me for help.

HELEN COHEN: Were White farmers having the same thing happen to them that had happened to you at New Communities?

SHIRLEY SHERROD: Yeah, I had thought that only Black farmers were losing their land. But in the Eighties, lots of farmers were having trouble, Black and White.

Black farmers were losing their land mainly because they didn't have access to credit. Or when they got credit, Farmers Home did exactly what they had done with New Communities. Once they got all available assets, they would move in to foreclose.

Black farmers were losing land at such an alarming rate. The US Commission on Civil Rights kept sounding the alarm, year after year. I think it was 1967 when the Commission said, "If you don't do something about discrimination in USDA, by the Year 2000 there'll be virtually no Black-owned farms." They kept trying to point out the problem with Black land loss. We would meet—I mean the Federation of Southern Cooperatives, Arkansas Land and Farm Development, and the Farmers Legal Action Group's Land-Loss Prevention Project—we would meet and we'd talk about the fact that we have to do something about Black land loss, we need to file a lawsuit.

People knew about the *Pigford* suit against USDA. So finally, early in the Nineties, we made the decision that we had to go for it. The Land Loss Prevention Project, which is located in North Carolina, and the Farmers Legal Action Group (FLAG), both nonprofit law firms, were chosen as the two law firms to file the lawsuit.

Their first action was to submit a FOIA request to USDA for complaints that had been filed. Our lawyers were told there was no information. The two law firms then filed a lawsuit to get that information. During the hearing, the judge really threatened the Farmers Home people, saying you either produce the information or you go to jail.

HELEN COHEN: Who is "we" at this point?

Shirley Sherrod: I'm talking about the Federation of Southern Cooperatives, FLAG, the Land Loss Prevention Project, and the Arkansas Land and Development Project. By then, New Communities didn't have anything. We kept the organization viable, but we didn't have anything to work with. So now I'm pouring all of my energies into the work I was doing as a staff member of the Federation of Southern Cooperatives and working with these other groups around the country.

HELEN COHEN: So, you demanded that USDA should produce the information you needed for your lawsuit?

SHIRLEY SHERROD: Right, the Federation's partners, the Farmers Legal Action Group in Minnesota and the Land Loss Prevention Project in North Carolina, filed a lawsuit to get the information. Then the judge, during the hearing, told the people from the Farmers Home Administration, "Either you provide the information or you go to jail."

So, at that point, Farmers Home sent fifty-five boxes of information to our lawyers. I think that half of it went to North Carolina and half went to the Legal Action Group in Minnesota.

We made the decision to start with six cases. These test cases in the original lawsuit included six farmers, but they were taken away from our law firms when a lawyer from Texas got them to sign with him. But these six test cases opened the door for the *Pigford* cases to be filed by a law firm in DC, led by Al Pires.

The years for *Pigford* cases would be 1981 to 1996. You had to have experienced discrimination between those years. The Federation and the others had worked to get Congress to use those years for the statute limitation, because when Ronald Reagan became President he had abolished the Office of Civil Rights at USDA.

USDA indicated they would be willing to settle, rather than go to court. In that settlement, there were two classes of farmers, Class A and Class B. Class A farmers didn't have to use a lot of instances of discrimination to prove discrimination. If they did prove discrimination, they would get $50,000. They would also get all of their remaining debt paid; plus the government was supposed to pay $12,500 as taxes on the $50,00. Most of the farmers decided to file a Class A claim.

For a Class B claim, you had to have more documentation of the discrimination. Then you would have your day in court. The award, if you won, could be unlimited.

HELEN COHEN: How did New Communities come to file a Class B claim?

SHIRLEY SHERROD: I was so busy helping farmers gather information, making sure the information was out there, that I hadn't thought about New Communities and our struggle. I was so busy working on other folks' struggles. The Federation has offices in Alabama, Georgia, South Carolina, and Mississippi. I had even gone out in Texas, trying to help some farmers with their claims.

But one night, I had been over in Alabama helping the farmers in that area. I was driving home, thinking about the day, the farmers, the work. I'll never forget. I was near Eufaula, Alabama when the light bulb went off. "Oh my goodness! We were farming in 1981. Oh my goodness!"

There were no cellphones then. There was no way I could talk to my husband until I could get home. It was another two-hour drive to get there. I walked into the house and I think I screamed, "We can file a claim under *Pigford!*" [laughter].

The Lawsuit Against USDA, Charging Discrimination by the Farmers Home Administration

SHIRLEY SHERROD: We got busy trying to pull that information together. We didn't really know what had happened to us. It was not just White people who had criticized us for what happened at New Communities, you know; it was a lot of our own people, blaming us for the loss of the land. They didn't do a thing to help, but they blamed us for the loss of the land. We were so hurt. We walked away, so we didn't know the real story about what had happened.

Gathering the information for this claim helped us to find out exactly what had happened to us. We had lost a lot of our information in the flood of 1994 here in Albany. We had stored some files in a building that was close to the Flint River. It didn't dawn on us, when the flood was coming, that we needed to move those files, so we lost all of them.

But we became very good at searching other records. My husband would be up there in that courthouse in Lee County on a daily basis, looking at records.

We finally learned the real story of what had happened. We had assets worth almost five million dollars. The government sold the land to a person in Atlanta, a rich person who was involved in the cable business. He paid a million dollars for the land, but three weeks after the sale, Farmers Home turned around and let him borrow $950,000 of that purchase price.

They didn't offer us options like that, which they were supposed to offer to us at the time. And there were other things that they did. They harassed us, my husband and me, for a few years afterwards, demanding payment, when they had actually settled the debt. It was just their way of still messing with us.

After all of those years, we saw had what happened to us. Finally, there was, you know, the real story of the things that they did to us. We had the documentation of it. So we were able to file the Class B claim for New Communities.

HELEN COHEN: That documentation was a comparison with how the buyer of your land had been treated by Farmers Home after the foreclosure?

SHIRLEY SHERROD: Well, the main documentation was that, while they were denying loans to us and while they would not finance irrigation for us, they were giving those loans to the big plantations around here. These were absentee landowners, operating plantations in the area, and those plantations were actually getting loans to finance their irrigation when Farmers Home wouldn't loan to us.

See, in filing your claim, you had to find a similarly-situated White farmer who got what you didn't get. So, in our case, we had to be compared to plantations, because of the size of the operation that we had. That meant we had to look to see what the plantations were getting that we didn't get. That's when we found all of this documentation that Farmers Home was actually letting them borrow, when they wouldn't let us borrow.

There was also the way that man made us give him the $50,000 for the timber we cut on land that Farmers Home didn't have a lien on. He couldn't do that, but he did. And, you know, there were many other things they did that we found out later they did not have a right to do.

HELEN COHEN: What was your reaction to those discoveries?

SHIRLEY SHERROD: We had a sigh of relief, just in getting the truth. We finally knew what had happened. Now there was documentation of what had happened.

The Long Road to Victory

HELEN COHEN: Okay, so you've gathered all this documentation of what Farmers Home had done to undermine New Communities. You filed a Class B claim. What was the next chapter in this saga?

SHIRLEY SHERROD: We thought, okay, we've filed this claim. It should be a short process. But it was ten years. Ten years! We filed that claim before October 13, 1999. Our hearing was not held until July 30, 2002.

If you had been sitting in that hearing, if you had been an observer, you would have said, "They won." It was very clear we had won.

The lawyer for the Justice Department seemed so incompetent. We found out two years later, she wasn't a lawyer after all. She was working for the Justice Department, but she wasn't a lawyer. She had been arrested in California. Someone out there had the sense to investigate her background and found that she wasn't a lawyer, but she had been working for the Justice Department. They sent a letter to us, saying that, "Yeah, she handled four cases for the government, but it won't have any bearing on your case."

Anyway, the original hearing officer denied our claim. Unbelievable. That meant we had to appeal. The judge set up a process so that there was a monitor. If you were not successful, you could appeal your case to a monitor. You couldn't present any new information, but the monitor could look at the record to determine if mistakes had been made. If the monitor found mistakes, the monitor could only pass those mistakes on to the chief arbitrator. She couldn't make any decisions, just point out the mistakes. In our case, the monitor had to recuse herself, because she was a friend of mine, so she couldn't handle the New Communities appeal. They had to find someone else to handle the appeal.

That individual took *four* years, but produced a document that fully documented the mistakes that the original hearing officer had made. The monitor's office then sent that on to the chief arbitrator. He sent us a letter in October of 2006. (Remember, we filed in 1999. We're now up to 2006.) He sent a letter to us saying that what they found had merit, but it was an extensive case and would take him some time to review it.

SHIRLEY SHERROD: We didn't hear anything else on our case until the night of July the eighth, 2009. That's when our lawyer called our house. I answered the phone. She said, "Shirley have you *heard*?" I said, "No." She said, "We won!"

She's all excited, you know. It's ten years now, so I said, "Really?" She said, "You want to guess how much?" I said, "Rose, is it at least a million dollars?" She said, "Shirley, it's twelve."

It was just, so . . . unbelievable. We didn't have the document. We didn't have the paperwork that she had, but she faxed it to us a couple of days later. When I sat down and read that decision, I couldn't do anything but cry.

That man, Michael Lewis, the chief arbitrator, had looked at the record. He saw the documentation of what had happened to us and he made a bold decision to award New Communities the money for loss of land and loss of income. He went on to give Sherrod and me $150,000 each for mental anguish. We also made sure that all of the people who were working at New Communities at the time of the loss, each of the families, got a hundred thousand each.

HELEN COHEN: What was the reaction in your household?

SHIRLEY SHERROD: We were happy and I think both of us cried. It was really, really something. We fought, we were hoping that we'd get something, but now we could continue with the dream. Now there was money to actually keep it going, to do something big, to do something great.

There were people who said we should just split the money up among everyone and move on. That was never a thought in our mind. No, we have worked so many years for this. So we immediately started putting things in place to start looking for land. We didn't know where it would be, but we knew we would find more land.

When you look at the amount of land Black people have lost, when you look at the land that *we* lost, when you look at all that we had tried to do . . . now we had this opportunity to really show our people, "Don't give up. Don't give up."

Who would have thought we would still have that organization, where we could still use it. They thought it was gone, it was buried forever, but we didn't give up. We still even had a bank account in name of New Communities [laughter], all from 1969. And here we were at 2009. We didn't give up the dream, and now we could really bring those dreams into reality. Those dreams and many, many more.

Cypress Pond Plantation

HELEN COHEN: That was quite a July!

SHIRLEY SHERROD: Well, a *couple* of things happened during that month of July 2009. You know, I'm on Cloud Nine about the land and the opportunity we have to rebuild. We received that call on the night of July eighth. On the night of July thirtieth, I received a call from the White House, saying we have selected you as State Director of Rural Development.

I said something like, "Really?" [laughter]. I knew that my name was in the hat, but it didn't happen in 1993 under Clinton. Even though I was willing to allow my name to be put in the hat during the Obama Administration, I didn't think it would happen. We've never had a Black person as State Director and here they are telling me I'd been selected. It's like, "Wow."

I'm a little slow and the guy says, "You're still going to do it aren't you?" And I said, "Oh yes, yes." And my mind was already going, "I've got to find an apartment in Athens. I've got to . . . gosh, New Communities, oh my goodness!" I felt like I needed to be here with New Communities and all that we needed to do, but I also felt that I had to take the position. We had never had a Black person in the position and who knows how long it would be before we could get another. I felt I had to do that.

That pulled me out of New Communities, because they were saying I'd have to disassociate myself from all the organizations, all the boards, and everything else I was doing. So I had to leave that to my husband and a few others.

We had decided to go slow. We had not received any money and I can't remember how long before the money actually came. So, I'm in it, and I'm not in it, you know [laughter]. That's the position I'm in.

I tried to do things through the government, with USDA. But we all know what happened. I was so rudely taken out of that position. But that put me squarely back here in southwest Georgia.

HELEN COHEN: I won't ask you to recount that awful episode of being forced to resign from the State Director's position because of false accusations based on a doctored video of a speech you had delivered. I think you are writing your own account, writing a book about that. We could make a whole film just about that. Instead, could you tell the story of how you got the new land?

SHIRLEY SHERROD: By then, we were looking for land and trying to decide where to go. We really didn't want to be in Lee County anymore, even though there was some land available there. Lee County, back during the early days of New Communities, was almost seventy percent Black. It's now only fifteen percent Black. If you think they didn't want us then, they certainly wouldn't now [laughter]. We didn't want to be there.

So we were looking in other places. We were learning through some local attorneys about plantations that were available. We had actually gone to look at one, just five or six miles outside of town and we were negotiating with the owners of that.

Then someone else suggested that we should look at Cypress Pond Plantation. So one Sunday morning, we came out here and got on this bird wagon they have on the plantation. We were riding all over the property. We went into that big antebellum home and I just had a problem with antebellum. Why would we want an antebellum home, a plantation? I really had an issue with that. I had to work through that.

I insisted that we get a consultant in to look at the other plantation that we were considering and to look at Cypress Pond. When that consultant finished, we had a meeting. We had a dinner where he showed up. He said, "You have to purchase Cypress Pond. When you look at all the improvements there, you can't go wrong."

I said, "Okay, this mind of mine needs to switch. Okay, it looks like we're going to own an antebellum home." I got over it pretty quick and then just jumped right into it. I realized quickly that it was the better buy. We purchased it on June 29, 2011.

HELEN COHEN: Could you describe the circumstances that allowed you to buy it?

SHIRLEY SHERROD: The previous owner developed ALS and died. I'm not sure, but I think he died in 2008. This was 2011, around March or April, when we came out to look at the property. Many of these plantations were kind of in trouble, because the economy was down. Hunters were not coming down to hunt and pay all of that money they had been paying. The housing market, you know, and the state of the economy was just not good. It affected the investors who had these plantations, so they were just ready to get rid of them.

Cypress Pond had been put on the market for twenty-one million dollars. By that Sunday morning when we came out here to look at the property, they had dropped the price to six-point-nine million. The corporation was just ready to get rid of it. The agent who drove up from Tallahassee, Florida kept saying to us, as we were going around the farm that day, "You all just need to make an offer. I can tell you now, they're telling me to sell this property. So just make an offer."

My husband said to him, before we left that day, "Well, see if they'll take five million for it." They sent us the contract the next day for five million [laughter].

When we got that consultant to come and to look at everything, one of the things he said to us that day was, "It's the better buy, but I think you can get it for less than five million. You can also negotiate and make them include the equipment."

So now we started playing hardball, you know. We don't want to pay five million for it and we need the equipment. We offered three point something for it and finally settled at four-and-a-half million.

We got this property for four-and-a-half million dollars. It just makes you know that it was destined to be. We got a property that was initially on the market for twenty-one; they dropped it to six point nine; and we got it for four and a half, with all the equipment.

HELEN COHEN: What are your plans for Cypress Pond?

SHIRLEY SHERROD: There are pecan trees here. The previous owner didn't really take care of them. One of the things we're trying to do is get the old growth back into production, but we're also expanding out to maybe five or six hundred acres of pecan trees. We planted three acres of orange trees. There's a variety that can grow in this area. We're thinking of muscadine grapes. You know, that was our signature crop under the old New Communities, so I'm certain we'll put in some muscadine grapes. We are looking at farming demonstrations and other crops, mostly vegetables that we could put in. And we have timber here on the place.

We have that big house; and, gosh, isn't that a house?! That house is 13,000 square feet with 3,000 square feet of porch. The previous owner didn't spare any expense in restoring that place. He put three million dollars just into restoring that antebellum home. That's going to become a great conference center.

He also built cabins, lodges, whatever you want to call them. They're kind of upscale just to be called a cabin. In one them, there's a steam shower in one bedroom and a clawfoot tub in another and granite tile topping. It's located flush on a lake. There's an 85-acre lake out there. It's just so peaceful. You can sit on the porch of one of the cabins and be in another world.

But if you drive out of those gates, you can be at the Albany Mall

Charles Sherrod at Cypress Pond Plantation, 2014.

in ten minutes. You can be at the Albany airport in five minutes. Our property line goes right up to the city limits of Albany.

HELEN COHEN: Could you talk about the others who are working here? What people have you gathered?

SHIRLEY SHERROD: Well, Donny was the first staff person we brought on. He was actually an agricultural specialist with the Southwest Georgia Project. That's the organization we started way back there in the Sixties, when we incorporated after pulling away from SNCC. The Southwest Georgia Project has this program of trying to bring women, Black women, back into agriculture, growing vegetables, marketing them to school systems and so forth. Donny was busy doing that work, but he came out here to the farm at Cypress Pond and we couldn't pull him away.

"Where's Donny?" "He's on the farm." "Where's Donny? We need him over here in Clay County." "He's on the farm."

You know, Donny just decided "I want to work on the farm at New Communities." So, finally, we just gave in. Okay, Donny is at New Communities [laughter].

Then there's Emery. He is someone who's worked in farming from early years. He and his sister, Rutha, sing. Emery was deeply involved in the Albany Movement, in the early years. It was only natural to bring Emery out here to work. And he loves it.

Robert is a mechanic. My brother who's on the police force knew him and recommended him as someone who could help deal with equipment and other things here on the farm. In addition to equipment, he knows the pecan business as well. I mean, the pecan work, working with the trees and so forth. So that was a plus.

Broderick was someone else who was a friend of the family and needed work, so he came out here to work.

Hilton, well, here's how Hilton came to us. I was doing a tour in

August of 2011 that included some USDA people. There was an Undersecretary in the group. Cypress Farm wasn't even on the tour schedule. They were touring the commercial kitchen that we had started in Baker County. I was taking them to a pecan operation that we started up in Leslie and another co-op I started in the earlier years. So one is like twenty miles away, the other one is about forty miles north. I made the decision to bring them by here, just to ride through. We were on a big bus that the University provided. So, I just decided to give them a ride through Cypress Pond. We didn't plan to get out, but people were saying, "You got to take us into this house, that antebellum home. You cannot bring us on this place without taking us in that house. We've never been in an antebellum house. You got to do it." So we did stop to go in there.

That Undersecretary was on the bus. He said to me, "We really need to get someone out here to help you. I'll try to find someone who can help look at this pecan grove to see what's possible here." They found someone locally to talk to us about pecans. Hilton Siegler was that person. Hilton came out to Cypress Pond and got hooked.

You know, he actually brought another expert in, who I think the locals ran off. That expert really wanted to partner with us on the pecan grove. He wanted to see us get up to about seven hundred acres of pecans and wanted to partner with us on doing that. We gave him access so he could map the trees and so forth. But that weekend he also went around and talked to some of the big landowners in the area who were very negative and didn't want to see him do anything to help us.

By the time we had our second meeting, before we could sit down, he said, "Shirley, I almost cancelled this meeting." He said he would continue, but three weeks later he called me and said, "It's not feasible for me to do it."

That's when Hilton stepped up and he's been out here just about every day. He's really an expert with pecans and he helps us. He's like an employee. He refers to this place as "ours," and we feel good having him here.

HELEN COHEN: It sounds like you are still getting some pushback from Whites. Is that so?

SHIRLEY SHERROD: Yeah. We're still dealing with some hostility on the part of White people in the area. Because of them, that expert, that first expert in pecan production, backed out and wouldn't stay in with us. There are also comments in the paper from time to time, like, "What is it with the Sherrods getting a plantation? How did they do that?" And maybe they would say something about taxpayers' money, or something.

In fact, just before we purchased the place, you have to sign an agreement to purchase. You then have thirty days to close. Somehow the local press heard that we were looking at buying Cypress Pond. A reporter called our house. I answered the phone and he said, "I heard that you and Charles are buying a plantation." I said, "Charles and I don't have money to buy a plantation."

He said, "Well, is it New Communities?" I said, "I wish you wouldn't print that. We're still trying to negotiate." He asked, "Is it the money you got from the lawsuit?" I said again, "I wish you wouldn't print that. We're still trying to negotiate on Cypress Pond." I said it that way, even though I knew we had negotiated the deal.

I knew they would probably make an attempt to keep us from getting it if they could. So, when we got off the phone, I called my husband and said, "Look, we got to hurry up, do what we have to do, to purchase this place within the thirty days. It cannot go beyond the thirty days, because I know they'll do whatever they can do to keep us from getting it." That's why we quickly got everything in place and purchased the property on June 29, 2011.

I was recently having lunch with one White person in the city.

The first thing he said was, "How are you enjoying your new home?" I knew what he meant, but I played dumb. I said, "What new home?" He said, "Cypress Pond." I said, "I don't live there." That's when I learned that was the perception throughout the White community, that my husband and I were living at Cypress Pond.

Even in 1969, we didn't live in the big house at New Communities. We could have, but we put the tractor driver in there who had the largest family. We didn't ever live in that house back in the Sixties and we have no intention of living in the house at Cypress Pond. I don't think I'd want to live there. That house has a lot of history, probably a lot of spirits [laughter].

Now, because of my ordeal with USDA, White people have learned part of my history and what I've done. They feel like they can approach me more. I've had so many of them come up to me to say, "We really appreciate you and all that you've done." I think they got a chance to see who I was and that I had also helped White farmers. That made them feel I'm more approachable. When I go to the grocery store, they come up and talk to me, where they wouldn't do it before. I went through all of that with USDA, but it helped in many ways. Whatever White people thought of us before, it helped them to be open to seeing another side.

HELEN COHEN: It sounds like you've become quite well-known in southwest Georgia.

SHIRLEY SHERROD: Yes, that's the other part of that [laughter]. I don't have to say, "Hey I'm Shirley Sherrod." I don't have to do that anymore. Even folks who haven't met me before say, "You look so familiar. I know you. Don't I know you?" If they can't think of it right away, I just say, "I'm the person that was fired." Before I can get any more out of my mouth, they say, "Oh yes, yes, yes, yes."

You still have the haters out there, but I get so many White people in the area who come up to me and say, "We really, really appreciate what you've done." That whole thing that I went through with USDA and the fact that a White family stepped forward to say, "Hey, she saved our land," it just helped to turn a lot of folks around.

The Past & Promise of Cypress Pond

HELEN COHEN: You said that big antebellum house "has a lot of history." What do you know about the origins of Cypress Pond Plantation?

SHIRLEY SHERROD: I didn't know the history at the time we bought it. While I was working on my book, the writer who was working with me rode out here one day. She was visiting and we rode out to Cypress Pond. Then she went back to New York. She later emailed and said, "Shirley, did you know that place was once owned by the largest slaveowner and the wealthiest man in Georgia?" No, I didn't. Then I started doing my own research.

I started looking at this former plantation and saying, "This is where we were supposed to be. What a statement to our people, that this could go from a slaveowner to descendants of slaves." It's like putting a crown on all that we've done.

We can do so much with this. We can do lots of healing here. There are so many opportunities for training, so many opportunities for New Communities to develop projects like the pecans and other farming to help support what's being done here.

HELEN COHEN: Is there also an opportunity to do training around community land trusts?

SHIRLEY SHERROD: Yes, I think we could do more in that arena. We could actually help people to understand land trusts, to help start land trusts. We have the setting for that.

HELEN COHEN: Do you still believe in it? Do you still believe in the land trust model of landownership that you and Sherrod and others tried to do decades before?

SHIRLEY SHERROD: Oh yes. Oh yes. This place is ideal for so much that we can do collectively to take our people from one level to the next. We can get our people to understand what it means to own land collectively. Each of us doesn't have to have a deed. That was the point before. We all own it together; it's ours. We can probably make that point and maybe get people to listen to us a little more when you bring them to this place out here. Now they know *everything* is possible [laughter].

We couldn't have done any better, I don't think, looking for a place after all these years, after the loss we've been through, to be fortunate enough to land a place like this. Now we can do even more, I think, than we could have in earlier years to help our people heal, to help get them training, and to get them working together for the good of all.

My mother was telling me about a young cousin. I think he's about ten or twelve years old. He went up to her at church one Sunday. He had seen me on the news a lot by then. He already knew me, but now people really pay attention because of what happened. He said proudly, "My grandmother took me to see the Plantation." They couldn't come on the land because she didn't have a code to get in the gate. But she had him standing out there at the mailbox, talking to him about this place, and that house.

It made me see how we can use this place, this Cypress Pond Plantation that was once owned by the largest slaveowner and the wealthiest man in Georgia, to help reach our young people, to help them know their history, and to help them heal and be able to move forward. This is a special place. These are special grounds.

2.

Mtamanika Youngblood

The Practitioner Who Promoted Equitable
Development, from New Communities to
Urban Neighborhoods

Interviewed by Helen Cohen
March 21, 2011 & May 3, 2012

Mtamanika Youngblood moved to Albany, Georgia in 1971. She registered voters for the Southwest Georgia Project and marketed farm products for New Communities Inc., a pioneering community land trust. She moved to Atlanta in 1977, earned an MBA, and went to work for Bell-South. Switching careers, she became a renowned community development consultant and practitioner. She was the first Executive Director of the Historic District Development Corporation and later served as Director of Neighborhood Transformation for the Casey Foundation. She convened and guided the committee that created the Atlanta Land Trust Collaborative to promote equitable development along Atlanta's BeltLine, the largest urban infrastructure project in the United States at the time.

HELEN COHEN: Let's begin with your personal history and your introduction to Albany, Georgia and New Communities.

MTAMANIKA YOUNGBLOOD: I was raised in New York City, in Jamaica, Queens. I attended New York University. I was the co-chair of the Black student organization at NYU. One of the things that we did was connect with other Black organizations on campuses around the country. There was an organization called the Student Organization for Black Unity, which had the idea of having students at northern universities and colleges connect with projects in the South and having students at southern universities and colleges connect with projects in the North.

I was at NYU, so I was supposed to be connected with a southern project. The project I was originally assigned to was in Washington, DC. While DC is southern in many respects, it wasn't in my mind. I told them to go back to the drawing board and to find another project for me.

They said, "There's a guy in Albany, Georgia with hundreds of acres of watermelons needing to be marketed." I knew almost nothing about Albany other than hearing about the difficulty Doctor King had encountered there. But, since I was a marketing major, I was fascinated by the idea. I eventually took about twelve other students from NYU on a trip to Albany in January, during our winter break. The vastness of New Communities was not understandable for me until I got there, particularly for someone who had lived on the corner of Eighth Street and Fifth Avenue. I was faced with six thousand acres of land, much of which was open. There were rather large stands of pine trees and lakes and ponds, but a good portion of the six thousand acres was actually open land, fields that had already been tilled during their previous ownership. I fell in love with the people and the whole idea and the notion of building New Communities.

Within six months of graduating from NYU, I found myself back in Albany. I was initially the operator of an African boutique. Like many places during that time, Albany had no representation of anything cultural for African Americans. If you wanted a dashiki or any African cloth, or even a note card that had an African or Black image on it, you couldn't get it. So, I operated something called the Harambee Shop which sold incense, dashikis and African jewelry, clothing, and books and that sort of thing.

I did that for about a year. I was also volunteering with the Southwest Georgia Project doing voter registration, marching, sitting in, rallying for civil rights, and talking to young people about being active and engaged, the whole gamut of marching and sitting in. During the day, I ran the Harambee Shop.

HELEN COHEN: Could you talk about being introduced to Charles and Shirley Sherrod. What was your relationship with them?

MTAMANIKA YOUNGBLOOD: SNCC had projects in Alabama, Mississippi, and all over the South. The Southwest Georgia Project was SNCC's presence in that part of Georgia. The home base was in Albany, but it covered all those counties in southwest Georgia. Charles Sherrod was the Project's director. I met Charles . . . hmmm, how did I meet Sherrod? Probably when I first came down to Albany, while I was still in school. I think that's when I met him. It's also when I met Shirley who was just beginning the development of a childcare facility at New Communities.

When I came back to live in Georgia, I lived with them for a few months. I was their house guest, and we became good friends. I worked with them for years. I'd like to think we're still good friends. They were, in many ways, my mentors, people from whom I learned discipline and commitment. They're inspiring. I mean, the things that they've endured, that they went through, the bravery of doing what they were doing in a very hostile place. You think of Shirley's history and what happened with the murder of her father in Baker

County. They have my utmost respect for what they've done. And they're *still* doing it, you know. Forty years later and they're still doing it. These are people who still love and care about other people and are simply trying to make things better. It's just remarkable.

Helen Cohen: You were soon working full-time at New Communities, yes?

MTAMANIKA YOUNGBLOOD: Because I was a marketing major at NYU, I was asked to become the marketing specialist at New Communities. I ended up being the person who negotiated with the large granaries for our soybeans and corn and the processing facilities for the peanut allotment. In addition to the row crops, I marketed the hogs and cattle. So, within a year of moving to Albany, I found myself on a 6,000-acre farm, managing the office at New Communities and marketing everything from collard greens to hogs.

HELEN COHEN: That was quite a contrast to where you had grown up.

MTAMANIKA YOUNGBLOOD: The situation in Lee County was in some ways similar to New York City and in many ways vastly different. Racism and segregation play out in all kinds of ways in cities and rural areas. I was used to the kind of poverty you experience in urban settings, but the poverty that I saw in rural Georgia was abject.

I remember the first time I got off Interstate 75, south of Cordele, and drove down the road towards Albany. As I was driving, I saw the shacks and I could see from the road that some had dirt floors. There was outside plumbing and an outhouse right next door to the house. Obvious signs of abject poverty. It was startling to me. I found myself asking over and over again, why? And what can I do about it, how can I fix it? Well, if not fix it, what part can I play to alleviate some of it?

To a great extent, that's what we were doing at New Communities.

It was not for everyone, but we had hoped the model could be used to address some of the issues that I saw. It was the rural South, a place that was very hard for African Americans.

HELEN COHEN: Could you say more about your role at New Communities?

MTAMANIKA YOUNGBLOOD: We had a very resourceful and energetic farm manager who saw this as an opportunity to do all the things that you can do on six thousand acres of land. We grew and raised everything from strawberries, collard greens, turnip greens, and watermelons to sugar cane and grapes. We made syrup, jelly and jam, and smoked the meat we raised on the farm.

We had a three-hundred-and-twenty-eight-acre peanut allotment and we grew hundreds of acres of seed corn and soy beans and everything that could grow. We didn't raise chickens and we didn't grow cotton, but we did everything else.

I have incredible respect for farmers. It is a very hard job. You do all this work, and you hope it yields something. Then you go to bed at night, and you wake up the next morning and there are insects, or there are floods. You are at the whim of nature. But it is an amazing kind of life. You grow to love the land and to respect the people who work it.

Community Ownership of Land

HELEN COHEN: How did you come to see landownership as being such a priority in the African American community?

MTAMANIKA YOUNGBLOOD: The thing that was facing us so bluntly in the Sixties and Seventies was the denial of civil rights. Most of our efforts were spent trying to address that issue and issues related to it. But, at some point, we recognized that economic opportunity was connected to civil rights and that economic opportunity also meant the opportunity for independence of a kind that we had never had, except within segregated communities. With the movement towards desegregation and the desire for civil rights, we recognized that was only half of the puzzle. Other pieces were connected to our economic viability as a community. If you continued the upward movement toward justice and equality, clearly you would come to the conclusion that economic justice and economic opportunity were just as important. You really couldn't have one without the other. You may be able to sit at the lunch counter, but if you don't have the money to buy a donut, does it matter?

The idea behind New Communities was to take civil rights one step further into economic independence and economic rights. New Communities provided an opportunity to create a self-sustaining community on land owned by the community, where the community owned the means of production, and the revenue and income could be utilized for the good of the folks that were there. It was to be a somewhat independent place for people who were low-income and people who wanted to come together in a place where there was not just a source of food from farming. As I said, there was a day care center that had been developed. We were eventually going to build housing.

So, we were really creating a "new community." We were on a path to building on this land, slowly but surely, the foundation for a community that involved local farmers, local businesspeople, local activists, and just regular folks who were all engaged in trying to make life better. The economic basis for that community was going to be farming. Using agriculture to form the basis for economic development, we farmed everything we could conceivably farm.

HELEN COHEN: How important was it to you and to the other people involved in building New Communities that you were pioneering a new model of land tenure that became known as a community land trust?

When I decided to join New Communities and found out about it, the concept was already established. I knew the land was to be held in trust for the benefit of the people who were there, and for generations to come. The notion of a community land trust is that the land is held in perpetuity for the community. New Communities was a different kind of community where there was collective ownership of land and, therefore, the collective responsibility that went it. I found that attractive and inspiring, and I wanted to be a part of it.

We didn't talk a lot about the fact that it was a community land trust once it was established and had the requisite legal form and structure that it would allow New Communities to operate as such. We were mainly concerned with trying to function in what I characterized earlier as a hostile environment. We still did those things that we knew were important, like school desegregation, voter education, voter registration, and those sorts of things, but we really had to do our best to ensure that this was a viable financial operation. The land had been acquired with loans from major religious institutions. It had a mortgage and mortgage payments needed to be made. We had the responsibility of operating a substantial business that happened to be a farm.

New Communities attracted a lot of folks, including me, mostly young people from all over the country, Black and White, who were drawn to the idea of building something that would better the lives of African Americans in southwest Georgia. We had young people who had gone to jail and who had participated in the Civil Rights Movement at a fairly significant level. The fact that we were operating a community land trust was of lesser interest to them and lesser known to them than what we were doing on the land and how we were doing it. That was what really attracted them.

White Reaction, White Resistance

HELEN COHEN: What was the response to New Communities from the local White community?

MTAMANIKA YOUNGBLOOD: We're talking about the late Sixties and, for me, the very early Seventies, around 1971. The progress that we were making in the South with respect to civil rights was still slowly unfolding in places like Lee County, Georgia, which was where the farm was located. There was a negative and nasty reaction to our being there.

There were African Americans from the area who were becoming empowered, and White folks didn't like that. You had people who had come to New Communities, many of us from the northern part of the country. African Americans, White people, low-income people, all kinds of folks were apparently coming together to work for good. It was resented.

I lived in a house in Terrell County when I first got to Albany, right outside of Lee County. The house had bullet holes in the windows and walls. The woman who previously lived there was an activist. The bullet holes were still in the house. Late at night, there'd be bright lights that would shine on that house and wake me up. It was a tough time. Of course, I didn't have to deal with the roughest of it, but many folks did and it continued into the Seventies.

The reaction from the White community was simply that you're not welcome; you're trying to change things; we like things the way they are; we're going to push back just as hard as you push forward. We were in southwest Georgia, you know. There was "Terrible Terrell" County and "Bad Baker" County. I can't remember what we called Dougherty County or Lee County, but it was scary. These were places where Black people had been lynched and killed. People were really taking their lives in their hands to do this work.

We were being activists and advocates at the same time that we were doing the kinds of things that you need to do to run a successful operation. We had to sell our seed corn to the local grain elevator, for example. It was, of course, owned and operated by White men who were not at all pleased with either our presence or with the activist side of our efforts.

It was a very tough situation. You know, there were African Americans, there were White people, there were all kinds of folks who were living together and working together in New Communities and at nearby Koinonia Farm. The local White population didn't like it at all.

You had to be careful when you went anywhere, especially at night. It was dangerous. It made everyone who was working at New Communities in those days very strong in terms of our relationships and the collective effort. You looked out for each other. You cared about each other. You wanted to make sure that everybody got home at night.

It was character forming and shaping. Those experiences taught me a lot about what it really takes to be effective, the notion of working with others and knowing that you can't do this alone. I got a grounding that I've never forgotten and that lives with me today about the value of land, of independence, of economic development and opportunity.

Losing the Land, Winning the Lawsuit

HELEN COHEN: You went to Atlanta after New Communities. Was it a tough decision to leave?

MTAMANIKA YOUNGBLOOD: Oh sure. You know, my perspective on these things is that when I think I can be helpful and give the best that I can and provide the most of me, that's when I do it. When I feel like things have moved on or that something has changed—or that I've changed—it's time to move on.

I was really looking to do something else. I was still young. I wanted to do some other things in addition to what I'd done at New Communities, but I didn't want to go back to New York. Despite everything, I decided that I really liked the South. It was a choice between Atlanta and Florida, and I ended up in Atlanta. I got married, had a life, and moved on.

But, in many ways, I stayed connected to the cooperative movement because of the work of my husband, so I always knew what was happening at New Communities. He'd come back from meetings at the Federation of Southern Cooperatives and tell me that Shirley said to say "hello." Or he'd say that Sherrod asked about me. So I was always aware of how things were going. I knew that the farm was having some difficulty. I hoped for the best.

HELEN COHEN: What was it like for you to hear that New Communities had fallen victim to discrimination and had lost its land?

MTAMANIKA YOUNGBLOOD: The loss of New Communities was crushing. Much of that, much of my feeling of being crushed, was for Shirley and Charles and for the folks who were there when I got there and were still there when I left. It was very, very personal. And then, of course, to have lost the largest tract of land owned by African Americans in the country to the same forces that had caused farmers of color to lose their land all over the country, was just hurtful. To have that happen twenty years after the Civil Rights Movement really took off and pressed against the racist structure was debilitating and very, very sad. It was like a scar in your soul, especially for Sherrod and Shirley.

I had a conversation with my brother the other night. He's still sorrowful about it. He looks back at the loss of the land and shakes his head. He's still very sad. You know, farming is hard. To lose the land, given the blood, sweat, and tears that go into it, was devastating. It was hard to let it go.

HELEN COHEN: Your younger brother worked on the farm?

MTAMANIKA YOUNGBLOOD: Yeah, once I got to New Communities and realized what the opportunity was, I was in frequent contact with my family. They would come to visit. My brother, who was at Malcolm X University in North Carolina, eventually became the hog herdsman, if you can believe it. Here's this boy from New York City managing hundreds of hogs! He met a woman and fell in love in Lee County and is still in Albany today.

HELEN COHEN: How did you learn about the loss of the land?

MTAMANIKA YOUNGBLOOD: I was getting reports that the farm was in trouble. I knew the reasons: the inability of Black farmers to get the kind of financial support that is given to White farmers when there's a drought, for example. You need irrigation and you need loans, the sort of financial support that agencies are set up to provide. I also knew very well the local political environment, that many of the decisions of those government agencies are made locally.

New Communities was a major farming operation. Just like all farms, it was dependent on the Farmers Home Administration and all those county services and state agencies that make farming a viable business for local farmers. New Communities was not seen kindly in that context. There was a very specific effort to undermine the work that we were doing.

When I heard about the farm's difficulties, there was a sense of helplessness about it. I was still hopeful that somehow something would happen. The Sherrods had been through so much and done so much. I had some hope they could somehow pull this out. But there was also a realization that this was going to be difficult. When those forces are aligned against you, it was going to be hard to overcome.

I didn't hear anything for a while. Then I got the news that they had lost the land. And it was crushing.

HELEN COHEN: Years later, were you aware of the lawsuit against the US Department of Agriculture?

MTAMANIKA YOUNGBLOOD: I wasn't closely involved during the time, but I kept up and I heard about the suit. As I said earlier, because of the work of my husband and his connection to the cooperative movement, I would get reports and hear about things. Shirley was working at the Federation. I thought that was the perfect place for her to be. And the Southwest Georgia Project was continuing to do projects, mainly for women—rural women. I felt good about that.

When I found out that Shirley and Charles were going to make New Communities a part of the Black farmers' lawsuit, I was delighted. I got a call from Sherrod, who asked if I had any information, any material, that could be used in the case. Even though I had managed the office, I didn't take anything with me when I left. All I could do was to recount some things that I remembered that had occurred. But I didn't have any documentation that could help with the suit. I could only give moral support from afar.

HELEN COHEN: What was your reaction when you heard about the lawsuit's outcome?

MTAMANIKA YOUNGBLOOD: I was like, "Wow this is amazing!" I was shocked when I first heard that New Communities had actually won. When I learned how *much* they'd won in the settlement, I was twice as happy [laughter]. This is wonderful. This is good. It's the right thing happening. It was incredible. I was very happy and delighted and thought that every now and then justice is done.

I then had a subsequent contact with Shirley, and she started talking about what had occurred. I later had the good fortune of riding back from a conference with Rose Sanders, the attorney who had tried the case for New Communities. I got all the background and all the inside dope on what had happened and how things had unfolded.

You know, one of the heroines in this story is Rose Sanders. Here's this African American attorney in Alabama, dedicated to the idea that this can be done and that this case was triable and winnable. She doggedly pursued it and did everything an attorney can do to make certain that the result was the right one, a good one. And she did it.

I knew all this from afar. But then to have the opportunity to spend those hours in the car with her and to hear the back story, it was wonderful. I remember getting out of the car and feeling really good.

Cypress Pond Plantation

HELEN COHEN: Could you talk about the process of purchasing the new property with the money that settled that lawsuit?

MTAMANIKA YOUNGBLOOD: Shirley and I had been in contact. Over the months after the case was won, we were emailing back and forth. I was really just staying in touch to see how they were doing. At some point she called and said she really needed to talk to me. I said "okay," so we made the time, just the two of us. She said that she and Sherrod really wanted to buy more land, use the money from the settlement to buy more land. I thought that was a good idea,

But she mentioned the word "farming" in the conversation and I'm thinking, "Hmmm, I'm not sure that is such a good idea." Racism and prejudice and all of that had a great deal to do with what happened to New Communities, but it also occurred in the waning years of family farms and the rise of agribusiness and huge conglomerate farming operations. The thought of trying to go back to that, thirty years later, just didn't make a lot of sense to me. I was really skeptical and told Shirley why farming seemed like a bad idea.

Shirley said, "We are talking about doing some kind of special organic thing, something that has a viable future market and would allow us to be competitive." But I wasn't really too high on that. She said, "Okay, we'll just keep you in the loop."

She later called back to say that they had identified a piece of property. When she said it had an antebellum mansion on it, I'm like, "What on earth are they thinking?" I had this vision of a big structure with white columns and a porch. All kinds of negative images flooded into my mind. I was respectful, lovingly of Shirley, but I was like, "Really, is that what you want to do? I'm not sure about that. Let me get on the website and look at this place."

I had difficulty getting to the website; the link wasn't working. We went back and forth about it, as they were getting closer to seriously considering it. Finally, I had to leave because I was going out of the country for a month. She said, "We need to make a decision." I said, "Well, you should do what you think you should do."

When I got back, she told me they had bought the land and she said, "You really need to see it." We then spent a great deal of time talking over several months, going back and forth about when our schedules would allow for a visit. Finally, I was able to go, and I've been hooked ever since. It's an amazing place.

HELEN COHEN: How long did it take you to feel that way?

MTAMANIKA YOUNGBLOOD: Well, when I first got there, I saw that it was clearly a well-developed piece of property. "Farm" is kind of a misnomer. This is more than a farm. In some ways, it's a preserve. You go through the gate and there are these wonderful pecan trees, and you can see the pond and the roads and the facilities. Then, when I got to the main house, I was like, "Okay [laughter], I get it. This is really an opportunity for special events and retreats and conferences."

I get to see lots of old buildings and facilities that are restored in my preservation world. This was a property the likes of which I had not seen. Understanding the economic development opportunity that the house would provide, and seeing the breadth and depth of the property, with the lake and fields that could be used for some kind of small and appropriate farming operation, I could see that this was something that was worth the effort.

They got a good price on it because of a slump in the real estate market. That was a sweetener, you know, not only to get the right property, but to get it at the right price was even better. All of that was combined, of course, with Shirley and Sherrod's enthusiasm. I'm listening to it and getting infected with their vision and opportunity for it. All of that helped me understand.

Before I went to visit for the first time, Shirley had sent an email that kind of characterized all of the opportunities. So, my interest was piqued even before I got there. I was replaying in my head what I had read, as I'm going from the house to the cottages that were all very well appointed. I could see how this could be a place that has resonance and lots of opportunity for economic development.

I should also say, however, that when I heard the history of the property, it was troubling. You know, understanding that there had been a slaver who originally owned the property. He became the richest man in Georgia because of the number of enslaved people he owned. That was troubling, so we talked a lot about it. We had to really come to grips with being able to get beyond the history of the place.

HELEN COHEN: The purchase of that property really turns history on its head.

MTAMANIKA YOUNGBLOOD: Yeah, it really does. Just think about the descendants of slaves eventually being the owners of the mansion and the land.

Life is interesting. You never know what you're going to end up with. Losing the land was torturous and very sad. But to have the settlement and to have what has happened to Shirley personally as a backdrop and then to have this land. Who could have predicted this road and this path and this destination? Who could have predicted that? No one, no one. But, in some ways, it really is the arc of justice.

HELEN COHEN: What do you anticipate your own involvement with this property might be going forward?

MTAMANIKA YOUNGBLOOD: Given my history with New Communities, my relationship with the Sherrods, and the work that I've been doing since I left New Communities, which is community economic development, historic preservation, and community revitalization, the board of directors of New Communities has asked me to become a member. Before I said yes, however, I wanted to make sure there were some things in place that I knew were going to be important. We're making decisions about sixteen hundred acres, which is not a little bit of land. But it's a *finite* number of acres. If we decide to do one thing, that may mean we can't do another.

I'm a proponent of good planning. It occurred to me that, before we get too much further down the road, we really need to do a master plan of the site. Then we'll know where we should put the conference center and what we should add, or how many more acres of pecan trees are really appropriate, or what kind of crop to plant as opposed to another, or where to site certain activities for the best use of the topography. I wanted to make certain that we are going to be good stewards of this resource.

Championing Community Land Trusts in Atlanta

HELEN COHEN: You've been a dedicated torch bearer for community land trusts during your many years of doing community development work in Atlanta. Why? What led you to become such an advocate for the CLT?

MTAMANIKA YOUNGBLOOD: The community land trust model, particularly as it was developed at New Communities, was basically about holding and preserving land for the community, especially the African American community. Obviously, there were others who were working with us, but the object really was to hold land for African Americans who had lost so much and been duped out of so much of their land, particularly in the South. We felt it was very important for us to be able to hold onto land for the African American community.

Having had the benefit of the experience of New Communities, one of the first things I did when I began doing community development work here in Atlanta was to seek out and talk to people who, at the time, were running community land trusts in Atlanta. This was the late Eighties, early Nineties. There were three that I can remember. The one closest to the King Historic District, the next neighborhood over, was in Cabbagetown. CRAFT was the name of the organization. It was a community land trust in Atlanta, but it was not catching on in Atlanta. That wasn't because the community land trust wasn't a good model. It was because CRAFT and the two other CLTs in Atlanta were nonprofit organizations that needed good leadership and resources. All the things that any nonprofit needs to survive, they just didn't have them. Therefore, these early efforts didn't succeed—not because the CLT was a bad idea; but because they were nonprofits that just didn't have what they needed to succeed.

When I began doing my community development work here in Atlanta in the King Historic District, in the Old Fourth Ward, I realized that you need to put mechanisms in place early on and up front. If you don't, market forces will do what the market does—seek its highest level. So, affordability becomes a problem. And you find that those who *were* able to buy, people who might be willing to hold onto their land, are bought out. Someone comes along with a very significant offer. The owners think that they're making a killing and they sell and leave. The land, once owned by African Americans or by other people of color, ends up being owned by others. We have a whole history around the country of all the kinds of things that have been done to African Americans to basically steal their land.

Being very cognizant of that, I wanted to make sure that we could improve places without that happening. We can revitalize communities for the African Americans who are there, and they have the opportunity to stay and to hold onto the land.

HELEN COHEN: When did you begin working in the Pittsburgh neighborhood?

MTAMANIKA YOUNGBLOOD: After doing all the work here, in the King Historic District, I began working in the Pittsburgh neighborhood in Atlanta. I remember taking a tour of the neighborhood—this was in January 2004 or maybe December of 2003. I was struck by how many houses there were in this relatively small neighborhood. There were small lots, all kinds of bungalows and craftsmen's houses and shotgun houses. It occurred to me then that, if the Pittsburgh community was going to revitalize itself, the first thing we needed to do was to get control of this land and put it in a community land trust.

I was consulting for the Casey Foundation at the time. I wrote a paper, sort of a memorandum, saying that if you are serious about affordable housing and community revitalization in this neighborhood, we really need to be thinking about establishing a community land trust. That was in February of 2004.

HELEN COHEN: What was their response?

MTAMANIKA YOUNGBLOOD: Well, at the time the Foundation was not really interested in doing development. The Foundation's work was around human development, not physical development. At that point, they were not willing to get into acquiring properties. It's not what they did.

I'm a big proponent of revitalization happening from the inside out, not from the outside in. I was mentoring the executive director of the Pittsburgh Community Improvement Association, LaShawn Hoffman's predecessor. I was helping him out with his board and getting him to understand what a community development corporation was supposed to do. I introduced the community land trust concept to him, to the staff and to the board. I explained why it was an important concept and why they should be considering it.

If they were thinking seriously about revitalizing their neighborhood, I wanted them to see what the implications would be. Right now, you look at the neighborhood and you might think, "This isn't going to be anything at any time. Nobody cares about this neighborhood." But you have to have the vision to look out twenty or thirty years and to understand that this will be a very attractive place for the people who are here and for their children. You need to be able to hold on to it. And holding on to it, frankly, is holding onto the land.

Any time that I had the opportunity to talk about community revitalization that was for the people who were originally the residents of a particular neighborhood, I always talked about community land trusts. It's a way to ensure affordability, not just for that first homeowner. My experience has shown that you can put a low-income family into a very affordable structure but when the unfettered market takes off, even this low-income family will want to take all the equity out of their property. It might have had an affordable price when they bought it, but when they sell it, it's a market-rate property. That's good for them, but it's certainly not good for maintaining an affordable community.

I've had to learn that the hard way. I feel very strongly about African Americans holding onto land. Whether it's rural or urban, the community land trust is a vehicle for doing that and for ensuring that, when neighborhoods change, the existing residents will get to hold onto their property. They get to benefit from the change that happens. It allows for their children, and their children's children, and the children of others who may also want to live in a neighborhood that's now nice, viable, and attractive. Low-income folks generally get pushed out of places like that.

HELEN COHEN: You were advocating for this during the boom years in the Atlanta real estate market?

MTAMANIKA YOUNGBLOOD: Oh yeah, 2004 was clearly in the boom time.

HELEN COHEN: Did you encounter opposition to the idea?

MTAMANIKA YOUNGBLOOD: Oh yeah [laughter]. The first reaction was, "Well, we tried that in Atlanta and it didn't work." Remember the earlier days I talked about, CRAFT and SALT and those earlier land trusts that were in Atlanta?

Beyond that, the notion of a community land trust really requires buying into the concept of community ownership. Which is hard, because it's contrary to the American way of owning your own piece of dirt. To get people to understand the value of a community owning land together has been a tough row to hoe. (That's a pun from my farming days, I guess.) They say, "Why should I buy a property in a community land trust when I can go somewhere else and buy not just the structure, but the land as well?"

That was the reaction. It just felt like a strange, foreign kind of concept to people. It was out of the ordinary. It was not in the mainstream of housing and development policy. So, there was a bit of pushback, even from people working on behalf of residents and communities who, you would think, would understand the value of it.

HELEN COHEN: Did your message eventually find more understanding and acceptance?

MTAMANIKA YOUNGBLOOD: As I was working with the Casey Foundation and AHAND (Atlanta Housing Association of Neighborhood-based Developers) and, later, with the Atlanta BeltLine Partnership, we spent a good deal of time getting to know what had happened with the first land trusts in Atlanta, wanting to understand what had caused them not to be successful. We wanted to come up with a way to respond when people raised the point that it had been tried before and had not worked.

We were also deliberate and thoughtful about trying to bring the broader community into the fold in terms of understanding the value of a community land trust. We've been somewhat successful in doing that, particularly as housing prices were increasing. It was looking like, if we didn't get a handle on some property pretty soon, the speculative market was going to make it impossible for people to stay in their neighborhoods.

We should have anticipated that all bubbles burst eventually, as the housing market did in Pittsburgh. But that just gave us an opportunity to acquire some property and put it into a community land trust.

HELEN COHEN: Have people bought into it now?

MTAMANIKA YOUNGBLOOD: Yeah. I think that we've had good support and good success in getting the broader community interested in the concept of community land trusts, mainly because of the lack of affordable housing in Atlanta. It's a real issue. The community land trust model is a mechanism for not just ensuring affordability for that first homeowner or that first renter, but for subsequent owners and renters. Government entities have come to understand that it's also a much better use of subsidies. I mean, you put in a subsidy, you provide downpayment assistance for a homeowner, and it's usually for some limited time frame like five years. They stay in the house and then, when they sell the house, they get all that equity. Housing prices are generally increasing. The equity accumulates and they take that equity, and they leave. So, the subsidy's gone and you've helped one homeowner.

With the community land trust, because the subsidy is technically in the ground, you allow that subsidy to have a much longer life and to support affordability for more than just one family. I think that governments—local, state and national—have come to understand the value of community land trusts as a way to recycle subsidy. There's never enough of it, so you really have to be smart about how you use it.

The Atlanta Land Trust Collaborative

HELEN COHEN: Could you talk about the Atlanta BeltLine and your own involvement in it?

MTAMANIKA YOUNGBLOOD: I was involved in a project when I was working here in the Historic District. It was called Studioplex. It was an old cotton compress warehouse that we developed into lofts and places for artists to live and work. It's right on what is now the

Atlanta BeltLine. It's right on the railroad track. You open your back door, and the railroad track is there. The idea at the time was to turn that railbed into a cultural ring. There would be electric buses that would run along this track and take you to various cultural sites around the city, whether it was Zoo Atlanta, the High Museum, the Carter Center, etc. There was going to be a charging station for the buses near Studioplex.

That was an early idea which was called the Atlanta Cultural Ring. I liked it, but for lots of reasons it didn't work out. Later, Ryan Gravel came up with the idea of the Atlanta BeltLine. He got the Atlanta City Council president, Cathy Woolard, interested. Then she got the mayor and other folks involved in it, helping to advance this idea of turning these old rails into trails and parks and development. Because of my community development work and because I had developed a project that's right on what is now the BeltLine, I was asked to be involved as well.

I was on the Atlanta BeltLine's Tax Allocation Task Force, which was the group of citizens that looked at whether you could have money from a district like a TIF or TAD to support the BeltLine. The task force decided, "Yes, you could do that."

Then I was asked to serve on the board of directors of the Atlanta BeltLine Partnership. This was kind of the social equity organization to ensure that this project would benefit all Atlanta citizens, not just those who were in the development community and those of greater means. If you think about the Atlanta BeltLine, it is going to be a world-class amenity. As a general rule, low-income families don't benefit from world-class amenities. The BeltLine was not going to be successful if existing residents and others of lesser means could not partake of it and share in the value of it.

I think the BeltLine is a great idea. It will bring green space and an opportunity to connect neighborhoods which are disconnected. I'm a strong advocate for the effort. But my advocacy is very clear. It is really around ensuring that it benefits all Atlanta citizens.

HELEN COHEN: Is that what led you to get involved in helping to create the blueprint for the Atlanta Land Trust Collaborative?

MTAMINIKA YOUNGBLOOD: Yes, the Atlanta Land Trust Collaborative has been put in place to ensure that the result will be the one I just described. It will be the first new community land trust in Atlanta.

HELEN COHEN: You sound excited.

MTAMANIKA YOUNGBLOOD: Yes, I am. I am excited about the fact that there is an Atlanta Land Trust Collaborative and that it's well supported. There are representatives on the board from the major public agencies that can make a land trust viable and feasible, including the Land Bank Authority, the Atlanta Development Authority, and the City of Atlanta. We've also received good representation from the BeltLine Partnership, the financial community, and the banking community. I think people understand that this is a good thing for Atlanta. Connecting it to the BeltLine was a very smart way to get Atlantans to buy into the idea of community land trusts. That was really smart.

HELEN COHEN: Is there genuine community participation as well, or is it just lip service?

MTAMANIKA YOUNGBLOOD: If you look at who's been involved from the very beginning and who's on the board, we have had community participation. We're trying to expand it, but we're being very deliberate about trying to find people who really have the same passion as the rest of us. We've spent a lot of time and effort trying to ensure that the community, writ large, is engaged.

One of the major efforts that I've got going on right now is in the Pittsburgh neighborhood. We've been looking at ensuring that residents really understand it, buy into it, advocate for it, and are engaged with it. I think we've done a good job of that. Can we do better? Yes, we can always do better.

While we are focusing on community participation in Pittsburgh, it's something that we really need to do across the city, because Pittsburgh is just the first one. We hope to have more community land trusts happening in rapid succession in other neighborhoods that are associated with the BeltLine. There's a very deliberate and strong desire to ensure that residents are really engaged in this effort and the neighborhoods really have a voice.

Think about the structure of a community land trust. Think about who's on the board of a community land trust. In order to be an effective, viable operation—which it needs to be because it's going to own land—you really have to have residents who understand it, who buy into it, and who are willing to work on behalf of it. To do that, you have to engage them. You know, folks have lives; they're busy. This board is a volunteer effort. To get to people to want to participate requires that you really engage them in a meaningful way and that they can see the benefit of it.

HELEN COHEN: You've suggested that it's important, in community development efforts like the BeltLine, to pay attention early on, right up front, to controlling land and putting restrictions on the affordability of housing.

MTAMANIKA YOUNGBLOOD: Yeah, you're going to regret it if you don't.

HELEN COHEN: If you were asked to describe succinctly why you've been such an advocate and supporter of community land trusts, what would you say?

MTAMANIKA YOUNGBLOOD: My experience in community

development, which is fairly long, says that you have to think about what you're trying to achieve and to put the mechanisms in place to ensure it at the very beginning. That is particularly true when it comes to retaining affordability and ensuring that low-income and moderate-income families can continue to live in a neighborhood once it's revitalized. You put resources, subsidies, and efforts into making the first round of properties, houses, or whatever afford-able. But remember, the market always seeks its highest level. Before you know it, the market comes into play, and you don't have the affordability that you had intended. You must address that up front.

A Follow-up Interview with John Emmeus Davis
January 26, 2023

JOHN EMMEUS DAVIS: Helen Cohen previously interviewed you in 2011 and 2012, back when we were filming a pair of documentaries, *Streets of Dreams* and *Arc of Justice: The Rise, Fall, and Rebirth of a Beloved Community*. Here we are again a decade later. Thank you for participating in our latest project, this time for a book rather than for a film.

MTAMANIKA YOUNGBLOOD: As I indicated in our emails back and forth, I'm just delighted that you're keeping on, that you continue to do this work.

JOHN EMMEUS DAVIS: Well, it's been informative and fun for me to collect the stories of unsung heroes who carried the torch from one place to another. These are people who took the lead in planting the seeds for new CLTs in the United States and elsewhere, encouraging the growth and development of the CLT model. You are one of those people. I'm so pleased that you're willing to return to issues and events that you touched upon in those earlier interviews with Helen.

Filming Arc of Justice, *Cypress Pond Plantation, 2012. Pictured: Shirley Sherrod (front); John Davis, Mtamanika Youngblood, and Ann Milton (2nd row); Mark Lipman and Rick Butler (3rd row); Alanna Milton and Helen Cohen (4th row).*

MTAMANIKA YOUNGBLOOD: I'm glad that we were able to schedule a time to talk.

JOHN EMMEUS DAVIS: I want to focus on your work in Atlanta, where you led efforts to revitalize the King Historic District and to plan the Atlanta Land Trust Collaborative. Before discussing those activities, however, there are a few loose ends from your time at New Communities that I'd like to ask you about.

MTAMANIKA YOUNGBLOOD: Okay.

New Communities Inc.

JOHN EMMEUS DAVIS: In one of the interviews that you did with Helen, you said, "We really didn't talk a lot about the fact that New Communities was a community land trust." At what point did you personally come to the realization that this was something extraordinary? Did you and the others at New Communities eventually realize that you were creating something that was quite new, quite revolutionary?

MTAMANIKA YOUNGBLOOD: Hmmm. So, there are two things there. As I said before, we didn't really talk about it being a community land trust. We talked about what we were doing and why we were doing it. But the legal form of it was not really relevant to us at that time.

I did feel like New Communities was something unique and so amazing. When I got there, I realized what the potential and the opportunity might be when I saw that land. That was early on. I got that pretty quickly. But I did not know it was the first community land trust in the country until I saw your presentation.

JOHN EMMEUS DAVIS: You mean later, around 2008, when we were working together in Atlanta?

MTAMANIKA YOUNGBLOOD: Yes, in Atlanta. You presented a PowerPoint about the history of the CLT. I was like, "Oh my God, I know the people in that presentation. That's amazing." That's when I learned that New Communities was the first, that it was a model for other community land trusts.

JOHN EMMEUS DAVIS: Interesting.

MTAMANIKA YOUNGBLOOD: It really is interesting. Because, as I said, we didn't think of it in those terms, that it's the very first one.

We just marveled and reveled in the opportunity and what we were trying to accomplish. The legal form of it was not anything we discussed. It never came up.

JOHN EMMEUS DAVIS: There was a book published in 1972 that held up New Communities as the prototype for a "new model for land tenure in America." Was there any discussion about that book?

MTAMANIKA YOUNGBLOOD: Well, there could have been a conversation that maybe Sherrod engaged in. It's possible. I was the office manager and the marketing specialist, so I had a very hard job. I was very focused. It's possible that there were board members or other people who were having those conversations, but I didn't participate in them.

JOHN EMMEUS DAVIS: Bob Swann and Shimon Gottshalk, two of the people who authored that 1972 book, were present at New Communities early on. But my impression from talking with the Sherrods is that they were seldom there after the book was published. Is that right?

MTAMANIKA YOUNGBLOOD: They were not. Clearly, if they were there, I would've known that. Now, the other thing you have to remember is that I didn't start working at New Communities until 1972. Before that, I had the Harambee Shop to run. I may have heard references to Bob Swann and Shimon Gottshalk. They were names that I might have heard in conversation. But the book? I didn't know anything about it. I kind of knew the origin story of New Communities. That part I knew: going to Israel and coming back and figuring this out. I knew that part. But more detail than that, I just wasn't privy to.

JOHN EMMEUS DAVIS: Here's another loose end that I've long been curious about. In *Arc of Justice*, there's a point where Charles Sherrod says, "We had 500 families who were lined up, who were waiting to move into the housing that we hoped to build." I've always wondered, how did those people get involved in New Communities? To have that many people on a waiting list, kind of watching and waiting to see what was going to happen on the land, is pretty extraordinary. What sort of outreach or messaging had been done by New Communities among the African Americans living in the surrounding counties to get them on that waiting list?

MTAMANIKA YOUNGBLOOD: Hmmm, I would say that "waiting list" might be a stretch. There were many people who expressed an interest in what we were doing. We counted those people, right?

Just as important as the number of people, you have to remember that New Communities was not happening in isolation. It was an offshoot of the Southwest Georgia Project. (Technically, I was employed by the Southwest Georgia Project at a whopping $10 a week.) All the stuff that we did was never disconnected from our organizing, which is what I talked about in those earlier interviews. We had a whole legion of young people getting people registered to vote, pressing for desegregation, addressing all the things that Black folks were suffering under. We did that constantly. That never stopped. Organizing was embedded in everything we did.

JOHN EMMEUS DAVIS: So New Communities was connected to all of the people who you were involving and engaging in other activities?

MTAMANIKA YOUNGBLOOD: Yes, we were meeting with people and talking to them and collecting their information. We'd talk about the Southwest Georgia Project, talk about what it does. We'd talk about the Harambee Shop, say that there was a place you could go to get the things that you couldn't find anywhere else in the area that we were selling. We'd talk about New Communities, of course, because it was such a significant thing.

But the point I want to make—and I'm sure you've figured this out, but I feel like I need to say it—people were afraid. It was so obvious, so prevalent. The counties where the Southwest Georgia Project worked were scary places in the Seventies. Many people were literally living on land owned by White people who did not want them to vote, who did not want them to participate in anything we were doing. They were hostile to that.

I remember being at a meeting and it was late. I stayed overnight with a family. They talked about how, if the person whose land they were on knew I was there, they would probably be evicted.

JOHN EMMEUS DAVIS: Because of your connection to the Southwest Georgia Project?

MTAMANIKA YOUNGBLOOD: Right, and my connection to this larger effort. The point of New Communities was to give those people the freedom to be and to do as they pleased without fear of retribution. That was pretty significant because it meant you would not lose the place you had to live.

In the counties surrounding Albany, we could have been in the 1920s, given the way those counties were run. Black folks were willing to participate in our efforts, but they understood what the repercussions could be. Our point was: if you are living with us, you don't have to worry about that. We are trying to make a place for you where you can be the person you want to be, a fully participating citizen.

From that perspective, the opportunity to live at New Communities was very exciting. That was one of the things we talked about. We asked if they would be interested and 90% of the people said yes. Some people said no, don't put me on that list. But 90% of the folks said yes. That's how we got this list. We didn't characterize it as a waiting list but, in many ways, I guess it was.

JOHN EMMEUS DAVIS: What you were selling was security of tenure, yes? A secure hold of your housing on community-owned land became the pre-condition for full participation as a citizen.

MTAMANIKA YOUNGBLOOD: That is correct. And depending on your circumstances, you could also work on the land.

JOHN EMMEUS DAVIS: It was an opportunity for a livelihood as well?

MTAMANIKA YOUNGBLOOD: Right. We had 6,000 acres of land. The plan was to do everything you need to do to have a community. That would've required the participation of all kinds of people who had all kinds of skills and all kinds of abilities.

JOHN EMMEUS DAVIS: The independence that comes from having a secure place to live and a secure livelihood is what allows you to participate politically as a full citizen?

MTAMANIKA YOUNGBLOOD: Yes, exactly. Frankly it was something I never thought about until I got to the South, and I realized it's like 1920. You register to vote, and you've got to be gone by tomorrow, or they'll come and throw your stuff out on the road and put you off the land. The ability of White landowners to do that is what kept people in fear. You could lose your life. That's a real thing. But you could also lose your job. You could lose your house. Then what do you have? What are you going to do?

The thing about New Communities is that it offered freedom. I don't know how else to say it. It offered freedom to be a fully realized person and to participate to the extent you were interested in participating politically.

Settling into Atlanta, 1977–1987

JOHN EMMEUS DAVIS: I want to shift the conversation to Atlanta, if I may. What year did you move there?

MTAMANIKA YOUNGBLOOD: I moved to Atlanta in January of 1977 in an ice storm. I was leaving New Communities. I was making $10 a week, so when I left I had nothing. I needed a car since I was moving to Atlanta and Atlanta did not have public transportation. My father gave me his old 1968 Pontiac Bonneville. It was the size of an ocean liner.

I slipped and slid in this car in an ice storm over to Georgia State. I had decided to take Sherrod up on his suggestion and get an MBA. So, I applied to Georgia State. At first, they turned me down and then they said, "Oh yeah, come." I was sitting in this big room at Georgia State. I had my transcript, and I was waiting to discuss classes with the counselor. I'm sitting there and I literally got a chill. I'm like, "You know what? I don't think I want to do this." I got up, I went outside, and I asked a security guard, "How do you get to Atlanta University?" He said, "Oh, okay. You go here, blah, blah, blah." I got back in the car and slipped and slid my way over to Atlanta University. I had my transcript and money that I had borrowed, and I enrolled on the spot.

There's a funny part to this story I will share, just because it's you. When I hand over my transcript from NYU, there's nothing on it but A's and B's. Then there's one D. I'm sitting in the Dean's office. I know when the Dean is looking at that D. He says, "Tell me about that course in Black history. There's a D there. All these As and Bs and then there's this." And he's looking at me, right? I told him, "Well, needless to say, the instructor and I did not agree on his perspective on Black history."

Anyway, that was that. I enrolled in 1977 and graduated in 1978. I went through pretty quickly. I did two years of graduate work in little less than a year and a half. Then I went to work because I was broke. I got recruited by Southern Bell. The telephone company was a good place to work at the time and I needed the money. So that's what I did.

JOHN EMMEUS DAVIS: You stayed with Southern Bell for a number of years?

MTAMANIKA YOUNGBLOOD: Yes, I stayed at Southern Bell. The job I had was involved in the court-ordered divestiture. A federal judge had forced the Bells to break up. They were under a consent decree to do that. They had to break up and they had to hire more Black people. I was one of those Black people that they hired.

I worked at headquarters. I did operational reviews and traveled all over the region. It was a pretty significant job. It got to the point where I either had to be willing to be pushed even further in terms of promotion or just let it go. I had a job that was very interesting, but I didn't want to do it. I felt like I can't spend this much time and this much effort enriching the telephone company. I need to do something else.

It was the late Eighties when there was a rash of corporate buyouts. You know, if you get rid of these middle management people, you can save all this money, blah, blah, blah, blah. But the buyout never materialized. Then finally they came up with a program called Career Alternative Plan. They were giving middle management an off-ramp. If you taught school, went back to school, or worked for a nonprofit, they would give you one-quarter of your salary and you could keep your benefits for three years, which was fabulous. I think I was the very first person in the Bell system to take them up on it.

JOHN EMMEUS DAVIS: Was that your transition into the world of community development?

MTAMANIKA YOUNGBLOOD: That was my transition. Initially I was consulting for the Southern Cooperative Development Fund. I was working with rural women on business development. Sometimes they'd ask me to help them do strategic planning and things like that. I was connected to them because my husband, George Howell, was very much involved in the Federation of Southern Cooperatives, the Southern Cooperative Development Fund, and the Emergency Land Fund. All those groups were a part of our lives.

JOHN EMMEUS DAVIS: Your husband was an attorney?

MTAMANIKA YOUNGBLOOD: Yes, he was *their* attorney. So, there was a connection, and I was involved with them too although obviously to a lesser degree.

I took the buyout and started consulting. But just before the buyout, I had moved into a very scary neighborhood.

We had a beautiful house. We lived in the suburbs, but I hated it. I spent my life in my car. We decided, "We can't do this. We need to move into town." So, we made a conscious decision to live in a Black community.

We were of the opinion that we could live anywhere. My husband was originally from Chattanooga and went to school in Knoxville. He went to Washington DC, got his law degree and lived in DC, and then moved to Atlanta. I came from New York. I can live anywhere, right? I'm from New York, what can't I handle? We can do this. We can buy this big raggedy old house in this very scary neighborhood.

JOHN EMMEUS DAVIS: This was in Atlanta's Old Fourth Ward?

MTAMANIKA YOUNGBLOOD: Yeah. It had been designated an historic district in 1979 or 1980. We bought the house in 1984, moved into it in 1985. My daughter was four weeks old when we moved in. I had a four-week-old baby, and we were in a scary neighborhood. We took a lot of ridicule from people because they said, "You have moved from that beautiful house to this, to the ghetto. What is wrong with you people?"

JOHN EMMEUS DAVIS: Talk about that "scary neighborhood." What were the conditions when you arrived?

MTAMANIKA YOUNGBLOOD: It was this little neighborhood between one of the wealthiest neighborhoods in Atlanta and downtown. It had some Victorians and craftsmen, but mostly a lot of shotguns and bungalows. A lot of the owners, many of them absentee, were renting them out for various reasons, none of them good. And there were a lot of vacant lots, because the structures had become sub-standard and were eventually demolished. Some of the dilapidated houses were vacant, some of them were occupied, but they were all dilapidated. The house we bought needed a lot of work.

Most of the residents, 95% of the neighborhood, were elderly, low-income women. When they passed away, their houses became vacant and drug dealers and prostitutes moved in.

JOHN EMMEUS DAVIS: It sounds a lot like the Dudley Street area in Roxbury before DSNI got involved. Dilapidated buildings. Arson for profit. Illegal dumping on vacant lots.

MTAMANIKA YOUNGBLOOD: Yes, I'm very familiar with Dudley Street. Ours was a similar neighborhood of dilapidated houses and vacant lots and prostitutes and drug dealers. I mean, it really was rough.

But there were all these elderly people who managed to live there, and they managed to do it. My thought was, "If Mrs. Goss can live here, we can live here." They became like my daughter's surrogate grandparents. We thought, "We've got these little old ladies still living here. We love them. They've become like our family, like our daughter's surrogate grandparents. We need to do what we can do to protect them." They were barricaded in their houses and they didn't want to come outside because it was the wild, wild West.

My husband started suing the landlords. I started raising hell. We just did it. We did what we could.

Historic District Development Corporation

MTAMANIKA YOUNGBLOOD: Our efforts became known. People found out. That's when my husband got the call from Ella Mae Brayboy, the community liaison person at the King Center.

Everybody knew my husband. He was in Maynard Jackson's law firm and a nonprofit law specialist, who incorporated many Atlanta nonprofits. He was a well-known person and we were raising hell in the neighborhood. So, he was asked to join the board of the Historic District Development Corporation.

I remember the phone call, because I could hear his side of the call. I knew who he was talking to. He was saying, "Oh, Miss Brayboy, you really want my wife." But I'm thinking, "Why is this man doing this?" Remember, I've got a baby. I'm still working for BellSouth at the time. I'm flying all over the country, leaving on Sunday and not getting back until a Friday night.

But eventually I joined the board of HDDC which, at that point, was five years old. No, by the time I got on the board it was 1987. So, the organization had existed for seven years.

JOHN EMMEUS DAVIS: What were the origins of that organization?

MTAMANIKA YOUNGBLOOD: It was founded by Coretta Scott King, Christine Farris, who was Dr. King's sister, and John Cox. He had been a senior manager at Delta Airlines and was involved in real estate and active in the neighborhood. They came together in 1980 and created the Historic District Development Corporation.

JOHN EMMEUS DAVIS: The one-sentence mission statement says the organization was created "to rehabilitate the residential and commercial property in the Dr. Martin Luther King, Jr. Historic District."

MTAMANIKA YOUNGBLOOD: Yes, that was the mission. The reality was that, once it was clear that the National Park Service was going to restore the houses in the birth-home block—which is the block that Dr. King's birth-home is in—Mrs. King and the founders just moved on. By the time I got to the organization, none of those people were involved and it was struggling.

JOHN EMMEUS DAVIS: You sat on the board for several years before becoming HDDC's Executive Director?

MTAMANIKA YOUNGBLOOD: Yes. I became Executive Director in 1992. I was the first staff person. Before that, I was on the board for five years. We were a working board. We didn't have a staff. My husband would do the applications for CDBG money. He would deal with the contractors. Mrs. Brayboy would go around and collect the rents. We were an all-volunteer board, but we still managed to renovate and manage 12 units of housing.

JOHN EMMEUS DAVIS: When you were finally able to start hiring staff did your activities increase? Did your program effectiveness increase?

MTAMANIKA YOUNGBLOOD: Oh my god, yes. We became the leading community development corporation in Atlanta over time. And a lot of that had to do with my previous experience at New Communities.

JOHN EMMEUS DAVIS: In what way? How was your redevelopment work in the King Historic District influenced by New Communities?

MTAMANIKA YOUNGBLOOD: I understood the importance of owner-ship, of not being subject to the whims of others. What I also learned from living in our house and from the work we had done with those 12 units of housing was that you have to have enough context—enough ballast I guess—to get people to buy a house and to live in this neighborhood. We were trying to get other people to do what we had done by moving into the neighborhood. But we had zero suc-cess at it. That's because our house was an island; we were an island in a very scary sea and nobody was interested in that.

As with those first 12 units of housing, we would buy a house be-cause it was horrible, and it was a real problem. We had to get the drug dealers out and the prostitutes out. We'd buy it and beautifully renovate it and put a family in. But it's a whole neighborhood that's the problem. Over there on Bradley Street is this beautiful house that HDDC had renovated, but you don't know that. Nobody knows that. We didn't have a real strategy.

I created an approach called "block-by-block," a revitalization strategy that people all over the country now use. You make a stra-tegic decision that this is the right block to work on and you then do everything all at once on that block. We felt that you couldn't do less than an entire block if you wanted to get people to see that we were serious and to feel comfortable about buying a house in this neighborhood.

JOHN EMMEUS DAVIS: So instead of distributing your efforts and your energies and your resources across the entire district in a scat-tershot approach, you were going block-by-block to rehabilitate an entire block and then move to another block.

MTAMANIKA YOUNGBLOOD: That is correct. And we had a plan. That was important. We had a plan that showed where we were going next so that people who were being asked to buy into this scary neighborhood could understand all that's going to be done.

The importance of that approach was that we had to deal with whatever we encountered, whether or not it made financial sense, whether or not it was something we'd ever done before. We had to figure all that out and make it work.

JOHN EMMEUS DAVIS: You are anticipating one of the questions I was about to ask. Am I correct that housing wasn't the only thing you were looking at in your block-by-block approach? The more comprehensive revitalization of the neighborhood was what you were doing, yes?

MTAMANIKA YOUNGBLOOD: You're correct. We had terrible commercial properties. We had terrible multi-family properties. We had a lot of scrapyards. You have to figure out how you are going to address this, because you can't skip over it and consider that you've done the work to revitalize the neighborhood.

You had to be working with the residents on their needs, whatever they were. There were a lot of elderly residents who were living in substandard, absentee-landlord-owned property. We would renovate a property, then move the tenant out of her house into the newly renovated one. We'd give her the opportunity to go back to her house once it was renovated. This was done at no expense to her and at the same rent she was paying, and in the same block. That was really important philosophically, because we wanted people to understand that we were not there to displace them.

JOHN EMMEUS DAVIS: Let's talk about that. This is not a neighborhood that was going to face gentrification, not for a while anyway. It was not immediately going to face market pressures that would push people out. Why was displacement an issue? Why was HDDC concerned about that?

MTAMANIKA YOUNGBLOOD: Because we felt that, as the neighborhood was improving, those little old ladies—I called them "neighborhood treasures"—had a right to a better neighborhood. They had a right to be able to stay there when things got better because they were what held the neighborhood together when things were bad.

JOHN EMMEUS DAVIS: Did you put protections in place to make sure that people were not displaced as things improved?

MTAMANIKA YOUNGBLOOD: No, not enough. We did not build in enough protections. I'll tell you that's my regret, which I'm still living with today. It happened faster than we could have guessed. The market just took off.

We would put low-income residents into a house that HDDC had built and made zero profit on. They would stay for three years or whatever and leave with all the equity that was in the house. We had no control over that because we were just so busy going block-by-block and trying to make sure that we could keep doing it. We didn't pay attention to keeping the homes affordable until it was too late.

JOHN EMMEUS DAVIS: HDDC was buying and renovating existing houses. Were you building new housing too?

MTAMANIKA YOUNGBLOOD: Not at first. We were renovating properties and whatever was there and, voila, 18 months later a block was done and we'd move on. We knew how to do historic renovations. We won awards for them. But we had never built a house. We didn't know how to do that.

However, we did form a partnership with Citizens & Southern

Bank, which then became Nations Bank and, ultimately, Bank of America. They had a community development branch of their bank that had done work in North Carolina building affordable housing. The Olympics were coming, and the Bank wanted to have a presence in Atlanta. They were shopping around for a partner. We had a good board. We had a strategic plan and we had a neighborhood plan. They could see themselves in our neighborhood. They were attracted to the idea that they could build on all those vacant lots, as part of our block-by-block strategy,

We formed a partnership and, because it was with Bank of America, we were able to buy up just about every piece of available property in the neighborhood. We owned over a hundred lots before we started on the first house.

JOHN EMMEUS DAVIS: Ownership of the land was by the corporation?

MTAMANIKA YOUNGBLOOD: The lots were owned by the partnership. It was the Bank's money but our strategy. We told them very clearly when we started that, "We like y'all, but we don't want you to be here forever. You are our partner until we learn how to do new construction on our own. Then thank you very much, goodbye." And that's exactly what happened. We ultimately dissolved the partnership. HDDC has been building houses ever since.

But we didn't figure out in time any kind of community land tenure strategy to stop gentrification. It was like a runaway train. Then we had big projects like Studioplex that were all we could focus on.

JOHN EMMEUS DAVIS: So, you were doing development, but you didn't really have the breathing space to focus on stewardship and protecting affordability and issues like that?

MTAMANIKA YOUNGBLOOD: Yeah. We did everything we could do to *make* it affordable. We just didn't think enough, at that time, about *keeping* it affordable. It was a hard lesson to have learned. That is why I say that you have to think about this from the very beginning. You have to know at the beginning what you want to have at the end.

We were just trying to fix a neighborhood that we were embarrassed about. People from all over the world were coming to see the King Center and Dr. King's birth home. When they went one block over, they found themselves in an abyss. It was just insulting to us, so our focus was to better represent Dr. King and his neighborhood. That was literally what drove us.

Our partner, remember, was Bank of America. Part of the reason they wanted to be our partner was to get all those mortgages on all the houses that were built. We built over a hundred houses. They're gone. Well, the affordability is gone. Someone who bought one of those houses for $75,000 during the Olympics sold it a few years later for $250,000. There are houses that we built that are now worth over a million dollars.

We didn't sell the properties we renovated. That's what's affordable today in the neighborhood. We own them and we're like a land trust. We only raise the rent if our costs go up. You get to stay as long as you pay your rent.

JOHN EMMEUS DAVIS: I recently listened to a webinar where Chenee Joseph, HDDC's current ED, was on the panel. She was talking about the commitment to permanent affordability. HDDC has now put a new shared equity homeownership program in place.

MTAMANIKA YOUNGBLOOD: We are trying to determine how to transition a lot of the single-family houses we own into this shared equity program, so that the residents can own their homes. We have a tenant, for example, who's been in her property since 1997. She's been renting. She was the first person that we said, "Don't you want to own your house?" She said she did, so HDDC said, "Okay, we're going to figure this out and do it."

JOHN EMMEUS DAVIS: She was your very first person in the new shared equity homeownership program?

MTAMANIKA YOUNGBLOOD: Yes. We don't really want to be in the single-family rental housing business if we can help it. The only reason we're in it is to make sure that it remains affordable. But, if we can do that another way and give somebody ownership, we'd much rather do that.

JOHN EMMEUS DAVIS: While preserving affordability for the next low-income homebuyer.

MTAMANIKA YOUNGBLOOD: Exactly.

Atlanta Land Trust Collaborative

JOHN EMMEUS DAVIS: Let's talk about the Atlanta Land Trust Collaborative, going back to its origins in 2008 and 2009. You and Valarie Wilson and Andy Schneggenburger led the effort to bring people together to talk about creating a new community land trust to promote equitable development in the neighborhoods adjoining the Atlanta BeltLine. Could you say why? What motivated the three of you to push this farsighted idea, especially in light of the fact that several earlier attempts to start CLTs in Atlanta had failed?

MTAMANIKA YOUNGBLOOD: Well, mine was the same motivation I'd had since 1971 when I went to New Communities. Remember, I had previously written a paper for the Casey Foundation. They ignored me when I said that a community land trust was going to be critical if they were going to do the work they were planning to do in the Pittsburgh neighborhood. The BeltLine was an opportunity to try again.

Valarie was Executive Director of the Atlanta BeltLine Partnership.

She was a fabulous person, but she did not come out of community development or housing. She's making all these presentations, trying to talk up the BeltLine, trying to get people interested in supporting it. But everywhere she went, it didn't matter who she was talking to, even in Buckhead, every time she started talking about the BeltLine, someone would ask the question about gentrification. They would ask whether they would be able to stay after there were parks and trails and all this new development. She didn't know what to say or how to deal with this problem.

I was on her board. I shared with her the approach to development that I had proposed for Pittsburgh. I said, "Why can't we do this? I know that the development industry doesn't like anything that looks like affordability. But if we are smart, we will begin to acquire property along the BeltLine to ensure that affordability exists."

JOHN EMMEUS DAVIS: Then there was Andy Schneggenburger.

MTAMANIKA YOUNGBLOOD: Andy, of course, was the Executive Director of AHAND, the Atlanta Housing Association of Neighborhood-based Developers. It was the trade association for community development corporations. Clearly, he had an interest in affordable housing.

The three of us started talking. We were trying to solve an age-old problem in Atlanta, which had two parts. The first part was unequal development. Everything was happening on the north side. Nothing was happening on the south side where Black people lived. A lot of those southside Black people were affluent, but it didn't matter. They were on the wrong side of the city, so nothing happened. No new development, no amenities, nothing. We were going to fix that problem.

Then there was the affordability problem. By the time the BeltLine was catching on, it was pretty obvious that gentrification was happening. The Historic District was already suffering from it and other neighborhoods around it: Reynoldstown and to some extent Mechanicsville where there were community development corporations doing neighborhood revitalization. We were our own worst enemies. Our success was creating the affordability problem we were trying to address.

We were hoping to fix that problem too, in part by getting supportive public policy. One of the things that I've learned, you know, is there has to be a requisite public policy to go along with your efforts.

JOHN EMMEUS DAVIS: I remember that first letter, the invitation to attend a meeting and to talk about possibly creating a community land trust. You and Valarie and Andy were the three people whose signatures appeared at the bottom of that letter.

MTAMANIKA YOUNGBLOOD: We were a good team. Valarie had all of that BeltLine energy from the mayor and the president of the City Council. She had all that energy behind her. I was famous as the community development person. I was also working for the Casey Foundation at the time. Andy had this cadre of neighborhood-based developers and community organizers. It was a good marriage in terms of constituents.

JOHN EMMEUS DAVIS: I don't know how Valarie found me or how the BeltLine Partnership located me, but being hired to support your team—and the talented group of people that you brought together— was a great opportunity that just dropped into my lap.

MTAMANIKA YOUNGBLOOD: Oh, it wasn't that complicated. You are kind of iconic, John, doing what you do. It wasn't a surprise that we found you.

JOHN EMMEUS DAVIS: Well, I was lucky to be asked. Here is the largest urban redevelopment project in the United States at the time. I get a call from Valarie inviting me to be a part of the planning process to figure out how the BeltLine might have an equitable impact, rather than fueling displacement. This was the opportunity of a lifetime, not only for Atlanta but for me as well. I loved working on that project.

Let me ask about some of the difficulties that were encountered. You had recruited folks from government, from business, the CDCs, and various civic associations to serve on what we called the "Atlanta CLT Development Committee." Do you happen to remember some of the controversies that arose as we were trying to get this diverse group of people to agree on a plan for the land trust?

MTAMANIKA YOUNGBLOOD: The first hurdle, as you'll remember, was, "Well, we tried this before and it didn't work." That was the refrain. We had to examine situations in other cities where CLTs were actually working and what was required for one to be successful.

Another thing that I remember as a difficulty was that we were going to have to deal with the State of Georgia trying to get tax assessments to be more in line with the fact that the land was not going to be sold and that CLT houses were going to remain affordable. That was very hairy.

The other issue I remember was, interestingly, "This is not going to fly because there's no bank in Atlanta that's going give you a mortgage for any of this stuff."

JOHN EMMEUS DAVIS: Somehow or another, after a year of meeting and planning, we came up with a document that everybody signed on to. How did we get there?

MTAMANIKA YOUNGBLOOD: Part of why it got done was because we were people to be reckoned with. Valarie was serious. I was serious. Andy was serious. So, we pushed it, and we had the premier CLT person in the country working with us. We *need* to do this. We sold the idea that the BeltLine was transformative. But you can't be transformative if you do the same thing every single time. You have an opportunity to do development where you don't get the same result as before, which is unequal development and lack of affordability. That's not transformative. If you say you're going to be transformative, then you have to do this.

JOHN EMMEUS DAVIS: In the end, everybody agreed on this nine-page blueprint for creating the Atlanta Land Trust Collaborative. They were excited about it. You went out and you sold it to the city government and to the banks and to the CDCs.

MTAMANIKA YOUNGBLOOD: It was really just because we pushed it, not because there was any great desire, frankly, to do a land trust on the part of many others on the committee. But there were very few voices raised publicly in opposition to this blueprint.

JOHN EMMEUS DAVIS: What happened after the blueprint was put out there and everybody raised their hand and said, "I like this idea, let's run with it." Where did it go? What did it achieve?

MTAMANIKA YOUNGBLOOD: Well, looking back—and looking at the interviews I did with Helen Cohen a decade ago—I'm struck by how naively enthusiastic I was. I was naive about the prospects for a community land trust movement in Atlanta. Not the movement writ large. I'm obviously still very much a proponent and advocate and supporter. But, as I was reading that earlier transcript, I'm like, "Oh boy, how naive." That is not how I would generally characterize myself. But 10 years later, 12 years later, we are in a different place than I thought we'd be.

I have to admit that the Land Trust Collaborative had some success, but much less success than we had hoped for. That was basically because the leadership fell apart. Valarie left to run for the State Superintendent of Education. She was required to resign from the BeltLine Partnership. Then in 2008, my husband got sick. I basically withdrew from public life.

I had been given the task of talking to the Executive Director of the Atlanta Land Bank Authority and the Director of Housing Finance at the Atlanta Development Authority, now called Invest Atlanta. I also talked to the Deputy Director for Planning and Development for the City of Atlanta. I remember calling all of them from the hospital and telling them they needed to join the board of the land trust. Because I asked, they said yes. It wasn't because they believed in it; they didn't want to tell me no. I think that's the truth. I mean, that's my assessment.

After that, I withdrew. I couldn't be this person showing up at meetings, pushing for the land trust while my husband was dying. And Valarie was off running her campaign, of course, so the push that was needed from the two of us wasn't there.

JOHN EMMEUS DAVIS: It was also the start of the Great Recession. CDCs all around Atlanta were dying on the vine. So Andy's constituency was going down the drain at precisely the time they were needed the most.

MTAMANIKA YOUNGBLOOD: Yes. We wanted the land trust to partner with them, but they were just trying to figure out how they were going to survive. I can speak for HDDC. We lost the commercial projects we were doing because the credit markets dried up. We also had a whole list of homebuyers who, under normal circumstances could get mortgages, but now they couldn't because the mortgage companies were tightening their requirements and they no longer qualified.

There was no push to keep things on track and on task, but there was also a context that made it difficult for what we wanted to do.

In all cities there are certain businesses—sometimes one, sometimes two or three—that run cities. If I said Los Angeles, you could tell me what the main business was, the film industry, Hollywood. If I said New York, the business would be finance, Wall Street. If I said Washington DC, you could tell me that politics is the main business. Right? What is the business that runs Atlanta? It's real estate development. Atlanta is a development town. Politically, private developers run Atlanta; it's where the politicians go to get money. And that industry did not like anything we were trying to do with the Land Trust Collaborative because every parcel of land that might be reserved for affordable housing means that developers can't make money on it.

JOHN EMMEUS DAVIS: I hear you. We were setting up this organization to take land off the market and to preserve the affordability of what was located on the land. We were pushing against the grain of the main business in Atlanta.

MTAMANIKA YOUNGBLOOD: Let me tell you the extent to which we were pushing against it. The person who was chair of the board of the Atlanta BeltLine Partnership was Ray Weeks, a major developer appointed by the mayor.

We were already pushing against that grain and then the bottom fell out of the market. It was the perfect excuse for people who said, "We can't deal with this right now." It wasn't just the housing market that crashed, if you recall. We had a major recession. The credit markets dried up. Portfolios dried up. It really provided our opponents with an excuse that they took advantage of.

The blueprint for the Land Trust Collaborative addressed the imbalance in economic development on the north and the south side. We addressed affordability. We addressed community engagement. We were trying to do all the right stuff that one would do to make this world-class amenity available to all Atlantans.

JOHN EMMEUS DAVIS: It was an intense educational process. I do remember members of the CLT Development Committee talking to people about it, saying this is why it's needed. The organizing, the education didn't stop as soon as we had that nine-page blueprint.

MTAMANIKA YOUNGBLOOD: No, not at all, not at all. But in the end, we were the only people interested in that.

The BeltLine has become exactly what we did not want it to become. It is exactly the thing we were trying *not* to have happen. Now you have people, all kinds of people, not just Black people, all kinds of people who can't stay where they were living. They can't afford it. The BeltLine is now Atlanta's beachfront property.

The leadership of our city and of the BeltLine, frankly, has no interest in affordable housing. No interest. I can say this unequivocally, they have no interest. They talk about it. They'll say they support it, because it's the right thing to say. But if you look at how many units of affordable housing were built in Atlanta along the BeltLine, it's a tiny number.

JOHN EMMEUS DAVIS: It's certainly a far cry from the days when you were talking to Cathy Woolard about starting a CLT for the BeltLine. That early vision of equitable development got diluted along the way.

MTAMANIKA YOUNGBLOOD: Well, you know, the number of new housing units inside the BeltLine Redevelopment Plan was 5,600. It's in the document. Remember, I was there. We were supposed to have built 5,600 units of affordable housing. It's in the document that was approved by the State of Georgia so that we could have a tax allocation district.

I don't want to mislead you. There are lots of people in Atlanta who care about affordable housing, but they're not in charge and they're not equipped to take on the development industry, which is the thing that runs the city. Where there's a will, there's a way. If there's no will, there's not likely to be a way. There just isn't the kind of political will in Atlanta that can move an equity agenda, even though there are many people who care about it.

Community Ownership of Land

JOHN EMMEUS DAVIS: I'd like to come back, at the end of this interview, to the question of land ownership—community ownership, in particular. It's a theme that's woven through several of the conversations that we've recorded for this book.

MTAMANIKA YOUNGBLOOD: Sure.

JOHN EMMEUS DAVIS: Some of the people we've interviewed have lamented the trend of many CLTs focusing only on the buildings, only on housing, so much so that land is diminished in importance. I want to raise that issue with you because it seems that, at New Communities, the common ownership of land by a group of African American activists was central to what you were doing. Does this matter only in a rural setting or is community ownership of land also important in an urban setting?

MTAMANIKA YOUNGBLOOD: I don't see how you can control whatever you do on top of it without owning the land. One of the things that I would often say during my community development days, when I was speaking to groups, is that you have to control the dirt. If you don't control the dirt, you don't control anything. You have to control the dirt.

You're asking me a confounding question. How do you even do a community land trust without the land? The house is on the land. The business is on the land. The community garden is on the land.

I don't understand. Without the land, what do you try to hold in perpetuity?

JOHN EMMEUS DAVIS: I have always admired that quote by Charles Sherrod in our film, *Arc of Justice.* He says, "All power comes from the land."

MTAMANIKA YOUNGBLOOD: It does. He was right. Unless African American people control the land, they don't have a place to stand to assert their rights.

JOHN EMMEUS DAVIS: We think about that in a rural context, but I don't know if that's the same way that people think about land in an urban context.

MTAMANIKA YOUNGBLOOD: It's the same. It is the same. You know, I was just thinking about Amazon in that context. This weird, kind-of-brilliant-but-obnoxious guy came up with this idea, you know? His genius was around internet marketing. That was sort of an intangible idea but, to make it work, he has warehouses all over the country, all over the world. His warehouses, those gigantic warehouses are sitting on land.

Land is land. If you don't own the dirt, if you don't control the dirt, you can't control anything. How does gentrification occur, right? It's pretty obvious that people who don't control the land can get pushed out.

JOHN EMMEUS DAVIS: I think we've also discovered that individual ownership, at least for low-income people, can be a rather fragile protection. Unless there is cooperative, collective, or community ownership of the land, it's too easy to move individuals out of a hot-market area and to gentrify the neighborhood.

MTAMANIKA YOUNGBLOOD: Yes. I think that's critical. Obviously, that's the conversation we're having. Who controls the land? What is it controlled for? Who is it controlled for, now and in the future?

JOHN EMMEUS DAVIS: One of the brilliant innovations for me, in looking at New Communities, was the farsighted understanding of the founders that, even if you had ownership of the land by individuals, people could still get pushed out. If you had community ownership of land, there would be security of tenure for everybody.

MTAMANIKA YOUNGBLOOD: Exactly.

JOHN EMMEUS DAVIS: It really came down to collective security for racially and economically marginalized people who needed an extra layer of protection, who would be vulnerable otherwise.

MTAMANIKA YOUNGBLOOD: Exactly. A current example for me is HDDC. All the property that we renovated, we still own. It is still affordable. We're the only entity in the Old Fourth Ward that is doing that. It's affordable because we own the land for the purposes we're talking about.

JOHN EMMEUS DAVIS: You're not speculating on it.

MTAMANIKA YOUNGBLOOD: Right. We own land in the Old Fourth Ward because we want to make sure that the kinds of people who are always the first to go when a neighborhood is revitalized will be able to stay.

JOHN EMMEUS DAVIS: That's a fine note on which to end. Thank you.

3.

Kirby White

The Writer Who Polished the Message
& Enhanced the Practice of
Community Land Trusts

Interviewed by John Emmeus Davis
January 2, February 11, and June 1, 2015

Kirby White worked for the Institute for Community Economics in the 1980s and 1990s, authoring and editing a host of books, scripts, and manuals about CLTs, including The Community Land Trust Handbook and The Community Land Trust Legal Manual. He co-edited ICE's newsletter, Community Economics from 1983 to 1996 and assisted several start-up CLTs. He later served on the board of Equity Trust and produced technical materials applying the CLT to the preservation of farmland. More recently, he has served on the board of the Honduras Community Support Corporation, supporting Fundación Eco Verde Sostenible, a regional land trust founded by his wife, Nola White, to assist mountain villages in Honduras.

JOHN EMMEUS DAVIS: You had a full life before getting involved with community land trusts and the Institute for Community Economics. Why don't you give a bit of background about where you were raised and what you did prior to ICE.

KIRBY WHITE: Well, I was born in Detroit in 1937. My father's father worked for the Ferry Morse Seed Company. My father also went to work for Ferry Morse a few years after I was born. They were both lifelong Detroit residents.

There was a small seed company here in Cambridge, New York that went back a century or so from the days when seeds were pedaled farm-to-farm with a horse-drawn wagon. It had gone bankrupt in the Thirties and was for sale. My father was interested in buying it, but Associated Seed Growers, a family-owned business in Connecticut, was also interested. In the end, they got together and bought it together. My father, as a minor investor, became the manager of the company in Cambridge.

So, I was moved at the age of not-quite-three and grew up in the Village of Cambridge on an old farm. My folks had lots of horses and I had some cows. I grew up between the ages of 10 and 18 milking cows. I loved the idea of being a farmer and having cows. I built up enough of a herd so that, when I was ready to go to college, I sold my cows and paid for several years of college.

JOHN EMMEUS DAVIS: Did you go to college expecting that, when you came out, you were going to be a farmer?

KIRBY WHITE: No, no. By then, when I went off to college, I thought I wanted to be a geologist. I'd always loved the outdoors. In high school, I had fallen in love with chemistry, but I didn't want to spend my days in a lab. I said, "Well, I can be a geologist."

I went to Wesleyan in Connecticut as an undergraduate and took a geology course. It was kind of fun, but the literature and humanities and history courses were much more interesting. I did the common undergraduate thing. I drank a lot of beer, drank a lot of whiskey, and read a lot of books, but none of the ones I was supposed to be reading. It was the era of Kerouac's *On the Road*. I went around with a copy of Ginsburg's *Howl* in my back pocket.

I had been in love with the idea of writing fiction for a long time. I wrote a novel at Wesleyan that people liked, given that I was just a kid. So I decided I was going to drop out of college and write. But then I got serious with Nola and wound up going back to Wesleyan and finishing up. We were married between my junior and senior year. We lived in Middletown in a $30-a-month apartment. It was quite comfortable married-student housing that was built after World War II for returning veterans.

I stayed for another year and went into the Master of Arts and Teaching program because I didn't know what else to do. Being an English teacher sounded like fun, so I got the MAT degree and took a job in Bennington. I was hired to teach creative writing and some English courses and to participate in teaching the more literary, cultural side of US history. I really loved high school teaching, but it was just overwhelming. A hundred students, five classes a day, five days a week, all of whom were writing things that you ought to read and grade.

After four years of that, I had a friend who had been teaching at a little college in Houlton, Maine. They were hiring an English teacher, so Nola and I moved to Houlton on the New Brunswick border. You'd drive northeast to Bangor, and then you'd drive another hundred miles north through the woods. It was potato country, very rustic.

JOHN EMMEUS DAVIS: When did you go west?

KIRBY WHITE: After three years. I was hired to teach at Colorado Alpine College in Steamboat Springs. In those days, the number of college students nationally had grown, following World War II, and all these little colleges had started up. This place had the most amazing faculty I've ever known. It was made up of one-third people from other countries, a lot of them political exiles or refugees; another third were young people without PhDs, like me; and the last third were ex-high school teachers from Aroostook County. It was great. A novel I wrote sometime later, my favorite novel, is somewhat about a place like this.

After teaching there for a year, I wound up as a faculty representative on the board of directors and then as Associate Dean of the College. I worked in partnership with a very impressive ex-geologist PhD who was running a summer camp. He couldn't be there all the time, so I was sort of the on-site Dean. This was the Sixties. My students enjoyed calling me "The Codeine."

The College was breaking even, but the board had an opportunity to bail. They arranged a so-called merger with a California university that wanted our real estate. When that happened, we all left.

JOHN EMMEUS DAVIS: Did you come back to Cambridge at that point?

KIRBY WHITE: No, I went to the University of Iowa Writers' Workshop and got an MFA. I was there for two years, having fun getting the writer's workshop experience.

By that time, it had become a question of whether I was going to get a PhD and become serious about becoming a college faculty member or start teaching at a community college. We really wanted to go back to the mountain West and I was trying to finish my next novel. So I took a job with a community college in Sheridan, Wyoming for a year. We loved it there. Going back to the land was in the wind at the time, but we could not afford to buy land in Sheridan on what I was making in a school like that. We couldn't have afforded it in Steamboat either.

So we came back to Cambridge and built this house. My father had retired from the seed company and started a little business of his own here in Cambridge. It was not selling seeds, but making the packets for seed companies.

I worked for my father's seed packet business for about five years. I became a dye press operator and envelope machine adjuster and truck driver, while also being a housebuilder and stonemason.

JOHN EMMEUS DAVIS: That was when you and Nola built this house together?

KIRBY WHITE: Yeah. We built this house on ten acres in the corner of the hundred acres my folks owned. We had a free piece of land that had access to electricity, a good spring with access to water, easy access from a road. Site development cost us almost nothing. We built a house for a little more than $5,000 and lots of sweat.

All during that time I did work for Cambridge Seed Packets, but I didn't want to spend the rest of my life running a small manufacturing business. It was not exciting work. It was convenient for the time but, after five years, I decided I wasn't gonna do that anymore.

We had finished building the house. We had no mortgage. We heated the house with wood. We had a big garden. We had chickens. So, I had a huge amount of freedom to do whatever was interesting. It left me with the feeling that I can go anywhere; I can do anything. I mean, it was a period of being totally independent of everything.

In 1980, I did a wonderful, summer-long canoe trip into the barren grounds west of Hudson Bay. I'd been doing a lot of canoeing with several friends for years, but nothing that big. It was just an absolutely pivotal experience in my life,

The Community Land Trust Handbook

JOHN EMMEUS DAVIS: That canoe trip would have happened right before you encountered Chuck Matthei, right?

KIRBY WHITE: Yeah. I came home from the trip and needed to do some work. SUNY Albany was looking for an adjunct teacher to teach a couple of writing courses. And I did that.

Nola had become friends with Jim Berger, Lisa Berger's brother, through her work with the Hudson Valley Co-op. Jim was working for Clear Eye at that point, a worker-owned business that distributed whole foods to co-ops. He was driving a route, delivering stuff that included the co-op that Nola was involved in starting in Cambridge. Often, on that loop, he'd spend a night here.

Jim and Chuck Matthei had become good friends. Jim brought Chuck Matthei to our house. They were going camping, but they spent a night here first. And, lo and behold, I heard all about community land trusts. I've never been the same since [laughter].

JOHN EMMEUS DAVIS: That would have been the fall of 1980, right after your canoe trip?

KIRBY WHITE: That's right. Then in January, I learned from Chuck that he was putting together a group of people to do this book, meeting in Boston. It sounded like something big and interesting, so I went to the meeting and volunteered to help. There I met you and Chuck Geisler and Perk Perkins. And maybe Bonnie Acker?

JOHN EMMEUS DAVIS: She came with Bob O'Keefe and Kerry Mackin on the second day of our meeting.

KIRBY WHITE: Oh yeah. So, I started getting involved with this group of people who did all this crazy stuff.

JOHN EMMEUS DAVIS: Other than the fact that you were independent and restless, what was it that convinced you to go to Boston? You spent two days in a meeting with a bunch people who you had never met before. And we're talking about writing a book. What was the attraction? Why did you volunteer to help with it?

KIRBY WHITE: Well, like a lot of people, I listened to Chuck Matthei describe something that sounded really neat, really interesting. I wanted to know more about it. I was free to do whatever seemed interesting at that point in my life. And the CLT was interesting. So I went and checked it out at that meeting. I met some really interesting people, including John Davis.

I also realized there was a ton of stuff I didn't know about a subject that I wanted to know more about. I was open to an approach to things that recognized the absurdity of private ownership of land. I had always had a feeling that land was such an important thing for people generally. But to cut it up into little pieces and treat land as property had never made sense to me. I hadn't developed the idea systematically, but I recognized that.

JOHN EMMEUS DAVIS: You ended up playing a larger role in producing that book than you had expected, yes?

KIRBY WHITE: We had a committee of people, including you, who were trying to put this book together. There was a friend of mine who was going to be the general editor, but he got busy with something else. It became clear that this group of people had all sorts of useful experience. But committees don't write books; well, they don't write *coherent* books. So I wound up, by the end of the summer of 1981, taking on the role of general editor. I had just been a volunteer up to that point, but I agreed to work for $3.00 an hour for a period of time, putting the book together.

That also meant writing parts of it; in fact, writing a lot of it. You wrote some chapters that I didn't have to write. So did Chuck Geisler. I wrote some chapters that needed editing and I helped with Chuck Matthei's writing. He was so organized about how he wanted to present things. I could sit down with him with the tape recorder and get his input. I'd then write it up, using his phrases.

I worked on case studies for Cincinnati and Tennessee and Columbia Heights without ever having been there. For most of those, I had badly recorded versions of interviews done by others. I did go to Maine and do an interview with Lucy Poulin for that case study. And I went to Cedar-Riverside in Minneapolis and interviewed a lot of people there.

JOHN EMMEUS DAVIS: How hard was it to find examples of CLTs when we were writing *The Community Land Trust Handbook*? How many CLTs even existed in 1981?

KIRBY WHITE: Oh, there were many organizations calling themselves a CLT. But most were what Bob Swann called "enclaves." Not many even roughly matched the ideal that we were talking about: a democratically structured organization with an open membership, serving an existing geographical community.

What most people were doing with the model, at that stage, was starting an intentional community and wanting that community to own land and for there to be individually owned houses. They were doing that with like-minded people who had the skill or the money to build their own houses. Earthbridge and the Valley CLT were early examples. ICE, under Bob, continued to work with those kinds of intentional communities. It was not where his *vision* saw the CLT going, but that is where Bob was really coming from in most of his work.

JOHN EMMEUS DAVIS: Where were CLTs to be found that more closely fit our working concept of a CLT?

KIRBY WHITE: Let's see, there was the Columbia Heights Community Ownership Organization. That was the first effort by Sojourners and other idealistic, theoretically-minded people to take the CLT model into an existing community where there was a need for housing affordability. It was a product of the Center for Creative Nonviolence and Sojourners and different radical organizations that wanted to do this thing. They had some very bright, talented people trying to do a CLT. But, by the time we wrote the book, it no longer existed.

Then there was Lucy Poulin and Marie Cirillo, two high-powered women, each of whom through their own energies and commitment had started rural community land trusts. They had a clear focus on problems of the rural poor who couldn't afford decent housing, who couldn't access land. Or, in the case of Marie Cirillo, people in the Appalachian region who had a land-based rural culture who had been pushed off the land.

In Marie's case, she got Bob Swann to come down to the Clear Fork Valley and talk about the community land trust model. Then Chuck Matthei and you and Mike Brown helped with that effort. ICE also provided some loan money and some people who helped to build the Woodland CLT's first houses.

JOHN EMMEUS DAVIS: There was Cincinnati, yes?

KIRBY WHITE: Cincinnati, yeah. Another set of dedicated people who were focused on dealing with inequality, dealing with economic injustice, and providing housing for people in a poor African American neighborhood. They were helping to create a structure that would allow people in that neighborhood to own something and do more for themselves and be more self-sufficient, not just be consumers of charity. That was an important goal for Mac McCrackin, Barbara Wheeler, and the other Dominican Sisters.

And we did case studies of the Quechee Land Trust, which is now the Vermont Land Trust, and the agricultural land trust in Marin County, which was thinking about doing a community land trust.

JOHN EMMEUS DAVIS: There was New Communities, of course, the first CLT. I was the one who traveled to Albany, Georgia and interviewed Charles Sherrod.

KIRBY WHITE: Well, we did include them in the book, although I have never been comfortable with saying that New Communities was the "first CLT." It was an impressive consequence of Bob Swann's talking with Slater King and the people in Albany about an approach to land reform that would address the kinds of terrible things that Charles Sherrod had experienced as a consequence of persuading people to vote and seeing them kicked off land they didn't own.

Their courage and passion for doing something about that is awesome. New Communities was philosophically congruent with the philosophy of the CLT model, but it wasn't a CLT. It was something different.

JOHN EMMEUS DAVIS: Bob Swann and the others who wrote that earlier book had described New Communities as an experimental "prototype." They admitted that the jury was still out as to whether or not it would develop along the lines they laid out in their book.

It's true that New Communities never had leaseholds, never built housing and, as far as I know, never had a formal membership that elected a majority of the board. It was, in essence, a cooperative agricultural enterprise on land held by a nonprofit corporation.

But the intention was to remove that land permanently from the speculative market. The nonprofit landowner had the active support of hundreds of people who were involved in planning for the use of that land or who were lining up to buy the homes that New Communities hoped someday to build.

I'd say that's certainly congruent with the CLT model, practically *and* philosophically. If Lester Maddox and the Farmers Home Administration and the White community in Dougherty County hadn't blocked them every step of the way, New Communities might have come to more closely resemble what we call the "classic" CLT today. Or maybe not. We'll never know.

KIRBY WHITE: What New Communities managed to do was wonderful. The loss of the land was tragic. And what they're doing today with the new version of New Communities is wonderful. But we should refrain from calling it the "first CLT."

JOHN EMMEUS DAVIS: Okay, so it's 1981. We're writing this book and we're working pretty hard to find fully functioning CLTs. Were we describing a paper tiger? Were we trying to make this handful of interesting experiments and innovations look like something bigger?

KIRBY WHITE: Yeah, something like a movement.

JOHN EMMEUS DAVIS: Even paper tigers have their uses, I guess. If you could portray this interesting idea as something that was spreading, seeding, sparking lots of interest, you could say to people that it's the **beginning** of a movement. I don't think it was complete hubris on our part, but we probably took it a little too far in claiming there was a "movement" that was already happening.

KIRBY WHITE: Well, it was consciously strategic on Chuck's part. It wasn't a bad strategy.

JOHN EMMEUS DAVIS: This was ten years after the book written by Bob Swann, Shimon Gottshalk, Erick Hansch, and Ted Webster had been published. Why did Chuck believe that a new CLT book was needed?

KIRBY WHITE: I can't say that I ever sat down with Chuck and asked him that question. He never explained exactly. But Chuck was very clear about what he wanted to do with the CLT model. It was not to provide land ownership for "enclaves" which is what most so-called community land trusts actually were at that time. Bob Swann had come up with this idea of a nonprofit landowner that included not only the residents, but also others who would be affected by that form of land ownership. In spite of his commitment to that idea, there really weren't many CLTs that had done that yet.

Chuck was working with Lucy Poulin in Maine, with Maurice McCrackin in Cincinnati, and with the Sojourners Center for Creative Nonviolence people in Washington, DC. All of these people were wanting to create an ownership structure for promoting social change. Chuck wanted to turn the movement in that direction, so he wanted a book that would reflect more of that.

JOHN EMMEUS DAVIS: How did Rodale Press get involved? What did they think they were doing?

KIRBY WHITE: It was Chuck Geisler who, as a Cornell Ag School rural sociologist, knew them. He contacted them and described the idea to them.

JOHN EMMEUS DAVIS: Why did Rodale agree to publish it? It wasn't exactly the kind of book they had published before—or since.

KIRBY WHITE: Most of the people who were thinking about community land trusts at that time—Bob Swann, in particular; Chuck Matthei too, to a lesser extent—thought of it as a rural way of owning land for a homestead kind of living, a working-land kind of operation.

Rodale got enough of that flavor to think, you know, "If we're going to make a point of the importance of gardening in a certain way, then this way of getting access to productive land would be interesting." And Chuck Geisler sold that idea to them.

When we eventually delivered a manuscript, they said, "Oh, this is not quite what we thought. This is about social justice! We believe in social justice, but that's not the kind of publisher we are" [chuckles]. But to their credit, Rodale went ahead with it: "We said we were willing do it, so we will."

JOHN EMMEUS DAVIS: That's a great story [laughter].

KIRBY WHITE: As I said, it was due entirely to Chuck Geisler.

JOHN EMMEUS DAVIS: To my mind, the most important ideas in *The Community Land Trust Handbook*, those that have stood the test of time, were contained in the opening chapters. We wrestled there with trying to find a balance between the "legitimate" property interests of individuals and the "legitimate" property interests of the larger community. I remember being here at your house with Chuck Matthei and Chuck Geisler and you, trying to frame the whole book around this idea. Could you talk about how we came up with that notion of balancing interests in a CLT?

KIRBY WHITE: I still remember how impressed I was at the time with the quality of that discussion among you three. I was just a listener, trying to get hold of it, so I could write it up. That was sort of the next stage of what hooked me. It was a really interesting process. I liked being part of that process with you and Chuck and Chuck. It was like those cut-outs that came with my chemistry set when I was a kid. You could say, okay, this is how things are **supposed** to go together.

Chuck Matthei was reluctant to talk about property in terms of interests. He wanted to talk about **rights** to security and equity and legacy as moral stuff. You and Chuck Geisler held off Chuck on that. I acquiesced, eventually. Rights were too hard to define.

Interests were defined in that book simply and accurately as things people wanted and needed. This is what people, as individuals, wanted and needed. This is what people in communities, as communities, wanted and needed. And there is a tension between those two sets of interests, which the CLT is able to balance. That was a wonderful discussion that made the whole book worth doing.

An Exaggerated Case for Homeownership

JOHN EMMEUS DAVIS: Looking back at that book more than 30 years later, what do you think we got right? What do you think we got wrong?

KIRBY WHITE: Well, we got those first two chapters right, setting a context for the book. We built a pretty good foundation for what a CLT was trying to do. If someone was asked to justify the CLT they could say, "That's what we're doing. We're claiming that individuals have legitimate interests and that communities have legitimate interests." Who can object to that?

With the case studies and some parts of the early chapters, I think we also made a pretty strong case for the link between land ownership and displacement, dispossession, and poverty, both in urban and rural situations. We talked about gentrification and disinvestment and we talked about absentee ownership in Appalachia and elsewhere. We identified the larger problems that this little model was trying to having an effect on. We got right the importance of the relationship between ownership and poverty—or non-ownership and poverty.

But we oversimplified the case for homeownership.

JOHN EMMEUS DAVIS: Let's talk about that. In what way did the 1982 book—and ICE's subsequent advocacy for the CLT—oversimplify the case for homeownership?

KIRBY WHITE: That was a lot of what Chuck Matthei wanted to emphasize, especially after the book was published. Chuck went on for years with his very persuasive talks about how tenants were paying over their lifetimes more than homeowners had paid on their mortgages during that same period of time. Well, that was often true, but that didn't mean it was practical to be trying, just like that, to make homeowners out of people who've been tenants all their lives and were not bankable.

That was a problem for the CLT movement for many years. There was this big, big focus on homeownership. You're going to help people in lower-income communities with no wealth to build wealth by making them homeowners. But they've never been homeowners before and they're not bankable. And CLTs themselves were not bankable in the beginning.

We were encouraging CLTs to try to do something that was pretty hard to do. Maybe it was still the right thing to do? It was probably better than just saying, "Okay, you can do anything at all with a CLT."

And, as you know, Chuck developed a financing mechanism in the community loan fund model to help finance resident ownership by people who CLTs were trying to serve. There was ICE's loan fund and the other little loan funds like the ones in New Hampshire and Vermont and the Capital District in New York, and especially the one in Boston.

JOHN EMMEUS DAVIS: Was some of Chuck's focus on homeownership a strategic calculation, a way of political positioning this unconventional model of tenure?

KIRBY WHITE: I remember, at one point, someone complaining about how difficult it was to make a CLT work. Chuck said, in effect, that he actually "hated" the model. But he saw it as a way to draw attention to the whole question of ownership and economic justice and everything that he really cared about.

JOHN EMMEUS DAVIS: He could challenge the ownership of property by *rich* people by talking about access to homeownership for *poor* people?

KIRBY WHITE: Yes. It was a rhetorical entree into the larger discussion about wealth and poverty that he really wanted to talk about.

JOHN EMMEUS DAVIS: I remember two people challenging Chuck on the homeownership focus, early on. One was Bob Swann. The other was Marie Cirillo. I remember Bob saying that the land trust was supposed to be about more than just homesteads and home-ownership. New Communities was a perfect example. It was going to be about cooperatives and economic development. I also remember Marie always saying to Chuck and to the rest of us, "Why are you community land trust people always talking about housing?"

KIRBY WHITE: Yeah, for Marie, housing was just a secondary dis-traction. What's important is the ownership of land. She was all about regaining control of the land for Appalachian people who were backed up into those hollers where they had no ownership or secure tenure. Yes, of course, it would be nice if they had better houses, but that's not the issue. They can build their own houses. They need access to land.

I feel the same way in Honduras, with the groups Nola works with. Land tenure, control of land, and community control of land are what's important, both for individuals and for communities. In Honduras, it's an Appalachia situation. People have been backed into the mountains and don't have much. They can provide some sort of housing for themselves, but what they can't provide for themselves is a way to deal with the people who are trying to take land away from them because they want to put their cows on it.

Multi-Media Projects in the 1980s

JOHN EMMEUS DAVIS: What were the various roles that you played at the Institute for Community Economics after the *Handbook* was published?

KIRBY WHITE: Well, writing and editing was the one continuous role that I had. In the beginning, it was the only role I had. I got in-volved with ICE because I agreed to help with *The CLT Handbook*.

Pretty soon there was another writing project. I agreed to edit, meaning mostly to write, *The Community Loan Fund Manual*. We also launched the quarterly publication, *Community Economics*.

JOHN EMMEUS DAVIS: Tell me about *Community Economics*. It was a significant ingredient in seeding and supporting the early growth of CLTs. It was also an important part of your own contribution to the CLT movement. What was your role in putting out this publication?

KIRBY WHITE: Well, my nominal role was editor for most of the history of the publication. My actual role was writer. I was the journalist. My medium, the field that I journalized in, was community land trusts and community loan funds and a little bit about housing co-ops.

JOHN EMMEUS DAVIS: Why was it named *Community Economics*?

KIRBY WHITE: Well, it was the newsletter of the Institute for Community Economics. And it was about community economics as con-

Kirby White and Lisa Berger, co-editors of ICE's newsletter, Community Economics.

ceived by that organization—or as that organization wanted the economics of a community to be understood in relation to land, housing, and capital. What we wrote about in *Community Economics* were CLTs as they were being developed here and there around the country. Community loan funds also became a major interest of ICE during that period. We told their stories.

We had a modest mailing list of people we sent this publication to. That number of people regularly heard about these odd little organizations, community land trusts and community loan funds, that were being created by a handful of people here and there.

JOHN EMMEUS DAVIS: You were also heavily involved with the talented people who ICE hired later in the 1980s to produce the first narrated slideshow about CLTs and the first video. Why were those projects important? What was the significance of doing the slideshow and the video?

KIRBY WHITE: It was very important in taking this rather abstract, theoretical idea of just land ownership and translating it into terms that many people could understand. Chuck was an organizer. He knew who he could influence with logic and words and who needed to be shown pictures. He found ways of getting the words out there, but he also worked very hard at finding ways to get the pictures up there too.

He attracted the interest of people like Tony Heriza, a talented filmmaker. A slideshow and cassette tape were what you could afford to do before the time when you could do video affordably. He got Tony interested. Eventually I got into it too and helped to produce a pretty good tape to go along with the slides.

He later got Helen Cohen interested who not only made a video for ICE, *Homes & Hands*, but also raised a lot of money to make it possible.

JOHN EMMEUS DAVIS: Helen came out of a planning and organizing background herself. It's not often you have a filmmaker who thoroughly understands what you're trying to do in terms of content and audience.

KIRBY WHITE: Yeah, for sure. She had been working at organizing CLTs on the West Coast before she teamed up with Deborah Chasnoff and did that film for ICE.

JOHN EMMEUS DAVIS: That's part of why they made such a dynamic film.

KIRBY WHITE: Yeah, absolutely. By that time, we had some pretty exciting CLTs to portray. We had some really powerful stories to tell. By then, there were stories that could be told in the past tense and the present tense, not merely in the future tense.

JOHN EMMEUS DAVIS: The video featured Durham, North Carolina, Albuquerque, New Mexico, and Burlington, Vermont. You had three very different CLTs, racially, geographically, and linguistically.

KIRBY WHITE: Yeah. It started to feel, by the time we did that video, that there really is diversity; there really is the spark of what might be described as a "movement." It's not just a small group of people with strong theoretical commitments to a certain approach to the ownership of land. It was becoming quite a lot more.

Burlington was ahead of the others in some respects, mainly because of the mayors who had supported the Burlington CLT, Bernie Sanders and Peter Clavelle. But in Durham and Albuquerque, we had CLT start-ups like quite a few at that time, which were coming out of a save-our-neighborhood sort of motivation.

There was that feisty little Sawmill group in Albuquerque. They wanted to save their neighborhood for the people who were already there. The neighborhood was tiny, intact, and effectively organized. There was a particleboard plant that was polluting the area. The residents organized and developed the political clout to deal with that plant. Then they dealt with the larger question of what was going to happen to that huge piece of blighted land. Once the particleboard plant was gone, that piece of land next to Old Town Albuquerque would have been valuable. There would have been developers standing in line at the City, asking for the right to do it themselves.

JOHN EMMEUS DAVIS: Most community organizations would have said, all right, we solved the problem. We've done our work. We've been advocates. We've been organizers. We got rid of the polluter. We've removed the menace, that's enough.

KIRBY WHITE: Yeah, the organizers in Sawmill didn't stop there. They formed the Sawmill CLT to develop the land themselves for their own people.

JOHN EMMEUS DAVIS: Durham, the third CLT featured in that video, was a different kind of case. It was an African American neighborhood next to a major university.

KIRBY WHITE: Yeah. The idea of the CLT had been seeded there by academics, people associated with Duke. It wasn't at all neighborhood-based in the beginning. But somehow, people in that neighborhood got hold of the idea and the Durham CLT became a save-our-neighborhood initiative, with some sophistication behind it.

Becoming a Technical Assistance Provider

JOHN EMMEUS DAVIS: I'd be interested in hearing how you began providing technical assistance to CLTs. How did you go from serving as a book editor, newsletter publisher, and script writer at ICE to serving as a TA provider?

KIRBY WHITE: When helping with *The CLT Handbook*, I was editing case studies based on interviews done by others. But we included a case study of Cedar-Riverside in Minneapolis and I went there myself. It was an important part of my education in the field. I was completely ignorant about community development at that point. Cedar-Riverside was a place where there had been effective community organizing, there was an effective community development corporation, and smart city officials were interested in what was happening and how a CLT might or might not relate to it. I learned a lot doing that case study.

Later, I went to Cincinnati. I went to Tennessee. I went various places with Chuck Matthei or with you and Chuck Geisler. I learned about technical assistance work by going along with people who had been doing that kind of technical assistance work.

When I was working on *The Community Loan Fund Manual*, I got to interview people like Julie Eades at the New Hampshire Community Loan Fund and a few other people who had succeeded in getting little community loan funds off the ground.

The other thing I did, while writing *The Community Loan Fund Manual*, was to play a central role in founding a community loan fund in Albany. I consciously decided that, if I'm going to write about this stuff, I need to find out what it's like to do it, to know what the issues are.

Once we had the loan fund up and running, we decided that we now could do a CLT. All of this was supported by United Tenants of Albany, led by Roger and Maria Markovics. I became the primary organizer of the Albany CLT and, then, its initial staff person for several years. I did everything from the bookkeeping to the hands-on rehab of old houses. My capacity as a technical assistance provider really developed as I did that work in Albany. I learned a lot about how federal programs work, how cities work, how neighborhoods work.

Editing *Community Economics* also gave me an opportunity to interview all sorts of people in different kinds of CLT-related or loan-fund-related efforts. I got to go out and look at places where they were trying to develop CLTs or loan funds.

I took on other writing projects for ICE over the years. I did a financial management manual for community-based housing organizations, including CLTs. So I learned a lot about accounting and financial management. I also learned a lot, of course, in helping to manage a newborn loan fund and a newborn CLT in Albany—and dealing with the city government with regard to both. That was my education.

JOHN EMMEUS DAVIS: Eventually you became ICE's director of technical assistance. When did that happen?

KIRBY WHITE: I became TA director in 1996 or maybe 1995. ICE had changed by that point. Chuck Matthei was gone and Martin Hahn was the TA director. Then Martin decided to take a job in North Carolina as executive director of the Durham CLT. I agreed to become ICE's TA director for two years.

ICE had just received a national grant from HUD to do extensive technical assistance with CLTs anywhere in the country. We went through the HUD money we had been given very quickly. That impressed the people in HUD's TA office because we had assessed all these groups and qualified them for CLT-specific technical assistance. We would visit groups and find out if there was any potential there. If there was, we'd provide TA. Most of their other national TA grant awardees weren't using the money as well. They were just taking canned TA packages off the shelf if groups requested them.

We impressed the TA people at HUD. We went through a lot of money very fast. At that point, they just gave us more money, without us having to respond to a NOFA, a "Notice of Funding Availability." Then, after several years, there was another NOFA and we got more than a million dollars out of that one.

That was a period when there was a lot of work being done, much of it by Burlington Associates—you and Tim McKenzie and Michael Monte, especially. I did quite a lot myself, trying to figure out what could be done in the early stages of a situation and what was needed. Then I would send you in, or send Tim or Michael in, to move along with it and to do new things.

Sawmill Community Land Trust

JOHN EMMEUS DAVIS: One TA job that you decided to keep for yourself was Albuquerque. When did you become involved with the folks in the Sawmill neighborhood?

KIRBY WHITE: Well, it was in the early days of ICE's funding from HUD. That funding allowed us to go anywhere in the country, wherever someone thought they wanted to start a community land trust. There was a guy in Silver City, New Mexico who had been interested for some time in starting a CLT there. I finally got HUD approval to work with Silver City. Nola was going to go with me on that trip.

A week or two before we left, I got a phone call from Albuquerque. They were looking for help in starting a community land trust—or, at least, they wanted to explore the possibility. I said, "Well, we're going to be flying into Albuquerque and renting a car. It would be easy for us to stop and see you all." Which we did.

At that time, the Sawmill Advisory Council was going strong. They had spun off another corporation that the Council controlled as a community development corporation. The Council's office and the CDC's office were in Max Ramirez's garage. We met Max. Dory

Wegrzyn was also there. So were Theresa Juarez and Debbie O'Malley. Theresa was doing community organizing. Debbie was running the CDC, which was constructing some infill houses in the old neighborhood.

It was a very old, mostly Hispanic neighborhood, although it was becoming more diverse. At the core of it was this group that had been active for some time fighting a particleboard plant that was polluting the air and water of that neighborhood. It was a long series of battles, which the residents eventually won. They got that plant shut down.

The Sawmill Advisory Council then wanted to get control of the big hunk of land owned by the City next to where the plant was located. But Theresa and Debbie had different ideas about how to go after it. Both of these women were committed and smart and strong. Both were Hispanic. Theresa wanted to fight the City for that piece of land. She was fierce. Her approach to getting that land was uncompromising, absolutely uncompromising. Debbie was more subtle. Her inclination was to get things done. Her feeling was, "We're going to need to be able to work with the City. Let's not alienate them. Let's see what we can work out to get the land on some terms that we can live with and can do what we want to do here over time."

It was a classic clash between an uncompromising organizer who was bent on challenging the City and a community developer who wanted to negotiate with the City. Debbie was into negotiating with the City because it looked like Sawmill could get an arrangement that would give Sawmill long-term control of the land on certain conditions that Debbie thought they could meet. Theresa didn't want to accept any of the City's conditions. So she and Debbie parted ways. Debbie stayed and Theresa left. It was really hard on Max. He loved both of them and respected both of them.

JOHN EMMEUS DAVIS: Did you know how Sawmill first heard about the idea of a community land trust? They had a traditional CDC that was doing infill housing. And the Council was doing community organizing. How did a CLT get added to the mix?

KIRBY WHITE: The idea of a community land trust was in the wind by that time. They might have heard about it from the Center for Community Change, which had supported an organizer in the neighborhood for a while. And Albuquerque had some people in the planning department who were fairly progressive.

Most importantly, Max Ramirez was sold on the idea of a CLT. Nola helped with that. She was there with me that first time and was able to converse with Max in Spanish. As a TA provider, I got the benefit of having a wife who talked with Max in Spanish, which Max liked.

JOHN EMMEUS DAVIS: What sort of technical assistance did you provide?

KIRBY WHITE: One of the things we worked on was questioning whether to start yet another organization that would be the community land trust. Do you let the old Advisory Council become the CLT? The CDC's board was appointed by the Advisory Council's board. And the Advisory Council, Max in particular, had control over what was happening in their tight little organization. They were reluctant to let go of that control. But Debbie worked out the idea of adopting new bylaws for the CDC corporation and adopting a new name. They became the Sawmill Community Land Trust.

JOHN EMMEUS DAVIS: Looking back on it now, what would you say that the Sawmill CLT accomplished?

KIRBY WHITE: Well, they built a brand-new neighborhood with some very nice features. You know, it was a complicated plan to put together and a complicated development process that needed to be staged over many years. I've seen other ambitious projects where they got phase one done, but ran out of juice at that point. Phase two and phase three never get built.

The Sawmill site got built. They had to move a railroad siding. They had to get a deal with the railroad and the City to get the siding moved out of the middle of the piece of land they wanted to develop. It was as challenging a development undertaking as I've ever had anything to do with it. I continue to be amazed that all of that development actually got done.

I didn't have that much to do with the development aspect of it. Tim McKenzie had more to do with it. My role continued to be a support for Debbie, helping Debbie to smooth out things between Tim and Dory Wegrzyn, who was the on-site development person. She was a feisty one herself and pretty good at what she did. My role was dealing with the interpersonal stuff and helping Debbie to clear away what was getting in the way of moving forward with that plan. It was a lot of fun.

JOHN EMMEUS DAVIS: Say a bit more about the role played by Debbie O'Malley.

KIRBY WHITE: The whole project was initially a hard sell to the City. They wanted to see that land developed. Once the site was no longer the dirty place that particleboard plant had made it there were certainly private interests who would have liked to get it, develop it, and make a lot of money off it. Debbie dealt with all that. She was a good politician. She dealt with the more progressive people in the city government. She dealt with the community development issues. And she got it done. Debbie was a very effective executive for the Sawmill CLT and later became an effective city council member.

The Complicated Culture of ICE

JOHN EMMEUS DAVIS: By the time you became the TA director, you'd been associated with ICE for 15 or 16 years. We talked earlier about what drew you to the CLT model. What attracted you to the Institute for Community Economics? What kept your loyalty and your involvement for almost two decades?

KIRBY WHITE: Well, Chuck did, you did. The people were interesting and the work was fun. I never worked primarily out of the ICE office. I lived here in Cambridge. I did the writing here and I travelled from here to do technical assistance work. I'd go to ICE periodically, have meetings with people, spend the night, and come home.

It was very unconfined and uncomplicated for me. Whereas for the expanding staff that grew up around Chuck, ICE was a very complicated place, as you know. That staff included some very good people, as well as some pretty useless people. I didn't have to be a part of the complications. I would just come in and be everyone's friend for a day or two and then go home. Or I'd go to Cincinnati and try to help people there or whatever.

JOHN EMMEUS DAVIS: Talk about the culture at ICE. You came in, you watched it, you experienced it. Then you left and came back a week later. You could observe it from the outside. What was complicated about ICE? What was the good and bad of the culture there?

KIRBY WHITE: Chuck created everything that was good about ICE—and everything that was complicated and difficult about ICE.

He attracted some very good people. But he also attracted a lot of young people who were awed by Chuck. They tended to be young men who were angry at their fathers, who were in rebellion against their fathers and, therefore, in rebellion against all authority and wanted a democratic workplace.

Chuck, of course, believed in democratic workplaces too—as long as he could run them, as long as they did what he wanted. That had an explosive potential and it blew up eventually.

Greg Ramm succeeded Chuck as the executive director. Greg was very bright and very effective in a different way, but he was not the ideal person. He was no Chuck Matthei.

Chuck left in 1990. When the Burlington conference took place, he had already resigned. Things were really rolling by then. I mean, there actually *was* a CLT movement—or something that people talked about as the CLT movement. There was a lot of smoke, even some fire, around the idea of CLTs.

We had a great conference in Burlington that year. Bernie Sanders, Gus Newport, and Winona LaDuke as keynote speakers. And African Americans coming in and challenging ICE to be something a little different from a bunch of idealistic White kids. What a conference!

JOHN EMMEUS DAVIS: Yeah, that *was* a great conference.

KIRBY WHITE: Greg Ramm carried on after Chuck left and started Equity Trust. A lot of good was done under Greg, including getting the HUD TA money. Working with Burlington Associates, we were able to help a bunch of CLT start-ups in many different parts of the country.

ICE was feeling big enough and strong enough and important enough to some of the people there, including Greg, that they felt now's the time to make a big investment and go to scale. There was a big strategic planning process that laid out, I thought, a totally unrealistic plan for getting big in a short period of time and trying to fundraise to support that kind of expansion.

Greg then left. I regretted his leaving, but he bequeathed to the organization this unrealistic, go-to-scale plan. Sarah Paige, the new executive director, struggled with it. She did what she could with that situation, but what she faced was just impossible. ICE went into a period of slow but steady decline.

The Laudable Contributions of Chuck Matthei

JOHN EMMEUS DAVIS: You've mentioned the "complications" that were part of Chuck's leadership and legacy. Lord knows, I had my own complicated relationship with him. In fairness, I believe we should also acknowledge his talents and accomplishments.

KIRBY WHITE: I got involved with ICE more or less at the same time you did. It was mostly Chuck Matthei working in communities around the country. He was on the road much of the time, telling the CLT story to anyone who would listen.

You know, years later, when I interviewed Julie Eades during the process of writing *The Community Loan Fund Manual*, she said, "A technical assistance provider is really just a troubadour who carries the stories from one community to the next." Chuck played that troubadour role better than anyone.

He was a great salesman. He impressed a lot of people who didn't start out agreeing with him. He made them believe that maybe they could make something happen that would never have occurred to them **could** happen, something they wouldn't have even **tried** to make happen. That was Chuck. He was willing to take risks and go for it. And he could sell the idea that you can do it too.

JOHN EMMEUS DAVIS: I remember interviewing Marj Swann a number of years ago and asking her a question about the difference between Bob Swann and Chuck Matthei. Without denigrating the skills of either one, she said something to the effect that, if Chuck had not come along, so much about the community land trust would have remained theoretical. It would have been an academic exercise more than a practical movement.

KIRBY WHITE: Bob was a theoretician. He was also an activist on a certain level, but he was not a community organizer. Chuck was certainly an organizer. If Chuck hadn't come along, the CLT model would have remained a nice theory or would have been limited to so-called enclaves, created by people who were doing it for people like themselves, people who were true believers.

When I sit down and think about how Chuck worked, I'm impressed all over again. He was a guy who made things happen. Bob Swann made certain kinds of things happen and was an effective voice in certain ways. But he was not the strategist that Chuck was.

JOHN EMMEUS DAVIS: We went from a handful of CLTs at the time we were writing *The CLT Handbook* to nearly a hundred by the early 1990s. There was a real growth spurt during that period, a proof-of-concept moment for the CLT. That didn't just happen. It was consciously, intentionally spurred by Chuck—and by ICE.

KIRBY WHITE: Well, the other strategic thing that Chuck was busy building at that time was ICE itself. Part of Chuck's genius was finding the right people, attracting the right people who came to ICE because of him. He was offering these "irresistible opportunities" to very smart, talented people who were going to be paid $50 and some vegetarian soup and a room to sleep in. Within a few years, ICE went from being an organization that had been whittled down to just Chuck with no salary, living with a little help from his friends, to a staff of 20-plus people. Some were just kids who liked the idea of CLTs and ICE and were willing to chauffeur Chuck around and whatnot. But some were extremely capable people: Louise Foisey, Chuck Collins, Greg Ramm, Mike Brown. You were a key part of the staff in those years. And people who served on ICE's board like Chuck Geisler and Michael Swack.

Chuck's strategic calculation was also that he got himself a couple of scribes: you and me. Well, you were more than a scribe. I mean, you came into that relationship with a PhD in a very relevant academic area and a lot of useful experience with housing and community organizing. I came into it with none of that. I was a pure scribe.

In the beginning, I would sit and listen to you and Chuck Matthei and Chuck Geisler and whoever else was there at the time and learn about stuff that I knew nothing about. Then I'd write up some piece of it. Later, the task would be writing a chapter for a manual or writing an article for *Community Economics*. I'd go to Greenfield and sit down with Chuck. He would have written some very precise notes about what points he wanted to have made. It was part of his old debating discipline. He'd know what points needed to be made in order to persuade his audience. He would give me those points and I'd ask questions. I'd get basic formulations, sometimes complete sentences out of Chuck or out of his little notebook. That's how he got quite a lot out there in written form.

Where Are CLTs Most Likely to Succeed?

JOHN EMMEUS DAVIS: I know you've been out of the game for a while, but I'd like ask you to reflect on the kinds of places that provide the most fertile ground for CLT growth. In your experience, where do CLTs succeed and where do they not?

KIRBY WHITE: I've been thinking lately about Baltimore in connection with CLTs. That got me thinking about Harold McDougall. Do you remember Harold? He was a young, African American Harvard graduate and Yale Law School graduate who was teaching law at Catholic University in DC. Somehow, he got interested in CLTs and attended the 1990 CLT Conference in Burlington. He challenged, very nicely, the CLT people and the ICE people who were there, who were almost entirely White, to pay more attention to issues of race. In 1990, it was still a pretty White movement. There was good work being done in African American neighborhoods like Cincinnati and

Albany and various places, but the people at the conference and the people on ICE's staff were mostly White.

Harold wrote a book a couple of years later called *Black Baltimore* which I reviewed in *Community Economics*. I also did an interview with him. He was kind of like your favorite Frenchman, Yves Cabannes, one of those people who is so excited about so many ideas that they spin your head.

Anyhow, he wrote this book which I just looked at again, 20 years later. One of his emphases in that book was "base communities." Do you remember that? It wasn't his term. It came out of liberal Catholic Church organizing in Latin America. Those were little, informal communities within a larger neighborhood, where people who you know get together and talk about what's going on and what the needs of the larger neighborhood might be. Harold saw base communities as being an important part of urban life and an important part of what was still good about West Baltimore and Black Baltimore.

Mindy Fullilove, an urbanist at The New School, talks about something similar. I don't know if this idea came from her, but she talks about "strong connections" and "weak connections" as a way of understanding how a city works. "Strong connections" are more obvious. They are the ones embodied in governments and established institutions that have political power and economic resources. But "weak connections" are important too. They are how people who are living in a particular place are connected with their neighbors on issues that concern them the most. My understanding of what she was referring to as "weak connections" is the same kind of thing that Harold was referring to as "base communities."

JOHN EMMEUS DAVIS: That brings us back around to the question of where CLTs are likely to succeed and where they will fail to thrive.

KIRBY WHITE: Well, they succeed most in the ways that I've always wanted to see them succeed, where they have been able to tap into "weak connections." If you look at CLTs that are obviously thriving, I think they have that going for them.

But they've also tapped into "strong connections." They've found financial resources and political support from outside their "base community." You can have all the "weak connections" in the world, but if you have no money and no political support, your effectiveness is going to be limited to your "base community." You're not going to affect things beyond that.

JOHN EMMEUS DAVIS: But the converse it also true. Unless a CLT pays attention to what you are calling the "weak connections" that bind a community together, the vitality and accountability of a CLT will be undermined. Whether or not there is a "C" in CLT is going to impact the quality of the organization.

KIRBY WHITE: Yes. But I don't see a lot of neighborhood-based CLTs being organized any longer. The number of relatively successful neighborhood-based CLTs peaked in the 1990s and then declined in the decade after ICE no longer had HUD funding to do TA around the country, going wherever there was interest and opportunity to start more CLTs.

CLTs are now becoming regional housing organizations or city-wide housing organizations. They are not neighborhood-based or community-based in any sense. Some organizations like the CLT in Burlington that started out as neighborhood-based became city-wide pretty quickly. And then became regional. They reached a large scale for housing development that was only available to a larger organization.

I feel like I should have been able to recognize that much sooner. Thirty years ago, we were trying to do neighborhood-based organizing and develop housing and find resources to develop housing and make it affordable for very poor people in blighted neighborhoods. That's pretty hard to do.

Bob Swann's original idea of a regional land trust that would have multiple community land trusts nested within it was a good idea. Marie Cirillo tried to do that in Tennessee, although she didn't get very far.

The most exciting CLTs today—the ones that have the most to do with community and a stronger sense of place—are not simply housing organizations. They don't just want to build houses on a vacant piece of land. They want an orchard; they want some commercial activity. They're doing whatever the neighborhood needs.

JOHN EMMEUS DAVIS: Well, you mentioned my favorite Frenchman a moment ago, Yves Cabannes. His manifesto, *Garden Cities in the 21st Century*, returns to that original vision of Ebenezer Howard. Garden Cities were complete urban economies. They weren't just about housing. They were also about stores and jobs and open space and transportation. They were about a community owning itself in order to have all the things that a community needs for quality of life and the sort of "weak connections" you've talked about. Yves would argue, I believe, that community land trusts should be doing that as well, going beyond housing.

KIRBY WHITE: I think that was the vision of the Sawmill CLT and the Dudley Street Neighborhood Initiative and those kinds of organizations. When dealing with the kinds of racial segregation and economic disinvestment found in urban neighborhoods like those in Baltimore, I think that focusing solely on housing is more sterile than it needs to be.

Land Versus Property

JOHN EMMEUS DAVIS: We've touched on the "C" in CLT. Let's talk about land, the "L" in CLT. Earlier, you said that one of the things that initially attracted you to the community land trust was that you had reached a point in your life where you saw the absurdity of land being treated as "property." Your long canoe trip in the Canadian wilderness, right before you got involved with editing—and helping to write—*The Community Land Trust Handbook*, seems to have nudged you in that direction.

KIRBY WHITE: That's right. I was struck by the idea that, in hunter-gatherer societies, the tools of survival that people made themselves or carried with them from place to place were personal property in a very real sense. The personal ownership of certain kinds of things for the Inuit and most other hunter-gatherers is not the idea that one would own land as an individual. That's absurd. The land is what you travel around on. It's not something you own.

When we were doing *The Community Land Trust Handbook*, there was someone, maybe Chuck Geisler, who had an old *New Yorker* cartoon. We wanted to use it in the book, but didn't know how to get the copyright, so we didn't bother in the end. It's a picture of two primitive guys wearing animal skins, holding clubs, sitting outside a cave. One is saying to the other, "I know what we can do. We can divide up the land into little squares and sell them." I've always thought that was funny.

JOHN EMMEUS DAVIS: You know, for years I believed that the biggest struggle in the CLT movement was going be to keep the "C" in CLT. But more recently we've had a hard time keeping the "L" in CLT. Given the importance of community-owned land in the Sherrods' conception of the CLT, the importance of land in Bob Swann's conception of the CLT, and the contrast we drew between individual property and community property in the opening chapters of the 1982 *Handbook*, I wonder if you would reflect on the place of land in the CLT. Why is it becoming more difficult these days to keep the "L" in CLT?

KIRBY WHITE: Well, the "L" is still really important for me. The idea of a ground lease rather than a deed restriction, as a way of dealing with land ownership, is far preferable for me.

But it has always been a struggle. The building that you're living in becomes so much more important than the land that it's on for most people. The home is your possession. How you deal with the ownership of land is far less important.

JOHN EMMEUS DAVIS: That's the irony, isn't it? As the importance of the house rises, the importance of the land diminishes, at least in an individual's sense of possessiveness. Even so, it is still a struggle for community land trusts to make a case for the separation of the building and the land. There may be a degree of indifference among homeowners with regard to owning the land, but there's still an unwillingness to countenance the separation of ownership.

KIRBY WHITE: It's been ironic, but understandable, that the people in my experience who have the most discomfort with the idea that they don't own the land in a CLT are African Americans in the South who've been pushed off the land. Owning the land that they're on has a kind of importance that it doesn't have for a Northern person in an urban neighborhood. That person may have spent most of her life in a condominium. Who cares who owns the land? As long as long as you can sell the damn box of air, it doesn't matter who owns the land.

JOHN EMMEUS DAVIS: It's striking to me that many of the advocates for urban CLTs in the North are less interested in fighting for community ownership of the land. Their focus is more on the building, more on the house, more on the resale controls, permanent affordability—and less on the land as something that is held in common.

KIRBY WHITE: Yeah. Yeah. You know, the people active in the CLT movement today are a different kind of people than when we started doing that work. The idea of what people should and should not own was an important idea for Bob Swann and for Chuck Matthei and for Mac McCracken and for the people who brought the CLT movement North into the cities.

Most of the people in the CLT movement now are housing people. They are people who feel strongly about housing affordability and doing something to provide high-quality affordable housing for lower-income people. *How* you do that is less important for them.

Impact & Influence of CLTs

JOHN EMMEUS DAVIS: Given the relatively small number of CLTs in the United States, compared to the number of community development corporations, Habitat for Humanity affiliates, and the like; and given the relatively small portfolio of land and housing that is held by CLTs, has there been much impact? What's the significance of this movement, given its modest scale?

KIRBY WHITE: I think the CLT movement has come to have a lot of significance in relation to housing policy, particularly in relation to how subsidies are deployed in the case of publicly subsidized homeownership. You know, 25 years ago when we talked about preserving affordability for the long-term, people would go blank. "What do you mean?" We'd have to explain it's where affordability that's a product of a government subsidy should not be lost. The owner of a heavily subsidized home should not be allowed to cash in the subsidy and remove whatever equity is in the home.

Woody Woodrow, the editor of *Shelterforce*, came to that first CLT conference in Voluntown, Connecticut in 1984. Back then, *Shelterforce* had been an advocate for not increasing governmental support for homeownership. If the CLT movement hadn't shown that you could handle ownership differently, people like Woody would still be against homeownership.

CLTs have slowly had an impact on the way that most community development people think about homeownership. I haven't heard a CDC person in a long time say that people in subsidized homes ought to be able to pocket the subsidy.

JOHN EMMEUS DAVIS: You do still hear that from many people leading local affiliates of Habitat for Humanity, although less and less. I remember being at ICE and trying to have a conversation with some Habitat people when Millard Fuller was at the helm. Any kind of resale controls on Habitat houses was anathema. Once Millard Fuller was no longer the leader of Habitat, however, there was a proliferation of partnerships between CLTs and Habitat affiliates.

KIRBY WHITE: So, there's been movement there as well. That's good. I have been annoyed with the way Habitat operates in neighborhoods at times. But they do subsidize homeownership for low-income people through a kind of communal effort that is a rare and important thing.

JOHN EMMEUS DAVIS: Their communal effort has always had more to do with how housing is constructed and financed than with how the housing is owned. Habitat has focused on production and finance. The CLT is focused on tenure.

KIRBY WHITE: There are a lot more Habitat affiliates than there used to be that don't want to see the first family cash in after all the effort an affiliate has made to get the house built or rehabbed. Whether it's through a ground lease or otherwise, Habitat is now much more careful not to allow that to happen. They don't want it happening under their noses. That's probably due, in part, to the influence of CLTs.

National CLT Network & National CLT Academy

JOHN EMMEUS DAVIS: By 2005, ICE had reached the limit of its usefulness—or, at least, the limit of its connection to the larger CLT movement which ICE had helped to build. Its unilateral cancellation of the National CLT Conference, planned for Portland, Oregon, was the last straw for many of us. You were involved in the meeting in the church in Portland, when we decided to create something new. Talk a little about what brought that on and what happened afterwards.

KIRBY WHITE: It was a matter of filling a vacuum that the decline of ICE had left. It was also exciting that the CLTs themselves had not let everything run down. The CLTs wanted to go on having national conferences, if nothing else. So they organized themselves to make that happen.

JOHN EMMEUS DAVIS: That was a pretty heady time. It felt like CLTs were taking control of their own movement.

KIRBY WHITE: Yup. CLTs were writing their own bylaws for their own association. We had a bylaws committee, which I guess I chaired. There were lots of conference calls with a bunch of people.

JOHN EMMEUS DAVIS: I remember that you went through a number of iterations before you brought the final bylaws to the Boulder conference for ratification the next year.

KIRBY WHITE: Yeah. The draft product was thoroughly vetted by CLT members and revised. It wasn't rubber stamped.

JOHN EMMEUS DAVIS: We were also creating the National CLT Academy on a parallel track. We were establishing the Network and the

Academy at the same time. The blueprints for two very significant initiatives were drafted by two different work groups, as we were getting ready for the National CLT Conference in Boulder in 2006.

KIRBY WHITE: I don't remember them as being two separate tracks. They were structured that way for practical reasons, but the vitality of the Network was expressed in the Academy.

JOHN EMMEUS DAVIS: A few years later, the Academy came calling again, asking for your help in editing and writing another CLT publication.

KIRBY WHITE: That was in 2010 and 2011, when we were doing that massive revision and expansion of *The CLT Technical Manual*. There must've been 50 people working on it. In the model lease working group alone, we revised the ground lease through more than a year's worth of monthly conference calls involving many people. There was a whole lot of legal and financial expertise included among those participants, as well as a lot of practical CLT experience.

I loved that work. It was great. We were seeing what all this real-world experience had generated and then bringing it together through those work groups. That was a blast.

JOHN EMMEUS DAVIS: After harvesting that experience, the Academy taught it and refined it as we interacted with CLT practitioners in the one-day and two-day trainings that we sponsored in various parts of the country. Unfortunately, the Academy had a short life. I won't say it was terminated, but it was absorbed by the Network in 2012 and split among several departments.

KIRBY WHITE: The Academy was the most vital part of the Network, really. It was compiling the collective knowledge and energy of a lot of people who were invested in the CLT itself, as we had described that model in the book that we wrote back in 1982. The Academy, in some ways, was the pinnacle of the CLT movement in the United States.

4.

Susan Witt

The Educator Who Showcased & Supplemented the Seminal Work of Swann and Schumacher

Interviewed by Lisa Byers
December 13, 2022

Susan Witt is Executive Director of the Schumacher Center for a New Economics, which she co-founded with Bob Swann in 1980. She has led the development of the Center's publications, library, seminars, and other educational programs, which has established the Center as a pioneering voice for an economics shaped by social and ecological principles. She helped to incorporate the Community Land Trust in the Southern Berkshires in 1980, a CLT that holds both agricultural and residential land. Then in 2015 she helped incorporate the Berkshire Community Land Trust, the sister organization to CLTSB. In 1985, she worked with Robyn Van En to form Indian Line Farm, the first Community Supported Agriculture farm in the country. In 2006, she co-founded BerkShares, a local currency program for the Berkshire region.

LISA BYERS: I want to thank you for agreeing to do this interview, Susan. I feel delighted that I get to be the one to be in conversation with you. I'm also grateful to John Davis for wanting to capture these stories for next-generation folks and activists.

The rhythm of today, the themes and questions that I'd like to explore, include some about you and your story, some about how you got into this work, some about the Schumacher Center, and some about how the community land trust is nested within the Center's larger mission. I'm hoping you'll reflect on the way that community land trusts have actually developed from theory to practice, so I'd like to hear your thoughts on that. We'll wrap up with your thoughts on where we might be headed and what you hope for the future.

How is it that you came into this new economics work? I understand that it was, in part, through Bob Swann. My hunch is you already had an inclination because you took a job at the Institute for Community Economics, right?

SUSAN WITT: Not exactly. I have no formal background in economics. In fact, I was a literature teacher in a small Waldorf High School in New Hampshire and I deeply love the world of great literature. However, I came to believe that the world's most pressing social and environmental problems could only be solved through fundamental changes in the economic system. In 1977, I heard Robert Swann on the Cambridge Forum radio program talking about his friend Fritz Schumacher's book *Small Is Beautiful: Economics as if People Mattered*, and my course was set. I decided to volunteer for the Institute for Community Economics to have a better understanding for this realm of new economic thinking.

Three years later Bob and I founded the Schumacher Center for a New Economics (originally the E.F. Schumacher Society) in the Berkshires of Western Massachusetts.

LISA BYERS: What insight did you find in Schumacher's work that moved you to change your life's course?

SUSAN WITT: In his book, actually a collection of essays, Schumacher offered a fundamentally different approach to conducting economic life. To arrive at this understanding, he was not reading books on economics; he was studying the great esoteric literature from all the world's religious traditions. His essays begin in spiritual principles and then lead to economic practice. This seemed to me the correct progression. At the same time such thinking is not dogmatic, but allows practitioners to explore their own solutions.

LISA BYERS: How would you characterize Schumacher's new economics?

SUSAN WITT: Schumacher offered a positive and locally-rooted way to respond to the problems of a global economy in which the processes of production are hidden from the eyes of the consumer—separating people, land, and community. He advocated for human-scaled economic systems, appropriate technology, cooperation between consumer and producer, and a re-thinking of the institutions of land and money.

LISA BYERS: Could you describe this need to re-think the institution of land?

SUSAN WITT: We've commodified land, enabling it to be sold on the market, resulting in the accumulation of land in the hands of a relatively few. Concentration of ownership prevents the poor from gaining affordable access to land to build their homes and earn their livelihood. The result is great wealth alongside unrelenting poverty. Without access to land, it is hard to achieve even modest self-sufficiency and a sense of a dignity. In the Berkshires we face the problem of rising land prices mostly due to demand from second homeowners, making home ownership and farming less and less affordable for local people.

Schumacher spelled out a philosophical framework for a new economics. Bob Swann then devoted his life to working out the operational details. What deeply impressed me about Bob's approach to creating the community land trust model was it was grounded in an economic analysis. Bob was a CO, a Conscientious Objector, during World War II. He spent two and a half years in a Kentucky federal prison with other COs. He later called prison his university. He and other COs, including Bayard Rustin who trained Martin Luther King in nonviolent tactics, shared books and had time to talk about what were the root causes of war.

Bob learned through his readings and his discussions with other COs that land, when it's commodified, creates an imbalance in the economy. New wealth is created when labor transforms the natural world into new products. These new products are appropriately owned and traded in the economic sphere. But land itself is nature-given and access should be by social contract, not through the market.

He went to Israel with Slater King and other founders of New Communities in Albany, Georgia to study the lease agreements of the Jewish National Fund. The JNF and the State of Israel own most of the land in Israel. The land is then leased to users who build homes and businesses on the land but cannot sell the land.

Of course, this is done to prevent non-Israelis from gaining land-ownership. It is a racist reason, but the lease itself is ingenious. The lease can be written to an individual homeowner. The lease can be written to an intentional community like a *kibbutz*. Or the lease can be written to a mixed community like a *moshav*, where there are private homes and cooperative farming. The lease of the land is independent of the social structure on top of the land.

That's what Bob brought away, an understanding for the genius and flexibility of the lease that separates ownership of the land from ownership of improvements on the land. He realized what was needed was a new community-based structure to hold land. If we were to start from scratch to develop a new economic system, then where would we place land? Not in private ownership or state ownership. Bob would have all land held in regional commons or community land trusts and then allocated via the social contract of a lease. Bob might have favored the term "trusteeship," a term used by his mentor Ralph Borsodi.

You can add anything on top of the lease. You can add subsidies to make the housing less expensive. You can add organic restrictions or restrict use to only full-time residents. You can designate the scale, the character, the ownership structure of a business leasing the land. The community land trust is just a platform for holding land off the market. The lease embeds the regional values and priorities for how the land is used—be that residential, office, manufacturing, retail, public building, or agricultural.

And Bob's innovation of the three-part structure for the board is brilliant. What's the organizational structure for a new way of holding land if designed from scratch? Well, you would want the users to have a say, but not a majority so as not to be able to arbitrarily amend restrictions. You would want the general public engaged to represent the still unmet needs for land use, so keeping the organization dynamic and forward-moving. And you need the experts who bring valuable skills such as legal, land-use planning, and financing in order to carry through projects.

LISA BYERS: Just to focus in on that a little bit. In Bob's *Autobiography*, he says that he thinks the most important thing that he contributed to the CLT movement was that idea of an open membership. Do you agree with that assessment, when you think about his legacy?

SUSAN WITT: Well no. In his conversations with me, it was the three-part board in conjunction with open membership which he understood as his most valuable contribution.

Through his work with Ralph Borsodi and from experience with his brother Jim and his family, Bob had known of a number of intentional communities. These were initiatives where people joined together to purchase land, establishing rules about ecological land use and cooperative living. All were very well-intentioned and noble in their origination. But by the second and third generations, if only users made up the board of directors, it was tempting to look at the rise in land value and suggest selling the land and splitting the profit. The three-part board structure of the community land trust was a way to address this problem of self-interest of users.

LISA BYERS: Do you believe that his addition to the model of the tripartite board is really the piece that was the most instrumental in the ongoing success of the community land trust?

SUSAN WITT: The tripartite structure creates a natural tension between leaseholders and non-leaseholders. Leaseholders would prefer that the organization turn its resources to improvements on land already acquired—removing invasives, improving the driveway, or reducing lease fees. They object to the ground rent being used to purchase new land. The non-leaseholders rightly push the CLT to find ways to increase holdings so that more people have affordable access to the land.

A seat on the board can thus be a coveted position. At the Dudley Street Neighborhood Initiative, there have at times been 30 people running for one open position. Thirty people! It can be a democratic nightmare.

LISA BYERS: Talk about splitting the ticket.

SUSAN WITT: It is that. Rosalind Greenstein, a professor at Tufts University and a longtime advocate of community land trusts, said she believes that the highest and best contribution of the CLT movement has been experience and training in direct democracy.

LISA BYERS: Interesting. And what do you think of that?

SUSAN WITT: I think the highest purpose of a community land trust has been in educating about the role of land in economics—an understanding that land should not be treated as a commodity, but "as a community to which we all belong," to quote Aldo Leopold.

But to be successful as an educator, the CLT must be structured to achieve its goal of holding all the land in a region. That's why I find OPAL so inspiring. Lisa, your community land trust currently holds 10% of the land on Orcas Island. You and your partners have built OPAL to hold all the land on the Island. That is OPAL's vision, even if not explicitly stated. Your goal is not just another housing project, but to stabilize land values on the Island to broaden access, create diversity, and narrow the wealth gap. Not that such a goal is achieved in year one of forming a CLT, or in year 20 or even in year 50, but that it could almost be achieved by year 75 is the point.

Yes, that is what I believe is the greatest contribution of community land trusts, as Bob envisioned them—that clear economic analysis of the benefits of decommodifying land.

LISA BYERS: I remember talking to you about what I would characterize as a disappointment you had about how community land trusts evolved to be focused on affordable housing and went down the charitable 501(c)(3) route. I wonder if you still feel that disappointment and how you're resting with that now.

SUSAN WITT: When we moved to the Berkshires and founded the

Community Land Trust in the Southern Berkshires, we did not want to incorporate as a 501(c)(3) for affordable housing. We did not want to exclude anyone from placing their land in trust based on income. Nor did we want the perception that decommodifying land is only for poor people and the rest of us can go on speculating. We were making an economic argument, not an affordable housing argument.

But, at the same time, without a (c)(3) designation the organization could not accept tax-exempt gifts of land or money. Income from the leases alone could not carry the costs of the organization. In the early 1980s, I researched and put forward the option of a parallel 501(c)(2) organization to a (c)(3) with multiple purposes—education on land use, affordable housing, preservation of natural resources, historic preservation, and economic development. As land is multiuse, the purpose of a land-holding organization, I argued, should reflect that complex, overlapping nature of uses.

The (c)(2) would be the actual "title holder" of the land and could lease it out to those of any income while providing equity in improvements. I called for a national meeting of CLTs to discuss this approach, which would open CLTs from being the narrow provider of affordable housing to a vehicle for broad land reform. But the idea was, at the time, rejected by those already deeply dependent on government subsidies for affordable housing.

Times have changed. Both community land trusts with the single focus of affordable housing and conservation land trusts with the single focus of preserving open space find that their structures are limiting. Conservation land trusts realize that taking land out of production for ecological purpose raises the cost of access for those that need housing and work purposes. Community land trusts are recognizing that subsidies for affordable housing are too narrow to meet the broad need for workforce housing and other land-use issues. More tools are needed. The (c)(3) and (c)(2) discussion is kicking open a lot of exploration, a lot of answers. That's tremendously exciting.

You've seen my proposal for a "Black Commons"? I wrote it at the direction of the board of directors of the Schumacher Center who asked me to explore how community land trusts could be applied to the question of reparations. I called for a national level 501(c)(3) Black Land Trust that could receive voluntary gifts of land and create a land-use plan for each site with a proposed lease that would specify the strengthening of African American cultural traditions. The national organization would then turn the land over to an existing or newly formed regional CLT to manage, with the 501(c)(3) having the right to repurchase buildings and other improvements when they come up for sale. The model has been adapted, in part, by the Agrarian Trust and by the Northeast Farmers of Color.

What Bob was calling for was new institutions, region by region, which would hold land and allocate land through a democratic process. His argument was not primarily focused on affordable housing nor conservation nor urban development. It was an economic analysis about the place of land.

LISA BYERS: You're reminding me that in the 1972 book, *The Community Land Trust: A Guide to a New Model for Land Tenure in America*, the authors laid out four pathways to pursue. One was new rural and urban communities, primarily to benefit the poor. Two was a broad-based effort with a legislative emphasis on the government as the funding source. Three was trusteeship of scarce resources, transferring control of natural resources to community land trusts, including coal beds and oil fields. Four was what you're referring to as regional land trusts, formed from existing communities.

If you think about the growth of the community land trust movement as it exists today, where do you think the most growth has occurred and why? And moving forward, where do you hope most of the growth will occur? Maybe those four concepts from the 1972 book are useful in that framing—or maybe they're not.

SUSAN WITT: Remember, that book was published by the Center for Community Economic Development which was formed to be a national advocate for creation of Community Development Corporations (CDCs).

LISA BYERS: Right, right. They were the funder for it, correct?

SUSAN WITT: Oh, it was more than that. Bob's Cambridge office for the Institute for Community Economics (formerly the International Independence Institute) actually shared space with CCED.

LISA BYERS: Got it.

SUSAN WITT: Bob saw CDCs as the nonprofit community developers on land held by community land trusts. He did not imagine CLTs as developers. If you think of the board of a CLT, it is a board to allocate and steward land. It is not a board to do development. He saw CDCs as doing the development, but the holders of the land would be the community land trust.

LISA BYERS: Got it.

SUSAN WITT: However, in the late 1980s and early 1990s, community land trusts were lured into a focus on affordable housing because there was a steady stream of government funding for administrative costs. That then created dependency and a bureaucracy. Community land trust administrators were professionals who did not themselves live on CLT land, but rather served the poor. The vision of having two separate organizations—the CDC as builder of homes and the CLT as land reform advocate—was lost.

You now have community lands trusts and community development corporations competing for the same money and the same projects and they're different. One is short-term. You build a house or a high-rise and it's over and done. Then someone else manages the long-term use of the land under the house. One's short-term. One's long-term. You need a mixture of the two, because you've got CDCs who don't want to be long-term managers and you've got CLTs who aren't equipped to do the short-term development.

LISA BYERS: Yes, although many CLTs have become community development corporations for that purpose rather than partnering. Yes, but it *is* a different skillset.

If you blend the aspect of the community land trust model that so resonates with you in terms of the keeper of the land, the steward of the land, what would be your thoughts about the current state of the mosaic of community land trusts around the country? What would you hope for the future?

SUSAN WITT: The Schumacher Center has invested a significant amount of time in creating a directory of community land trusts. It is a very "high touch" procedure, meaning we review materials— website, articles—about the CLT, create a profile, then reach out to see what changes/additions the CLT would like to include. That kind of respectful engagement gives us credibility with what are often grassroots groups.

LISA BYERS: And connection, yes. Probably almost more than any other organization, the Schumacher Center has insight into the current state of play as to the way that community land trusts are showing up.

SUSAN WITT: Right, and we're good at it. We are story tellers and documentarians. Our library contains books and papers on the theory, evolution, and practice of building new economic institutions for holding land. Our newsletters draw from that vision. We bring in speakers like George Monbiot who provide a new lens on the old question of how to achieve land reform.

And all those accumulated resources are available for free to these old and emerging CLTs as they build their boards, build their membership base, and learn to tell the story of what it would mean if land in their region was removed from the market to be replaced by a democratically structured citizen group that oversaw allocation through a lease.

I am a champion of the idea that concerned citizens, working together in communities of place, can solve problems of the community. A community land trust is a tool for activating that concern and addressing problems.

Byers: I have two more questions. First, one going back in time. You and Bob sponsored E.F. Schumacher to come to the United States, right?

SUSAN WITT: Bob, not me. In 1974 Bob organized a US tour for Schumacher to bring greater attention to *Small Is Beautiful*. During that trip Bob and Schumacher became good friends. They recognized that they approached this economic work in similar ways. Schumacher asked Bob to found a companion organization to his British Intermediate Technology Group (now Practical Action), but Bob declined. He was not prepared to take on a new organization.

LISA BYERS: Okay, that was before you were involved much. Did you know him personally? Did you meet Schumacher?

SUSAN WITT: No, I started working with Bob in September of 1977, the same month that Schumacher died, Erick Hansch died, and Ralph Borsodi died—all who were close to Bob.

LISA BYERS: Oh wow. Wow. This is my final question and I'm going to bridge the two questions together a little bit. What keeps you going? If we recognize that the pace of change is slow, what is it about the writings, the teachings of Bob Swann and E.F. Schumacher that keep you going?

SUSAN WITT: I think of Wes Jackson at the Land Institute who has not a five-year plan or a seven-year plan, but a hundred-year plan to grow a perennial grain. He is breeding a perennial grain so that the prairies no longer need to be tilled, so there's a rich enough content in the grain to feed 8 billion which is the task before us. And there was no doubt in his mind that that's a long-term goal.

So, it's this picture of a new economics that is moving me. I have just such confidence in the approach Bob brought forward out of his years in prison to decommodify land, to democratize money issue, and to build thriving place-based economies. There is such an urgency to it.

This outline for action that Schumacher shared in *Small is Beautiful* and that Bob confirmed through a lifetime of work is further strengthened by what I learned from Jane Jacobs and from my readings of Rudolph Steiner's economic lectures. I have confidence in the direction we've set. So I'm not discouraged by the length of time.

I see the vitality of the concepts. I see how they light up the young people who come to work with us. I see how it radicalizes them. Land reform. Monetary reform. This is work that can transform the whole economic system to one that is more just, more socially accountable, more ecologically responsible. A vision that gives hope in a time of crisis.

LISA BYERS: Got it. That's great. Thank you, Susan.

SUSAN WITT: And thank you, Lisa. Not just for today's interview, but for your decades of leadership in the community land trust movement. On Orcas Island where the OPAL community land trust, which you founded, is such a fine example of a CLT well-applied. But also nationally in the creation of the Community Land Trust Network, now a part of Grounded Solutions, in the development of educational modules to provide training in the theory, history, and practice of CLTs. You set a tone, set a standard for this work for which I'm most grateful.

Bob Swann & Susan Witt, 1980s

5.

Gus Newport

The Mayor Who Embraced
Community Land Trusts in the
Third Act of the Storied Career

Interviewed by John Emmeus Davis
September 21, 2020 & November 1, 2022

Eugene "Gus" Newport was a renowned social justice activist and community development consultant who became a high-profile advocate for community land trusts following two terms as Mayor of Berkeley, California. Introduced to the CLT by his friend and fellow Mayor, Bernie Sanders, Gus went on to serve as executive director of the Dudley Street Neighborhood Initiative and as Executive Director of the Institute for Community Economics. He assisted numerous grassroots organizations, worked for several foundations, and taught at multiple universities. He served on the board of the Center for CLT Innovation from its founding in 2018 until his death in 2023.

―――

JOHN EMMEUS DAVIS: Good morning, Gus. Since I am sitting here in Burlington, Vermont, I want to begin by asking you about your

153

long-time friendship with our favorite US Senator. You were elected Mayor of Berkeley in 1979 and served until 1986. On the other side of the country, Bernie Sanders was elected Mayor of Burlington in 1981, serving until 1989.

Your terms overlapped. Your politics were similar. In fact, you were two of the *only* progressive mayors in the US during a period when a reactionary President, Ronald Reagan, was dismantling every social program he could get his hands on. (Thatcher was doing something similar in England at the time.) Is that when you and Bernie first got to know each other?

GUS NEWPORT: We actually got to know each other right after Bernie was elected in 1981. Bernie, as you know, was the co-chair of CORE, the Congress on Racial Equality, when he was doing graduate work at the University of Chicago.

Berkeley was the first city to divest from South Africa when I became Mayor. We had it on our ballot. Bernie called me to inquire about that, and we sort of started exploring each other's politics and we became very good friends. Then, we would go to the Conference of Mayors meetings twice a year. A small group of us—Bernie, Harold Washington, Dennis Kucinich—we'd pull ourselves aside. We didn't pay attention to the general meeting. We'd compare notes on public policy, community planning, and organizing.

During that time also, Bernie, Dennis, and I were invited to be on panels at eastern universities like MIT, Harvard, UMass-Boston, and other places to talk about our policies because, as you said, we were considered the most—and the only—progressive mayors in the country.

So Bernie and I became close friends.

JOHN EMMEUS DAVIS: When Bernie later ran for governor, he asked you to come to Vermont to campaign for him. Why in the world did he think a Black Mayor from Berkeley, California could win votes for him in Vermont?

GUS NEWPORT: That's really interesting. I flew in the night before we were to go campaigning. They picked me up at my hotel and took me to his office the following morning. There were two reporters there, one from the UPI and one from the AP. As we started talking, the woman from The Associated Press pulled out a long sheet of paper, the old print-out stuff you had to have for the old computers. Bernie said, "What the hell is that?" She said, "Well, you know, we can put a public figure's name into a computer. We put Gus Newport's name in and we've got 90 stories." She said, "Bernie, we want to know why you, a Jew from Brooklyn, who's a socialist, invites Gus Newport, a former Black nationalist and a socialist, to campaign in a state that's 97% White." Bernie sat back and said, "Because we want to talk about the issues." They had no more questions from that perspective. We then went through, generally, what those issues were.

Of course, you know those issues as well as anybody, having been the head of housing for Burlington when Bernie was Mayor. I first learned about community land trusts by visiting Burlington and meeting you guys.

JOHN EMMEUS DAVIS: Did you also get involved, later on, in Bernie's national campaigns when he was running for the Democratic nomination for President in 2016 and 2020?

GUS NEWPORT: Yeah, in 2016 my good friend, Danny Glover, wrote an Op Ed piece for the *Huffington Post*. Right after it was published, he called me and said, "Gus, I wrote this piece about Bernie Sanders because I'm really impressed. You know him personally. You think we could get in touch with him and maybe do some work for the campaign?"

I was in Kansas City doing some community engagement and organizing. I said, "Sure." So Danny said, "Well, how soon can you contact him?" I said, "Let me try today." I called Bernie and got him and said, "Look, my friend Danny Glover wants to meet you and campaign for you. Can I give him your contacts?"

Before the day was up, Danny Glover called me back. He said, "Look, I know you're in Kansas. I know you're planning to go back to Oakland, but let me reroute your plane ticket. We're going to South Carolina and meet up with Bernie." So we went to South Carolina and started campaigning. He, James Early, Danny, and I went down there—and Cornel West. We started campaigning in South Carolina for Bernie in 2016.

JOHN EMMEUS DAVIS: You continued in 2020, the next time around?

GUS NEWPORT: Yeah, in 2020. Matter of fact, Danny and I were campaigning in South Carolina, North Carolina, and Oklahoma right up until March, when the Pandemic grounded it all.

Early Days in Rochester, New York

JOHN EMMEUS DAVIS: Let's go back before Bernie—and before you became Mayor of Berkeley. I am pretty sure that you are the only person I know who once heard Paul Robeson and Marian Anderson sing when you were a child. I believe it was your grandmother who took you to concerts featuring them. Tell me about her.

GUS NEWPORT: Well, my grandmother, she was unbelievable. My grandmother grew up in a place called Horse Pasture, Virginia. When she was in the fourth grade, she went to school late one day after picking cotton. She walks into the classroom. The White teacher didn't even ask her a question. She just slapped her. My grandmother just walked out of school and never went back. But she was an avid reader.

In those days, people got married real young. She got married at the age of 16. When they went on their honeymoon, just to show you how bad things were in the South back then, they got stopped by the Ku Klux Klan. The police put them in jail for two days and took all their little wedding presents.

Her husband was later injured in a mine accident in West Virginia. My grandmother, after her husband was injured, decided to pick up and move to Pittsburgh, where she had cousins. My mother and her mother, they moved together to Pittsburgh. And then she moved from Pittsburgh to Rochester, New York where I was born and where she had a sister.

My grandmother was so attuned to community development and stuff. Rochester was well known for the Eastman School of Music. Paul Robeson and Marian Anderson used to come there to perform often. Whenever they'd come to the Eastman School of Music—or within a few hundred miles of Rochester—my grandmother would take me to see them.

But the other thing that was interesting about her was my grandmother took me to all kinds of church events and various organizations she belonged to. Although we were living in the North, the community was still segregated. A lot of single White female teachers started moving into our neighborhood because it was more affordable. My grandmother would host a reception for them to introduce them to the community. From a Southern perspective, she'd have us kids call these teachers "Aunt Jones" and "Aunt Jenny" and things like that. It created a sense of the beloved community, the commonwealth, the kind of thing that Martin Luther King talked about. That was part of my early development.

JOHN EMMEUS DAVIS: It sounded like she was very socially aware, politically conscious. Right? She introduced you to that?

GUS NEWPORT: Well, yeah, but that's what happens. Kids had to understand what Blacks were going through, the kinds of situations that she went through. Only when I was active in civil rights did my grandmother tell me that her own mother had been a slave. After learning that, I looked at her as a model of what kept her going. She lived to be 98, as did my mother.

JOHN EMMEUS DAVIS: Tell me about becoming active in civil rights.

GUS NEWPORT: I was head of the biggest civil rights group in Rochester, the Monroe County Nonpartisan Political League. There was police brutality going on, as it is now. I was in charge of a case, the Rufus Fairwell case, which was the first police brutality case in a federal court in the United States.

The police also invaded the Black Muslim mosque. Daisy Bates, who had integrated schools in Little Rock, Arkansas when Eisenhower was President, was in Rochester organizing for the NAACP. Malcolm X called Daisy and says, "Daisy, I got to come to Rochester to find out about this police invasion of the mosque. Who should I be talking to?"

She gave him my name and phone number without letting me know. Malcolm X called me and, as you can imagine, I was taken back when he called. We spoke for about two hours. We then did that every night for two weeks.

He flew into Rochester on a cold February day. It gets very cold in Rochester, New York. We're on Lake Ontario, right across from Canada. In those days, planes parked out on the tarmac. I'm standing inside the airport, surrounded by a lot of White men in felt hats and white shirts and ties. The plane stops and lets the stairway down. Malcolm walks down the stairway and comes into the airport. We hadn't seen each other yet. He says, "Who is Gus Newport?" I raised my hand and said, "I am." He said, "Young blood, you got the best-tapped telephone in America. This is FBI all around you, all these people here" [laughter].

JOHN EMMEUS DAVIS: Well, you always *could* draw a crowd. Even in those days you could draw a crowd.

GUS NEWPORT: Right? So we're surrounded by the press. Some people laughed and other people were just in shock. We went right from there to the County Courthouse to get the eight Muslims who had been arrested out of jail. We went to court and got them out.

Let me tell you one thing about politics. After Malcolm came to Rochester that first time, the State Legislature passed a law. Malcolm X would not be allowed to speak at any government-financed institution or any nonprofit foundation or financial institution in New York State. They passed that law in 24 hours. I'd never seen anything like that before in my life, or since.

From then on, I became quite friendly with Malcolm. As a matter of fact, they put so much pressure on me in Rochester I had to move to Harlem. That's how I got mentored by both Malcolm X and Adam Clayton Powell.

JOHN EMMEUS DAVIS: What was your impression of Malcolm X? What is your memory of him as a human being, as an individual?

GUS NEWPORT: He was the greatest person I think I ever knew— next to my grandmother. Malcolm X always had some comedy about him, but he was so intelligent. You know, during his 15 years in prison he'd read everything he could get his hands on. He always had a sense of wanting to upgrade everybody that was a participant.

Here's an example. When we used to go into restaurants, we'd sit down. All the waitresses, Black or White, they'd come running to see if they could wait on his table. They wanted to get into the conversation. He included everybody. He'd say to Blacks, to White people, "Look, I'm a Black nationalist. It's not because I'm anti-White. I want to prepare my people to be able to sit at a common table with you White folks to create a common agenda, a common plan of what our society should be going forward." And, you know, all the White people would stay right there and ask questions and whatever else.

He was just great. I remember when he came back to Rochester like the second or third time after I first met him. We were meeting with the first Black elected officials and some other people, a couple of Rochester police and whatever else. A couple of Blacks, who were not as hardcore as I was, were going off on some stuff. And I said, "Stop that bullshit. You know, let's talk about the real things and make a better society."

He reached over to me and said, "Brother Eugene, let me tell you something. You're very intelligent. You got a great mind. Cool down a little bit. Why are you busting people? I want you to process this meeting out of the left side of your brain, while on the right side you're planning what's going to be our next steps out in the community."

Well, he was a great teacher.

JOHN EMMEUS DAVIS: What I like about that story is here's Malcolm X, who had a reputation as this firebrand, and he's turning to you saying, "Uh, Brother Eugene, cool it. Calm down a bit." There's a certain irony there. *You* were the young firebrand.

GUS NEWPORT: Right, right. But he knew when, where, and how to do that.

Dudley Street Neighborhood Initiative

JOHN EMMEUS DAVIS: After six years as the Mayor of Berkeley, you moved to Boston and were hired as Executive Director of the Dudley Street Neighborhood Initiative. How did that connection originally get made? How did you become acquainted with the folks at DSNI?

GUS NEWPORT: Following my term as Mayor in 1986, I was invited to UMass-Boston to be the first senior fellow at the newly founded William Monroe Trotter Institute. I was teaching a course on alternative economics and public policy. I was supposed to be working with Black and Latino legislators, helping them examine public policy that was necessary and whatever else.

Quite a few people from Dudley Street started coming down, monitoring my class, including Peter Medoff. After two or three visits, Peter Medoff pulled me aside and said, "Gus, why don't you come out to Dudley on the weekends and participate with us in some of our discussions?" I said, "No, I ain't got time for that." And Peter, with his little sharp self, he's telling me, "Goddamn it, I thought you were a real revolutionary." So I went out there and it was love at first sight, the kinds of things that Dudley was doing.

You must remember what preceded the Dudley Street Neighborhood Initiative. There was an initiative put on the ballot for Roxbury to secede from Boston.

JOHN EMMEUS DAVIS: Yeah, I do remember. Say what were they going to name that new city.

GUS NEWPORT: They were going to name it "Mandela."

JOHN EMMEUS DAVIS: Take a quick detour, because I believe that you met Nelson Mandela when he was released from prison after 27 years.

GUS NEWPORT: Right. Remember, as I said, Berkeley was the first city to divest from South Africa. By that time, I was in Boston. After Mandela was released from prison, when his first trip was planned to the United States, Boston was one of the cities that he was coming to.

The elected officials in Boston were so mixed up, each trying to make a name for themselves at the expense of his visit, rather than organizing it correctly. I was participating in some of those meetings. Some of the people knew that Berkeley was the first city to divest, so they turned to me and they said, "Gus, will you coordinate Nelson Mandela's trip to Boston?" So I did.

Of course, I knew both Danny Glover and Harry Belafonte, who were escorting him on this trip. I was taken to the airport and was able to get behind the scenes, going out on the tarmac and whatever else. The Governor, Mike Dukakis, was there and his wife. My wife Kathryn was with me. When the plane landed, oddly enough, it was Trump Airlines [laughs]!

They let the stairs down and Danny Glover and Belafonte walked down together. Of course, Danny and Belafonte greeted me and introduced me to Mandela. They let him know that I had been Mayor of Berkeley and been made an honorary member of the African National Congress because Berkeley was the first city to divest. I was also on the Committee Against Apartheid at the United Nations.

I got to escort Mandela all that day to various venues. After, we went to the JFK Library where there was a big event. He was one of the kindest, most generous people I've ever met. He was still with Winnie at that time. I have a picture with both with them.

JOHN EMMEUS DAVIS: Back to the ballot initiative. What had sparked the campaign for Roxbury to secede from the rest of Boston?

GUS NEWPORT: It was because the City of Boston, like most cities, would use all the Community Development Block Grant money and other kinds of money for downtown development, rather than using it to build up inner-city neighborhoods that were poor.

Well, that ballot initiative failed. But then, the city government was going to start re-planning and rebuilding the Dudley Street area. At one of those early meetings run by Steve Coyle from the Boston Redevelopment Authority and some other people, a couple of Black women who were in the Nation of Islam stood up and said, "Wait a minute, you got this panel up there planning for what the Dudley Street area is going to be and whatever else. Do any of you live here?" Well, that was a "no" and the women said, "Always, we got somebody planning for us that doesn't know a damn thing about our area. Here you go again, proposing that."

That's when they started organizing, put together a small non-profit, and hired Peter Medoff to do some of the planning and things.

The community started out wanting to clean up all the vacant lots. I mean, they were used for illegal dumping by private developers. We found out that was happening to Black communities all across the country, because developers didn't want to pay any tipping fee or anything. They knew that these Black communities didn't have any political clout. If you ever saw the vacant lots in Dudley in those days, they were just covered with rocks and dirt and debris. Meat packing companies would drop off loads of meat that was spoiled and things.

So, the first thing we did was challenge the City to pass a statute that would cite these developers. Then the City started sending out trucks on the weekend and we went and cleaned up those things. At the end of the day, we would have a barbecue and celebrate. Then we went to some flower companies and got seeds and planted flower seeds. Where there was blight, it became beauty.

Later, when I was on board, Steve Coyle was aware of the fact that there's a statute in the Commonwealth of Massachusetts that goes back to the 1800s. It says that a nonprofit organization could get the power of eminent domain over certain areas of land if they could create a master plan. It had only been done once before and that was by some insurance company, which must have been a nonprofit at the time in the 1800s.

We were able to hire a couple of guys who helped us create a master plan. We engaged with the community. MIT helped us, the Department of Urban Studies and Planning, and Tunney Lee, who was one of the greatest community planners.

Our master plan was accepted and we got the right of eminent domain. But we still had to have legal help, so that we could legally take the land. That's where David Abromowitz, our first attorney at Goulston & Storrs, came in. The City conveyed some land to us because they had taken it by tax arrears. But other parcels were owned by private individuals. So we had to get the legal right to purchase that land at the right cost. Goulston & Storrs made that analysis.

The Ford Foundation then gave us a $2 million Program Related Investment. We used that PRI of $2 million to purchase those vacant lands. We were also able to convince the City to mitigate all outstanding taxes on the properties they owned.

I want to say, before I forget, that David Abromowitz is probably the finest nonprofit lawyer in the country. He worked for Goulston & Storrs, which gave Dudley Street pro bono assistance when I was there. David is one of the greatest people I've known.

David Abromowitz and Gus Newport, Boston, 2008

A Community Land Trust for Dudley

JOHN EMMEUS DAVIS: Once you started getting land, once you had the power of eminent domain to get more land, you then had to figure out: How do we hold it? What do we do with it? How do we develop it?

That's the point at which DSNI started exploring creating a community land trust. You were the Executive Director at that time. Why did you believe that a community land trust might be a good strategy for holding the land and improving conditions in this area of Roxbury?

GUS NEWPORT: In the beginning, I had no clue what would be the best process. But through engaging the community, through organizing them, community people said, "Look, we'd like some kind of housing that is permanent, that allows us to keep it affordable."

We began working with this group of organizations that was helping us with that kind of planning. But once they starting talking about CLT housing, I had to go out and learn more about the community land trust.

I knew some of the people at the Institute for Community Economics. And I got to know the history, the role that Mahatma Gandhi had played in proposing community land trusts for people who were victims of the caste system. We thought that was the sort of thing we needed in Dudley.

At the time, all the nonprofit housing professionals in Boston were opposed to community land trusts. They said, "My God, people own the house, but they don't own the land. How can that be?" But they didn't understand that it stabilized lives. The affordable housing that the nonprofits were providing, when it came to the end of the term, the housing would get brought up by the private sector and whatever else. The nonprofits hadn't thought through the distance. They weren't creating something that would last in perpetuity like the affordable housing on a land trust.

JOHN EMMEUS DAVIS: I imagine you also had some skeptics in the Dudley neighborhood itself. I mean, *you* may have become convinced that a community land trust was the right way to go. Your *staff* may have become convinced. But I would imagine that you had some convincing to do out there in the community. What did you say to folks?

GUS NEWPORT: A lot of the existing homeowners were certainly opposed to it. I mean, homeowners are generally opposed to anything that benefits renters anyway.

Well, here's what we did. We looked at all the land that was available. We said, "We're going to beautify this whole community." So, we gave homeowners access to part of the land we were taking, allowing them to extend their yards and whatever else. And we showed them the master plan, that we were *not* just talking about housing. We're talking about small businesses. We're talking about upgrading the quality of education, health care, and transportation, so the working poor would have access to the jobs and all those kinds of things. The plan wasn't just around housing.

As they began to learn more, they got more and more involved. And then, of course, we had to elect a board. We created both the DSNI board, which included people who were going to be homeowners, other community people, small businesses, religious institutions, and some representatives of local government. We also created a sub-entity called Dudley Neighbors, Inc. to hold the land and to maintain it, to pay the taxes, and all those kinds of things.

JOHN EMMEUS DAVIS: Even after DSNI created its community land trust subsidiary, Dudley Neighbors, Inc., DSNI kept doing community organizing. That's one of the things I've always admired about

DSNI. Unlike many nonprofits that do less and less community organizing and leadership development as they start doing more and more development, DSNI continued to be *both* an organizer and a developer.

GUS NEWPORT: Right. Well, we recognized that, if you're going to develop a community, you do development for the people who live in that community. In order to keep on top of it, if you're doing a good job, you need to know what are the community's ongoing concerns. You have to keep the community involved.

An example. Every two years, DSNI has an election for the board. This past year, 61 people ran. Can you imagine? This many years later, 61 people running. Right?

JOHN EMMEUS DAVIS: DSNI had 61 people who ran for the available seats, the open seats on the board?

GUS NEWPORT: Yes, this past year. And it was really interesting, because people began to understand more what it meant to have a functional community, affordable housing, affordable businesses.

JOHN EMMEUS DAVIS: I imagine that many people may have first learned about the Dudley Street Neighborhood Initiative by watching the video that Mark Lipman and Leah Mahan produced a number of years ago called *Holding Ground*. If I'm not mistaken, *Holding Ground* was made under your watch. And, if I remember correctly, you made a guest appearance in that video. It was your first performance as a rapper. So, tell us, how did *Holding Ground* come to be?

GUS NEWPORT: Well, I happened to give a lecture at the Kennedy School at Harvard about Dudley Street. Leah Mahan and a young man named Derek were both there. They were working as interns on *Eyes on the Prize*. The very next day they came to my office to visit me. Leah walked in and said, "You know, Gus, we heard your lecture yesterday. We love that story. We'd like to make a video documentary about it."

I had always felt that nonprofit communities should be making more documentaries so that people could see what was happening. So I said yes and took them to a meeting of our executive committee. I said, "Look, these two young people want to make a video documentary. They're just getting started. I'd like for us to appropriate some money for them to buy a camera and just start engaging and interviewing people around the community." And the board went along with it.

Then she got together with Mark Lipman, who knew the film business. And they started interviewing and coming to all our meetings and they were accepted. No questions about them.

The way the rap happened, some of our young people had written the rap about Dudley Street with Paul Yelder. We were going to have a meeting and the young people said, "Well, we're not going to do

Gus the Rapper in Holding Ground: The Rebirth of Dudley Street, *a film by Mark Lipman and Leah Mahan, 1996. Paul Yelder is pictured on the left.*

the rap unless you do it with us, Gus." So, we get there and they start going, "Bup, bup, bup," and I noticed I was the only one rapping. But it was caught on video tape. [Laughter]

JOHN EMMEUS DAVIS: It was one of the highlights of *Holding Ground.*

GUS NEWPORT: Right.

Institute for Community Economics

JOHN EMMEUS DAVIS: Years later, you became Executive Director of the Institute for Community Economics, an organization founded by Ralph Borsodi in 1967. Over the years, it had considerable success in supporting the growth and development of CLTs. By 2005, however, ICE had run out of steam. You had been hired to turn things around, but you made the difficult decision, along with Chester Hartman and other members of the ICE board, to wind things down at ICE. You began the process of distributing the Institute's assets and programs to other nonprofits, including the newly formed National CLT Network. Reflect on the last days of ICE, if you would.

GUS NEWPORT: Well, you know, ICE was a great organization. Borsodi and those early people were very committed. You had worked there too. But, by the time I arrived, some people had come on the staff who had no real commitment to the work. For them, it was just a job.

Remember, it wasn't only CLTs that got started out of ICE. Community Development Financial Institutions also started there. Before the CDFIs got set up, however, ICE was doing a lot of lending. I didn't like how the data was being kept on some of the money and some of the lending. I got a feeling that what was going on wasn't all straight.

When I challenged people about it, they got upset. "Who is this guy? Why is he coming in here with all this?" But I was able to get Chester Hartman on my board after I was hired, and a few other people. Chester has always been a sharp analyst.

I began to say, "Look, under these circumstances, I don't want to stay in charge. I think we ought to transfer the assets and the programs for land trusts to another organization." Chester and various other people on the board helped me do that. It took a while, but the transfer was fairly smooth. And of course, as you said, a new organization was being put together, the National CLT Network, which kept the community of people doing CLT work involved. It was a smooth transition.

Center for Community Land Trust Innovation

JOHN EMMEUS DAVIS: Even in the middle of the Pandemic, you had lots of invitations to serve on boards and to do long-distance public speaking via zoom. I'm interested in why you were drawn to the Center for CLT Innovation. What was there about the Center's mission of encouraging the growth of the world-wide CLT movement that appealed to you? Why did you say yes when we invited you to join the Center's founding board?

GUS NEWPORT: Well, when I was running the Dudley Street Neighborhood Initiative, we began getting visits from people from different countries, including Russia and Japan. They wanted us to translate for them what a CLT was. Where they were getting the information from, I'm not quite sure, but they were so hungry for information. I began to recognize this as a need throughout the world.

It's amazing to think that Mahatma Gandhi thought about CLTs as something to help people who were victims of the caste system. If we're going to create a world of peace and love and harmony and understanding, then we have to have flexible and workable communities that people feel good about. They can look to each other as aspiring to a greater society. I began to recognize that people throughout the world aspire to this.

When I heard about World CLT Day, I wanted to be a part of that. And of course, John, I have to give you credit because of your many writings, including your most recent, *Community Matters*. That's what made me aspire to continuously want to be a part of the international CLT movement.

JOHN EMMEUS DAVIS: This is a depressing time in world affairs. We see discouraging signs of rising authoritarianism and a resurgence of White Christian nationalism in the USA and in other countries. Where do CLTs fit into this gloomy picture? Where does the Center fit?

GUS NEWPORT: Since I've become an amputee, I'm around home a lot. Watching television, I've gotten so turned off by the news. It speaks only about things that underwrite their stations; it's about money. They don't ever look at the success of land trusts or communities working together. They don't expose that stuff to the greater world, so we the people have to do it.

JOHN EMMEUS DAVIS: Those are the kinds of stories that we wanted World CLT Day to lift up, right? The successes and the victories of these small neighborhood-based, community-based organizations can be inspiring in the midst of the pretty dark times that we're in politically.

GUS NEWPORT: Right, and I think that more people are maybe finding out about these stories than the mainstream media ever covers.

JOHN EMMEUS DAVIS: Sharing these stories and best practices are definitely commitments we've made at the Center. But it's not just about taking ideas from the Global North and sending them to the

Global South. There's a lot of innovation and activism and creativity that's happening in the Global South that can be taught to groups in the Global North. Cross-pollination is what we're trying to foster, spanning national boundaries and the North-South divide.

GUS NEWPORT: That's what's so good about the community land trust movement. That's why it's taking birth across this country and across this world. We freely share the great new ideas we hear from our friends across the international community, right?

CLTs in Communities of Color

JOHN EMMEUS DAVIS: Last night I rewatched *Arc of Justice*, the film that Helen Cohen, Mark Lipman, and I produced a number of years ago. In that documentary about the rise, fall, and rebirth of New Communities, Charles Sherrod says at one point, "All power comes from the land. And the land comes from God. All power comes from the land." Why would a Civil Rights activist of Sherrod's generation believe land to be important for the empowerment of African Americans?

GUS NEWPORT: Well, he'd gone across the country during his time in the Civil Rights Movement, and he'd raised money for New Communities. Remember, he was part of that group that was sent to Israel to study the environment for land trusts, the financing, and everything else. This led to New Communities becoming the first land trust in the United States.

I was fortunate enough to be on the board of New Communities for a while. Charles was a brilliant man. He knew it took money and financing. He went around the country raising funds for that first land trust. And of course, his wife, Shirley Sherrod, was his great right hand. She saw her own father get assassinated in their front yard during the Civil Rights days by a right-wing redneck. All this stuff they had seen, but they believed in God and they believed in the land.

JOHN EMMEUS DAVIS: You've played a continuing role in planting seeds around the country—and around the world—about community land trusts, particularly in communities of color. I periodically get calls from places as different as Delray Beach, Florida or Seattle, Washington. I pick up the phone and someone will say, "Gus Newport was here last week and he said we should create a community land trust. And he told us to call you." Many times, those folks are young African American activists or Latino activists who are hoping to do something similar in their neighborhoods to what you and DSNI accomplished in Roxbury. Do you really believe that CLTs can help to solve some of the serious problems that plague African American communities and other communities of color in the United States and in other countries?

GUS NEWPORT: Very much so. I ran a project called the Partnership for Neighborhood Initiatives in Florida in the mid-1990s. That's when I came across Delray Beach and various other places. They were going through the same kinds of things that communities of color were going through in other places. They could use more affordable housing, permanently affordable housing, so I introduced them to the community land trust.

And, of course, whenever anybody shows interest, then I give them the name of John Davis, the man who knows more about land trusts than anybody in this world. And of course, Jason Webb was on my staff at Dudley Street, so I give them Jason's name.

I plant the seeds wherever I can and I stay involved with places as they learn about the CLT. And, of course, we show them *Holding Ground* and other kinds of things to get an idea of it. I get people doing their own videos too, so they can record their progress as they go forward.

JOHN EMMEUS DAVIS: What's the appeal? Why are young activists in communities of color drawn to the CLT?

GUS NEWPORT: I met Martin Luther King on several occasions. We did some things together. I was with Malcolm X quite a bit, and I saw him change. I was traveling with him four days before he was assassinated. Martin and Malcolm always looked for the good in people. They worked for the community, the process to raise something so that we could learn to live side-by-side and everybody could grow, that education would grow, that the people would grow.

The CLT underwrites all that. It's not just about affordable home-ownership, where land is owned by the organization, et cetera. It is looking at the total needs of the community.

I've spent a lot of time recently in Tennessee. I've gotten to know quite a few ministers. They are some of the biggest critics of the Black church, which doesn't play the role today that it did during the Civil Rights Movement. They're spanking the churches because they don't look at land trusts and things like that.

JOHN EMMEUS DAVIS: You're saying that Black ministers are criticizing the Black church?

GUS NEWPORT: Oh, yes, very much so. They see a few Black ministers who've gotten very wealthy. They're driving big cars. Some of 'em got their own airplanes and stuff. But where is their focus on community, like it was when I was a kid?

There are now more young people who are coming back into the church. They want to be movement kind of people. It takes a movement—the CLT is a national and international movement—and the churches should be part of that.

Being in the South has been amazing to me. Everybody seems to know the term "CLT." They don't know all the approaches, but they're learning about it. They aspire to it, because they connect it with building the beloved community.

JOHN EMMEUS DAVIS: You are co-chair of the Diversity, Equity, and Inclusion Committee at the Center for CLT Innovation. Given the Civil Rights origins of the CLT model, do you think the CLT movement has fallen short in making racial equity a priority? Can we do better?

GUS NEWPORT: I know we can do better. I've recently spent a lot of time, like I said, in Tennessee. One of the ministers there named Tucker asked me early in the month, he said, "Gus, have you ever thought about what it was like just before the Civil War?" I said, "No I haven't." He said, "Well, that's what America is about right now."

That's why, having known that history, we gotta think differently as we go forward, so that we don't allow something like that to happen. Even though we've got Trump and people like that, we've got to stay involved. Our people have the vision. They're not aspiring to just being recognized in some high office and making loads of money. They want to live. They want a future for their children. It's people doing things together for the good of everybody. It's all about coming together collectively as we approach this work.

I remember hearing Bishop Tutu after a meeting of the Copenhagen Accord. All these countries had come together and voted to enhance the environment. Bishop Tutu was asked by a television anchor, "You come out of a country going through apartheid. Yet you're still believing that the whole world can do this. Why?" He answered, "Look, you find differences in races in all neighborhoods, countries, whatever. Eventually, they can negotiate around their differences. We ain't got but one planet. If we don't take care of that, we can kiss everything else goodbye."

Those things give you a vision of what is best to do. If we believe in the future, in a greater place for our children, our next generation will prosper.

JOHN EMMEUS DAVIS: Is there a place for CLTs in the larger conversation about reparations for African American descendants of slavery? Young activists, in particular, those associated with Black Lives Matter and Right to the City, have raised the question of whether community land trusts can be a vehicle for reparations. What's your view on that?

GUS NEWPORT: Not only should community land trusts be tied into that conversation; a master plan has got to be tied into reparations as well. Just giving money to people, without them knowing how to spend it or how to raise the quality of life, would end up with people having nothing in the long run.

My point is that we would need to have a plan for how to invest reparations money to make sure that people have functional communities. Remember the 2008 financial fiasco? Blacks lost 72% of their wealth when the economy went down and because of predatory lending and all that stuff. They need the education and knowledge to plan how this money can be invested in creating stable communities.

JOHN EMMEUS DAVIS: I've read that, during the mortgage meltdown and Great Recession of 2008, something like $7 trillion in home equity was stripped from American families. And *half* of that was taken away from Black families, Black homeowners. There was an article published last week in *Shelterforce* by a wonderful writer named Anne Price. She called this "the greatest confiscation of economic assets from Black people in modern American history." That's quite a statement.

GUS NEWPORT: Yeah. There's got to be a master plan for reparations.

There's got to be legislation. I mean, I'm just thinking about the leg-islation that the US House passed to give money to people who were unemployed during the Pandemic. The majority of that money went to millionaires and billionaires.

Community Acceptance of Community Land Trusts

JOHN EMMEUS DAVIS: You've been doing this for a long time. You've been preaching the CLT gospel for many years. In the early days, I would expect that people scratched their heads and said, "What is a community land trust? What is that Gus Newport talking about?" And I would imagine there was a lot of skepticism and pushback. Do you think that people are more familiar with community land trusts today? Do you think they're more receptive to the message?

GUS NEWPORT: I think they *are* more receptive. When I first began discussing the CLT, it was because I had gone through Dudley in the early days. I remember what that community went through. But I also went up to Burlington, Vermont and you and Bernie Sanders and people like that were aspiring to transform what was a fairly poor, White, working-class community. That's why I got involved with land trusts and will always be involved with community land trusts.

You know, the neoliberals and extreme progressives think they know it all and can come up with the vision and ideas themselves, but the people often know what are the missing pieces. They know what *shouldn't* be done.

As I looked at how affordable housing was being normally built in the United States, people were just doing affordable housing proj-ects and all that kind of crap that came out of HUD. There was noth-ing to complement them: no open space, no small businesses, none of the kinds of things that make a community sound and complete. They were doing what they thought was best, but they didn't have the time or the energy to engage the community. We have to engage the people—as you say in your new book, *"community matters."*

JOHN EMMEUS DAVIS: How do we keep "community" at the center of the community land trust so it doesn't become just another afford-able housing gimmick?

GUS NEWPORT: I think you have to be able to show examples. I was on a zoom call with Marin County a couple of weeks ago. Marin County is considered the most racist county here in California. But they've now recognized that they've gotta have some communi-ty-owned land, not just in parts of the city that are predominantly Black, but throughout the city.

They're going through a planning process right now. I've told them, "Take your time." They were first trying to get that Coast Guard property. Some people responded to the RFP. Four groups came forward who want to do the work. The group we selected was called CLAM [Community Land Trust of West Marin]. Now, the in-teresting thing is, the women who operate CLAM are three White women. But their vision and their process are so great. I spoke out for them and said, "I think they're the best choice."

We'll have to get some other folks to complement them, but it's about engaging the community first. Not just going in there and saying, "We'll do this housing and implement this and that." It is understanding the totality of how you want this stuff to work, not just accepting government financing, whatever. If that had been the case, Dudley Street never would've made it. It takes time, but the community is ready to take the time. If you can get some short-term goals accomplished very early on, that can lead to long-term accomplishments.

JOHN EMMEUS DAVIS: Well, that was the brilliance of Dudley. DSNI took the time to build a base of support. They educated people, so there was familiarity and acceptance of the community land trust *before* they started building housing and separating the owner- ship of land and buildings. They were organizers before they were developers.

GUS NEWPORT: Right. That's what organizing is all about. Peo- ple don't understand the necessity for achieving short-term goals, which lead to the long-term goals. That's the kind of stuff we have to be structuring and teaching.

JOHN EMMEUS DAVIS: You've said that you encountered some re- sistance to the community land trust idea when you were at DSNI. I would imagine that was also true, later on, when you introduced the CLT to folks in other places. How did you get past that skepticism?

GUS NEWPORT: Well, at first, they just couldn't understand how they could become a homeowner but not own the land. And profes- sionals who were developing affordable housing were saying, "Well, if people can barely make rent, how are they going to be able to pay a mortgage?"

We had to explain that they get title to the house and don't have to buy the land. And in the future, if they sell the house, they can make some money off it, despite the resale formula that's been set up.

But see, nobody else ever thought about that. They're thinking through the minds of capitalists and through neoliberalism. It was interesting. Boston has more colleges and universities than anyplace in the world. And people from Harvard, MIT, and the like would come to Dudley and say, "My God, some of the stuff you're doing, we never thought about that." I would say, "Now isn't that something? The world thinks you all are just the greatest for educating people and here is this community that has come up with this."

Then they would start sending over graduate students to go door-to-door with us to get the statistics and the data. We then used that to create GIS maps to put the data on our "wall of wonder" to share with bankers, politicians, educators, and business people. "See, this is what a community is all about." And each of them began to recognize that and to say, "Oh my God, I never thought about that."

That's the sad thing, the individualism of people coming from various arenas thinking they know it all. But if they do, why aren't we in better shape than we are?

JOHN EMMEUS DAVIS: What's the prognosis for the growth of the CLT movement in the years ahead?

GUS NEWPORT: I think the prognosis is great. Stop and think about where CLTs were at, John, back in the Eighties, when you and I first got involved with them.

JOHN EMMEUS DAVIS: Yeah, we had only a handful of organizations like Dudley that we could point to and say, "See, that's what a community land trust looks like." Now they are maybe 550 around the world. What fueled that growth? How did we go from a handful of community land trusts in the Eighties to hundreds today?

GUS NEWPORT: Annual peer-to-peer meetings, I think, people hearing more about the CLT, video documentaries, books, all those things. I don't think we've had time to stop and to put that in perspective and to see how we manifest that and allow it to grow even greater, how we can get the word out there so it grows from one place to another. Maybe we need to do more documentaries of success, along with the books, et cetera. I think that documentaries should be another element on our international wish list.

As I went through the South last year, I was surprised at how many people generally asked for stories about community land trusts. People already knew about community land trusts. I mean, it's just like a regular conversation.

JOHN EMMEUS DAVIS: Compared to when we started out, that's pretty amazing. There would be like five people in a church basement asking me, "What the heck is a community land trust?" Right? There's certainly a lot more familiarity with the CLT today. People may not know the technical details, but they have a general idea of the meaning, the message, the purpose of a community land trust.

GUS NEWPORT: That's why you gotta keep writing, John. Cause all the books you write help to explain that more and more.

Role Models Provide Inspiration
to Us to Keep Going

JOHN EMMEUS DAVIS: Gus, I want to ask a personal question as we end our time together. What keeps you going? You've been doing this for a long time. You've continued to fight the good fight year after year, decade after decade. How do you remain hopeful? How do keep your eyes on the prize?

GUS NEWPORT: Well, I'm fortunate. My grandmother started taking me to see Paul Robeson and Marian Anderson when I was five years old, and she took me to all kinds of community meetings. She practiced the beloved community.

My minister used to take me and a couple of the guys in my neighborhood across the state of New York on debate teams. We'd debate other young men in the Baptist church about the various problems we were given.

Then I went to college, the first in my family. I dropped out and got drafted. But I got put out of the military early. They gave me an honorable discharge, but I was asking too many questions. I was stationed in Heidelberg, Germany, which is a coincidence because I later went to Heidelberg University as a student.

All these things were a learning process. It's just something that grows on you.

You know, I saw those Blacks who aspired to become middle class, et cetera. They separated themselves from the rest of us. It wasn't a good feeling for me. The good feelings I got were a function of the community, the growth of the community, the spirit of the community.

After I was Mayor of Berkeley, I went to UMass-Boston. The Dudley Street Neighborhood Initiative starts inviting me down on weekends and I'm realizing, "My God, this is a dream I've been looking for." It wasn't even very developed yet. The process was just beginning. And that beginning has grown and grown and grown.

Our committee at the Center for CLT Innovation is now dealing with the race thing among community land trusts at the international level. We talk about that. We've gotta get more people of color aware of land trusts and such, and more young people.

JOHN EMMEUS DAVIS: It seems like you've drawn inspiration from your elders, but you also continue to draw inspiration and energy from the people you're interacting with, particularly young activists. You're involved in mentoring that next generation.

GUS NEWPORT: Well, I guess mentoring goes two ways. My granddaughter says, "Papa, you're four years older than baseball. You know everybody." But I listened to my grandmother who told me, "Don't think you know it all, boy. No one of us knows everything. Learn something new every day."

You have to have role models. One of our greatest role models just died, Ruth Bader Ginsburg. Even though she had all kinds of cancers, she kept doing health workouts and continuing her social interactions, and whatever else.

Of course, I've also been inspired by the other elders I've met. Right now, I'm a member of the National Council of Elders, a group of people founded in 2011 by Vincent Harding who was Martin Luther King's speechwriter. You have to be 65 or older. These are people who were part of the Civil Rights Movement, the environmental movement, the free speech movement, the feminist movement, and people like Delores Huerta, co-chair of the United Farm Workers. People like that.

We get calls from a lot of young people who are out there demonstrating now with Black Lives Matter and whatever else. They want to know how we planned and how we did stuff. They want to know how we dealt with some of the problems of dissension and stuff within our own organizations. We share with them our successes, as well as the mistakes we've made.

I reorganized the police department when I was Mayor of Berkeley. That's come up now. So, I'm able to share with young people how we did that. Also, when I was Mayor, I began seeing all these homeless people. Ronald Reagan was the Governor of California at the time I got elected. He closed all the mental health institutions and all those people started flowing to places like Berkeley and San Francisco because they felt we'd be more sensitive to their needs. I went down and engaged them. I let them use my conference room to have discussions and I gave them the first hour on my city council.

Then we bought some old yellow school buses and put them on our marina, with port-a-potties in them. We put portable showers outside and gave each person, the homeless, a post office box so they could apply for Supplemental Security Income. And we began planning with them, because you've got to know what the needs of any community might be.

Well, I've been through a lot of that. I've been with a lot of people, including yourself, who know what to do about things like CLTs. Together, I think we can engage the community and make us a better society going forward. I know that together we *shall* overcome.

JOHN EMMEUS DAVIS: I'm glad you're still out there, Gus. We need elders like you to keep guiding and inspiring "young fellows" like me, showing us how to stay hopeful and engaged.

GUS NEWPORT: Thank you, brother John. Always appreciate you.

6.

Stephen Hill

The Surveyor Who Expanded
the Dimensions of Democracy in the
Development of Affordable Housing

Interviewed by Dave Smith
March 28, 2023

Stephen Hill is an independent public-interest practitioner in planning and housing development, advising central and local governments, developers, housing associations, and community housing groups. In 2014, he visited the USA and Canada as a Churchill Fellow, reporting on approaches to the co-production of housing and neighbourhood development by the "state" and citizens through community organising. In 2021, he retired as a trustee of the National CLT Network (for England and Wales) and as Chair of the UK Cohousing Network, but he is still active in supporting community groups and getting the law changed to help them. In 2017, he received the "John Emmeus Davis Award for Scholarship" from the Grounded Solutions Network in the USA and has a lovely wizard's hat to prove it.

DAVE SMITH: I'm delighted to be joined this afternoon for an interview with a colleague who, I'm also very pleased to say, has been a friend of mine for a number of years: Stephen Hill.

STEPHEN HILL: Hello. Nice to see you.

DAVE SMITH: Stephen, the purpose of this interview is to take in the history of your career as a public interest surveyor and the history of your significant contribution to the CLT movement, not only in England, but across the globe.

I thought we should start, however, by having you describe the broad range of roles that a "surveyor" plays in the UK, since that profession tends to be more narrowly focused in the United States and in other countries. Then we'll turn to the path you followed in finding your way into this career.

STEPHEN HILL: Well, that's a rather large question to start off with! So, I am a planning and development surveyor, but that is just one of over 100 different surveying disciplines in the UK. My professional body is the Royal Institution of Chartered Surveyors, which was founded in the middle of the 19th Century and incorporated with a Royal Charter in 1881. Since the end of World War II, a number of smaller professional bodies have been amalgamated into it. You have the kind of surveyor that is familiar in the US, someone who surveys and measures land, but we also have "quantity surveyors" who measure and cost all the components of new buildings or any form of new development, and "building surveyors" who design and construct buildings, "valuers" who survey the market and will tell you how much your property is worth, surveyors who manage completed buildings or agricultural estates, project managers who coordinate everything from briefing to funding to building, and even fine art auctioneers and valuers for the beautiful things that might go into a building!

My particular planning and development discipline was invented by the institution in the late 1960s, as part of a programme of modernizing the profession. What was felt to be missing was a synthetic skill of integrating all the technical expertise in the many different disciplines into an overarching strategic perspective. Much of the conceptual thinking that led to these changes came from the university teachers under whom I studied during my Land Economy degree. So, you could say that I was coincidentally indoctrinated into the "planning and development" way of thinking from an impressionable age . . . which didn't stop me trying to be an architect a few years later, as I expect we'll discuss!

DAVE SMITH: Any chance of you explaining that doctrine, in a nutshell?

STEPHEN HILL: OK, I'll give it a go. One of a number of the tasks listed for surveyors in the 1881 Charter was "to secure the optimal use of land and its associated resources to meet social and economic need." I would take that as being a pretty accurate job description of my approach to surveying, but in the 1960s no one was taking responsibility for that idea. It was a pretty advanced public interest idea, probably a reflection of the classical economic thinking that was dominant in the 19th Century: David Ricardo, Henry George, Thorstein Veblen and others who recognized the importance of land alongside labor and financial capital in ordering a well-working economy.

This was an idea that the Chicago School of neo-classical economists, funded by Wall Street, successfully trashed in the 20th Century, although poor Henry George was simply ignored. The Chicago School promoted the idea that land was just another commodity whose price was solely determined by market forces. That was to the great detriment of every developed economy round the world. It is one of the reasons why housing is so expensive and unaffordable today. We are experiencing the ultimate realization of their vision of economic theory. They have a lot to answer for!

Against the backdrop of the affordability problem which they left in their wake, it becomes obvious why CLTs became so central to my professional practice . . . and why professional practice can't avoid being political. Perhaps we'll cover that later.

Background & Education

DAVE SMITH: Where did you grow up, Stephen? Where in England were you born?

STEPHEN HILL: I grew up in rural Hertfordshire in a small village between the county town of Hertford and the small market town of Stevenage. During my childhood, Stevenage was being developed as one of the post-war New Towns, and was very instrumental in my personal urbanization. You could go to Stevenage and get the real urban highlife of Wimpy (coffee) Bars and bowling alleys and even Cecil Gee hipster trousers. That was unlike Hertford, where you could go to the Gents County Outfitters and the Shire Hall Tea Rooms, and that was about it. Going to Stevenage was definitely the exciting part of my life.

It also introduced me to the character of new development. We had friends who lived there. Once, when we went out into the town center in winter, it was a very foggy night. When we came back, we found ourselves trying to get into the front door of another house that looked exactly the same as our friends' house, but wasn't. We eventually found our way back, but it was quite hard to work out where you were on a foggy night. All the roads and houses looked much the same.

That must have been a memory that's been stuck in my mind all this time. I thought, "We have to do better than this."

DAVE SMITH: I'm a New Towns boy as well. I was born in Crawley. I didn't think it had anything to do with my choice of career or my interest in housing afterwards. But, when I look at it now, the idea of these small neighborhoods, which each had their own essential local shops that served the basic needs of the community: that was place-making, as we now call it. Perhaps these things do have a have an influence on you as you move forward.

STEPHEN HILL: Yeah, but I couldn't get out of there quick enough, thank you.

DAVE SMITH: We did, we both got out. Unlike a number of people in our field, you actively chose to study housing and land economy.

STEPHEN HILL: Well, yes and no. I mean, part of the childhood experience was not quite knowing what career you wanted. I was at a school that had a Careers' Master. He asked, "What do members of your family do?" I said, "Well, my father's a civil servant. He has told me, 'You definitely should not become a civil servant.'"

Then the Master asked, "What else do people in your family do?"

I said, "My brother's in the Army, but I'm not going in the Army. And I have a cousin who's a solicitor." He said, "Ah, solicitors. Now that's a good career. Why don't you talk to them?" That was it. That was as helpful as it got.

I went to university with the idea that I was going to study the law. But at Cambridge you can do your degree in two Parts: Part One in one subject and then Part Two in something else. So, I went up with the idea of doing Part Two in Law. But for Part One, I thought, "Well, I'd just like to do something I'm really interested in." So, I studied archaeology and anthropology.

I'm very glad I did read archaeology, because you get a bigger perspective on how civilizations develop; how they come and go. And in anthropology, social anthropology, you learn the characteristics of different kinds of social organization and how societies organize themselves to survive and to adapt. That was really fascinating.

I then switched to law in my second year. You had to do an eight-week summer vacation conversion course to get yourself up to speed. I struggled through my first term, not really getting to grips with it. I found it so abstract. Topics like international law, which are more like the topics that you read about in the news, seemed much more accessible and interesting, but that wasn't the heart of the course.

I shared a room with a friend who was reading Land Economy. I was beginning to be really interested in architecture, but I thought the whole business of becoming an architect was very long and drawn out, and I couldn't imagine spending so much time getting qualified. My friend was telling me, "Well, we do a bit of architecture and planning and design, alongside all the other topics about land use management." That sounded really interesting. There was a lot of law in that, which was also quite attractive, as it was law that was very specifically related to a particular activity that you could get your head around. So, I switched to Land Economy.

DAVE SMITH: I always thought of Land Economy as the "thickos" subject to which they sent a university's rowers and rugby players. But you very consciously chose that subject.

STEPHEN HILL: I think the discipline of Land Economy gives you a very particular perspective on the various roles of landowners, landlords and tenants. You get a perspective over the whole business of freehold and leasehold ownership in English property law, which is very unique across the world. It's actually quite an efficient way of allocating capital, risk and reward. There was a lot to learn from that.

DAVE SMITH: You graduated from Cambridge in which year?

STEPHEN HILL: 1970.

DAVE SMITH: And you went off into the big wide world doing what?

STEPHEN HILL: Well, I first went to a property development company as a graduate trainee. They were unusual as a development firm because they had an in-house town planning team. It was headed up by a man called Ernest Powdrill, who was well known as an adventurous and imaginative planner.

At that time, a whole series of measures were being put in place by government to try and direct new development, particularly industrial and employment, to other parts of the country, not to London or the South East. There were incentives or disincentives being applied to landownership and planning.

Part of my graduate traineeship was to spend time in each bit of the business, but I spent most of my time in the planning section. It was the most interesting part and where projects get started.

I was exposed very early on to some quite big projects in London. I was basically told to go out on my own initiative, and to make assessments of the development potential of these sites. Wow! Do some research about the planning context, try to understand the market and things of that sort, and then make recommendations.

DAVE SMITH: Can you remember any in particular?

STEPHEN HILL: Yes. Well, there were some interesting semi-derelict sites up behind Kings Cross Station which are only being redeveloped now. And another big development was on the south bank of the Thames. This was a very large site called the Green Giant. It was highly contested and no one really knew what to do with it. The owner of the property development company that I was working for, the Lyon Group, had recently acquired it. Ronald Lyon just had the cash, so he bought it. At that stage it seemed like an incredibly long shot. My amateur judgement: it was premature and poorly located. But a generation later, after completion of the Victoria Line, it eventually became the highly developed area that we now call Vauxhall Cross and New Covent Garden, very well-connected by over-ground and underground trains.

DAVE SMITH: That was a huge scope of work, a huge amount of creativity for a young person to be given in their early days of their career.

STEPHEN HILL: Yeah, it was an amazing opportunity. Everybody was grappling with the challenge of "what to do with London" in the 1970s. I won't say it was a shithole, but it was pretty bad. Housing conditions were terrible. Even in the private ownership sector, people didn't look after their houses. People were still living in a post-war period state of mind. There were still undeveloped bomb-damaged sites well into the 1980s. Nobody was coming to invest in London. The population was still declining. People were moving out of the city; rather like New York at the same time. The idea, back then, that these big development sites had any kind of potential was completely alien.

I did my graduate traineeship for about six months. Then they offered me a position in project management. But I wasn't very interested in managing industrial projects. What next? My supervisor at Cambridge on the Land Economy course was a Mauritian called Sylvio Prodano. He'd been an advisor to the National Federation of Housing Associations. It was then in its very early days. So, a lot of his coursework and our conversations during supervisions were about housing, particularly council housing (now social housing) and colonialism.

That's how I got interested in affordable housing.

The property development company did have a housing arm,

but it was building suburban housing for sale. Not really very inter-esting, although it was pioneering what we would now call "mod-ern methods of construction" in its family houses. But I left them and applied for a temporary job working for the London Borough of Islington in north London, on their council housing management side. They were involved in a very substantial redevelopment phase of building on bomb-damaged sites and slum clearance.

On the housing estates that I was managing, they were continu-ing to build, but nobody was ever looking at the bits that had already been finished. Nobody was seeing how they were working. There was no feedback, no consultation with the residents whose direct lived experience might have told them something about what was working and what wasn't working.

I think, mainly, what this experience did was to reignite my inter-est in architecture. I started thinking, "How do we do better build-ings? Maybe I should go back to college, go to architecture school, and learn how to be an architect."

In a matter of about three weeks, I rang up what was then the Ox-ford Polytechnic Architecture School. There was a term beginning in about four weeks. I asked, "Is it possible to apply at this late stage?" They said yes. So, I sent in some material, had an interview, and they took me on. That was quite extraordinary. I had an interview with the head of the school and explained to him what I was interested in. And he said, "Well, I think you come to this training with a very dif-ferent perspective from anybody else I've ever met who wanted to be an architect. Let's give it a go." He was great.

It was a school of architecture that had grown out of architec-tural firms operating in the city, back in the pre-war period. Most of the teaching was done by practicing architects, which gave it a very practical feel. It wasn't highfalutin'. It was a very grounded, down-to-earth approach to architecture, which I really appreciated. But despite that, what I was beginning to find was that in the way that projects were briefed, there was no systemic way in which you were drawing on the needs and wants of the people who might live or work there.

I think the crux came when we had to design a community center. It was in a little suburb on the outskirts of Oxford, quite near the College. We went to a church hall and met some of the parish council who were thinking they would improve the parish hall and then turn it into something bigger.

We did get some elements of a brief from them. But what I learned from that was that the experience of running, or trying to run, a multi-purpose multi-user building community facility was hard to capture in a brief. People had so many ideas of things that they wanted to do. It was very difficult to crystallize them down into something very precise.

Indeed, the very idea of being precise and prescriptive was quite alien to the way in which they would be using the building in the future. They needed something that was very adaptable and flexible. So, you needed both a user-led brief, but also user-control of the building, and it all needed to be very adaptive.

That was in tune with some fashionable architectural ideas that were around in the early 1970s called "Long Life, Loose Fit," which is now right back at the forefront of architectural thinking. How do you create some basic structural components of a building that have a very long life and, within that, how do you have "loose fit" elements that could be moved around and were more disposable? My ultimate solution to this was not to design a building, but to design a construction system that could be moved around with relative ease by the users of the building. So, you can see aspects of the CLT starting to take shape in this kind of situation. Citizens in charge!

DAVE SMITH: Did you qualify as an architect in the end?

STEPHEN HILL: No. I did three years, and I did a "year out" working in an architectural office. I had a great year working with a firm of architects near where my parents lived. The job I did there was to run a project for the firm, converting some existing farm buildings into the firm's own design studio.

I had to learn how to design every component of the building. But they also gave me the job of making a lot of it. There was another architect in the firm who was a really good carpenter. So, everything we designed we then made: all the windows, all the doors, and other bits of the work. I learned a lot about the practicalities of putting buildings together, learning from mistakes and putting them right the next time, which a lot of architects don't get until much later in their careers—or maybe never!

Having completed that, I could see that I wasn't really going to be a very good architect of the kind they were training people to be. But I thought I could be quite a good *client* in the sense of knowing how architects work and the way in which they approach their work in relation to a brief.

Bringing Resident Voices into Housing Design

DAVE SMITH: I'm interested in your drift towards the CLT model. I suppose my question is what was the golden thread running through those times that led you to the CLT?

STEPHEN HILL: Nothing directly to do with CLTs, but what was most striking when I briefly worked on housing management was the attitude of the people working for the local authority, which was absolutely deplorable. I mean, they were contemptuous of their own tenants. They treated them with disrespect, as people whose opinion was of no real value.

DAVE SMITH: Have you got examples? Or was it just a general, pervasive thing?

STEPHEN HILL: Something particular would be the experience of people coming into the council's housing office, either to pay their rent or to ask for some repairs to be done. The attitude across the counter, rigged up as a security grill, was just terrible. I thought, "Why is this? Why can't they be treated with respect? You treat other people badly and then you don't listen to them. You don't even try to find out if they might have useful things to say, which could help you to do better buildings and to do better neighborhood revitalization."

After architecture school, I went back to working for a local housing authority. Initially, I got a research job at the London Borough of Haringey, also in north London. Then an opportunity came up on their development team. They were setting up a new client-side function, which astonishingly they'd never previously had. They'd been building thousands of new council homes since the end of the war, but it had never been done with the Housing Department as a client.

At the time, the council had decided to hand over the management of some completed projects to tenant management cooperatives. Some of the projects had been completed for many years, and the choice to turn them into tenant management co-ops arose from established tenants' associations active on the project. However, for some of the newly completed projects, the new tenants were suddenly confronted with a situation they may not have been prepared for. In fact, most tenants were very pleased to take up the challenge. So, it seemed a small, logical step to think about recruiting a tenant management cooperative from potential future tenants for the design stage.

Part of what I'd learned, when I was at Oxford Poly, was about the Byker Wall redevelopment area in the east end of Newcastle. This was an area of antiquated housing being redeveloped by the city council. They employed Ralph Erskine, an English architect working in Sweden. Uniquely, he insisted on setting up a design office within the area, and he then designed each phase with the residents who were going to live in that phase.

I thought, "Well, why don't we do that here in Haringey?" If you're going to have tenant management of properties that have already been developed, why don't we set up a tenant management co-op of people who will live in and manage this place in the future? They will be the client for it. That goes back to my experience of thinking, "How do you bring the resident voice or the user voice into the design of new places?"

My director brought in a guy named Tony Gibson, a very eccentric academic at Nottingham University. On first meeting, we thought of him as very unworldly and unrealistic. He had been working on ways to help people who were at the margins of society to have a greater say over their lives. That was not just in relation to development; but also in relation to all sorts of situations, like people who get into debt. How do they find ways of managing themselves to get out of debt? His approach was to devise techniques that were very accessible and approachable, allowing people to take some control of their situation and not be dependent on external professionals who may or may not know what it actually feels like to be in that position.

What he called "The Game," which later became known as "Planning for Real," was a technique for involving residents affected by development. If you were doing a major redevelopment project, or something where people are going to be affected by new transport infrastructure or whatever, it was a way for professionals and communities to be engaging with each other, using language that was very accessible.

His idea was that you come together around a model or a map or photographs, something that people can see that represents the place that you're talking about. Then people simply tell stories about that place. Anyone can tell a story: What happens on that street corner where those annoying kids hang out, where old Mrs. X tripped on that paving stone that's never been fixed, and so on? That becomes the language of interchange between professionals and lay people for ideas about what you think this place is now, and what it could be like in the future.

It was incredibly successful. It amazes me how little it's used as a technique today. It still exists. It's a trademarked technique. Lots of similar games have been devised since then for the same purpose. The Prince's Foundation developed something called "Enquiry by Design," but it was much more focused on helping design professionals. It doesn't really address the basic idea of "How do you get everyone talking to each other on an equal footing, with a shared language?"

"Planning for Real," on the other hand, is really straightforward. It appeals to children because they can tell you a story about what it was like to play in that part of the street, or there's a big old tree down in the park where they meet their mates even when it's raining. It was just a great, great technique. Everyone can tell a story. Having done that, there was no looking back. Why can't we do this all the time?

DAVE SMITH: How did you come across the CLT model?"

STEPHEN HILL: My touchstone was the Dudley Street Neighborhood Initiative. Pat Conaty had visited Dudley and written it up for a pamphlet published by the New Economics Foundation in the late 1980s. Dudley was still quite a young organization then, only about six or seven years old. But they'd already gone through the experience of working with the city council, who had "lent" them compulsory purchase powers (eminent domain) for assembling land in the middle of their neighborhood. That made it possible to develop a neighborhood where economic, cultural, and social activities could happen in a way that wasn't possible before.

Here was a community of people deciding to do something for themselves, doing this in the public interest for the benefit of their community. And they had an organizational form that gave them some democratic legitimacy, as it described to other people *what* they were trying to do and *how* and, therefore, *why* they should be accepted and supported in doing that.

That seemed to be such an extraordinary achievement. I thought, "How could we learn from that? How could we embody that here in an organization that citizens had set up themselves and could represent everybody?"

The Land Question

DAVE SMITH: In the chapter you contributed to *On Common Ground*, you quoted a statement from a 2019 conference that proclaimed, "What oil was to the industrial age, urban land is to global capitalism." You clearly believe land is the central question we've got to address.

STEPHEN HILL: Yeah, yeah, yeah. Certainly, there was a toxic effect from global financial deregulation in the mid-1980s, coming very shortly after the introduction in the UK by Margaret Thatcher of the Right-to-Buy of our social housing. Those two events in combination caused a significant value uplift in a more liberalized housing market. There were bags of wholesale money going into mortgages, previously constrained by sensible income criteria and lending from savings. It made urban land a global speculative commodity.

Obviously in places like Britain, which are well-regulated and quite stable, our land markets were much more attractive than in many other parts of the world. It wasn't really any surprise that so much footloose and some quite dirty money poured into London property.

The global value of residential property today is something like $165 trillion. All the gold that has ever been mined is only $7 trillion. It's extraordinary. We're hooked on the value of our housing.

DAVE SMITH: You've used another phrase in your writing, which I really like. You talked about the community land trust as problem *defining*, rather than problem *solving*. What did you mean by that?

STEPHEN HILL: I can't claim any originality for that. That's lifted straight from John Davis!

DAVE SMITH: What did you both mean by that?

STEPHEN HILL: It's a really important idea. Let's take as an example a village in the West Country, where the perennial problem is people moving out of London to buy holiday homes. Capital that's been generated in one place in urban land markets is being exported by people who have the ability and the discretion to do it. Global capital is being put into a local rural housing market with very particular characteristics.

That kind of movement of capital from one market to another, from global to micro-local, is deeply problematical. There are no formal land management systems that we can put in place to control it. So the community comes together. They can see that their village is dying on its feet because most of the houses are now being bought up by second homeowners and are empty for 80% of the time. There are no homes that are affordable to local people. The village shop and the local school are under threat. What should they do? So they have defined the problem as being the future of their village.

The reasons why the CLT idea started off so quickly in Cornwall, a prime holiday destination, was that it was part of a study by the Carnegie UK Trust, which was looking at two rural areas, one in Scotland and one in England. The research question of the project was, "What would make the most difference to local quality of life?"

The villages in Cornwall were saying, "Access to affordable housing" because, without that, these villages will die. They'd already worked out what the problem was. They defined it as the future of

our village. How do we solve the problem? We need affordable housing, but neither local authorities nor housing associations could or
would help.

They looked around and they found the CLT model. People like
Bob Patterson and Steve Bendle, who both lived in the West Country, had been to the United States with Pat Conaty. They'd been to
the Institute for Community Economics, and then to Dudley and to
other places. They'd seen the CLT at work and they brought the idea
to England in that particular form. You have to find a mechanism
for taming your local land market, which was essentially what those
Cornish people were trying to do. That then provided the opportunity for the local authorities in Cornwall to put their support behind
communities who wanted to take this path.

DAVE SMITH: You've played a major role in taking the seeds planted
in Cornwall and scattering them across the UK. Part of that has involved explaining the CLT in terms that different audiences could
understand.

STEPHEN HILL: In the late 1990s, Catherine Hand (a solicitor who
was later involved in drafting the statutory definition of CLTs in
2008) and I were first thinking about how we should describe CLTs
in the context of English law. We called the papers we wrote "Rein-
venting the Feudal System." This was a risky thing to do, as feudal-
ism is generally thought of as an exploitative system through which
rich and powerful landowners kept "the peasantry" under their
thumb. It's more complicated and interesting than that!

The Feudal System was not just a set of economic relationships;
it was also very much about social relationships and the kind of mutual obligations that exist between people who hold different interests in land. In English law, it's possible for there to be a whole range
of different interests in the use of the same bit of land. It's not just

about a singular landlord and tenant. It's also about a range of different people or organizations who might own easements across a parcel of land, rights to hunt, or who have particular rights to things that might lay under the land, such as minerals, or the water that flows over the land. These rights can all exist in the relation to the same bit of land. That's completely unique in the world.

We have a fantastic system in the UK that allows us to do things so simply, in such a well-ordered way. So, if you like, the Feudal System, if managed properly in the public interest, is actually rather a good one.

DAVE SMITH: The focus on land and the focus on land economy isn't just an abstract philosophy for you. It's not just a nice story to tell. It's absolutely essential to the work that we do in the CLT movement. From a philosophical perspective, nothing translated that story better for me than the story of David Ricardo and him previously living at the St Clements site in East London. I wonder if you could briefly tell that story.

STEPHEN HILL: Well, David Ricardo was a classical economist, working at the turn of the 18th/19th Centuries who came up with the idea of "economic rent." Essentially, economic rent is the return that you expect to make, if you invest in something, that justifies your investment. If the returns are higher than expected, however, or even excessive—that is, more than you need to justify the investment—it becomes extractive. It deprives other parts of the economy of capital.

That is particularly true with land, because it's a scarce, finite resource. Ricardo assumed, in fact, that the state would do something to ensure that economic rent related to land did not become damaging to the rest of the economy. In the 19th Century, that meant taxes directly related to land ownership. Landowners were more or less the only people paying taxes. That gradually changed, of course, as income taxes and corporate taxes grew larger, and the taxation of land became negligible.

Henry George was the natural successor to David Ricardo in thinking we have to tax the underlying value potential of land. That was his single tax or site value tax. Doing so removes the perverse incentive to invest in land at the expense of everything else.

DAVE SMITH: Ricardo is an under-discussed part of the history and philosophy of the CLT movement. He deserves more discussion than he gets. You discovered the phenomenal coincidence that he once lived on the site of the London CLT's first project.

STEPHEN HILL: Yes, I think it was called New Grove Villas. It was a row of very posh Georgian townhouses built for wealthy sea captains in the 1790s, which would have then been a genteel rural setting on the outskirts of the City of London.

DAVE SMITH: But, come 1848, that row of houses was knocked down to make way for what was first a workhouse and later a psychiatric hospital. It became known as St Clements Hospital and now proudly stands as London's first-ever community land trust.

People can read about that project and the history of the London CLT in other places, but I think it is fair to say that, where it not for you, the St Clements project would never have happened.

STEPHEN HILL: That's very kind, Dave. But I'm going to make sure that anyone who's reading or listening to this interview knows one thing about St Clements. I might have had a bit to play, but actually *you* were the person who did all the hard work, all the legwork, all the donkey work: pestering politicians, doing the business plan, negotiating with developers. You did all the things to actually make it happen. Everybody needs to know that.

The Theory of "Massive Small"

DAVE SMITH: It was 15 years ago that we met for the first time and started working on St Clements. The London CLT developed its first 23 homes there. This weekend, the 2nd of April, we're opening our next 11 homes down in Lewisham.

That's 35 homes in 15 years, an average of only two a year. You could look at that and say, "Well, the impact is negligible. Our efforts didn't lead to the creation of thousands of units of London CLT homes. We haven't gone to scale." The question that I'm getting to here is you don't believe the impact to have been insignificant. You have this theory about "massive small." I'll let you explain what you mean by that phrase.

STEPHEN HILL: St Clements was important as a symbolic trailblazer. All the other urban CLTs in England that have followed, as in Bristol and Leeds and Liverpool, draw their inspiration from St Clements. It was the first significant urban CLT. Prior to that, all the activity was in rural areas.

CLTs stand out as an uncomfortable truth. They make it clear to policymakers and public authorities that, if you're talking about proper affordability, this is what it takes. It's not cost free. In terms of the public interest, if you want genuinely affordable housing that relates to what people actually earn, you can precisely define the affordability criteria and then calculate pretty exactly what the price of the land should be. That ought to be of assistance to a local authority where private developers are resisting providing affordable housing at all, or where housing associations are unwilling or unable to provide housing that is properly affordable. But, for all sorts of reasons, they have not been as exacting in enforcing affordability policy requirements as they could and should have been.

CLTs are a reminder to people in power that government is not really solving the problem. CLTs say: "That's not good enough. You are playing around the edges of the problem." CLTs get to the heart of the problem by saying you have to do something about the price of land. If you're not doing something about land prices, you are not doing anything meaningful about the affordability problem. Politicians and public authorities don't like to be told that, do they?

DAVE SMITH: What are your feelings about the challenge of "going to scale," the implied critique that unless CLTs are bigger or more numerous, they will not have the impact that citizens are after?

STEPHEN HILL: I've always had mixed views about the question of scale. I think there are two ways of looking at it. When I would go to a young CLT to talk with their local authority, you'd often get the raised-eyebrows treatment that implies the question, "Why are you doing this? This is what we do!" Except they don't!

We will never deliver large numbers quickly and easily and cheaply. I've spent my life doing development, and I sometimes feel I've been very unlucky; I must have missed out on these quick, large, cheap, easy-to-do schemes that CLTs are always told about when local authorities or government officials give reasons for not supporting CLTs. These are the fantasies of people who have never built a house in their life! All housing development is difficult in the UK, and it all takes a long time, and it nearly always costs a lot more than you have planned.

So, I'm just wondering whether delivering large numbers of housing is a false ambition. The one thing that CLTs do really well is to do something that's absolutely right for their community, their place. We've seen, for example, how the housing association movement (which are like community development corporations in the US) started off very local and doing things that were welcomed by their community, fixing particular problems that nobody else was fixing. Now look at them. They're multi-million-pound enterprises with very little connection with their locality, and are now often deeply resented by communities when they come and do developments near them, and too many are not too hot at managing and maintaining their homes once they've built them.

It just feels there has to be more openness to different ways of doing things. Clearly there is a need for large-scale producers, but there are also very particular things that communities need, which nobody else seems to understand. Then CLTs came along and, uniquely in the UK, opened people's hearts and minds to the idea that new development is a good thing. Whereas, so often, new house-building is seen as something to be resisted and sometimes deeply resented, because the producer doing the development doesn't have any connection to the community. So, you just feel there ought to be more tolerance and acceptance of the idea that we need many more different kinds of housing and organizations who build new homes and help to build communities. CLTs build housing to meet a very particular community need.

So, on that question of scale, I'm still of two minds about it. What the CLT movement is trying to do is to provide hyper-local solutions that are right for each community. Very often, these are very small communities. Cities are obviously starting from a different place. Even here, however, there are very different identities in different parts of the city, and it is quite wrong to write off CLTs as only necessary and appropriate in rural areas.

So, what I think of as "massive small" is the combined power of many small actions, in many different places, with CLTs and housing cooperatives and cohousing organizations and other forms of community-led housing all working together. You know Arlo Guthrie's words in Alice's Restaurant? Much cleaned up, the lyrics say something like, "If one person does it, they may think he's sick. If two people do it, they may think they're crazy. But if fifty people do it, my friend, it's a movement." And that's what CLTs are. They're a movement.

DAVE SMITH: The London CLT is still the biggest urban CLT in the UK. We have examples in Liverpool and in new developments around Cambridge and in other places as well, but don't CLTs still remain a predominantly rural venture in the UK?

STEPHEN HILL: I'm not sure about that. There's so much activity bubbling up in Liverpool and Leeds and Bristol. I think cities are getting the idea—and , in those three large cities, there are Labour Party civic leaders who have "got it." Particularly in Leeds and Bristol, I think there was a recognition by the political leaders that there were jobs that needed doing in the housing market that might historically have been done by housing associations or by themselves, but they are no longer active in those fields.

Those jobs still need to be done for the health and wellbeing of the city, particularly picking up the renovation or rebuilding of poor private rental stock, and housing for mostly single people who are particularly vulnerable. These are people needing social care, needing to live in an environment where there's an immediate relationship with the landlord and a sense of belonging in a place they know. These are people with low-level mental health problems, loneliness, things of that kind. All these jobs need doing for places to work well.

City leaders in those places have given the impetus for municipal officials to work differently with the community, or the many different communities across the city. Some of those leaders are mayors, like in Liverpool and Bristol, and in Leeds there's a traditional city council leader. Manchester, too, is coming along now, building on a strong cooperative tradition. That's also happening in Liverpool where a new generation of people is drawing on those cooperative and self-help traditions to drive the renaissance of community-led housing in the city. The city council there has now very strongly backed a community asset transfer policy to enable these groups to buy city land at sensible prices.

DAVE SMITH: This land issue is a central concern. CLTs are about land values ultimately. And land values are just so much higher in UK cities than they are in rural areas.

STEPHEN HILL: Sure. But what you get in rural areas, too, is a much closer identification between landowners and all members of the community. Particularly in those rural areas in the West Country, there's been a strong tradition of local landowners putting their land into CLTs on very generous terms, sometimes for nothing, because they say, "Well, this is our community too. We want it to survive and thrive."

You are completely right about urban land prices, though, and there are no philanthropic community-based landowners there! But, as you were able to achieve at St Clements, every development over a certain size has to have a policy-compliant amount of affordable housing. On the St Clements site, the affordable homeownership element was undertaken by London CLT, with the land priced accordingly.

It is true that urban CLTs are more reliant on sourcing public land for their work, as that offers greater scope for buying at a sensible price. The city councils in Bristol and Liverpool, as I just mentioned, have designed special policies to facilitate that. In theory, all councils could do the same. They have the legal powers. They may not all use them, and some feel nervous about selling at below-market value. That is a subject on which I could talk for hours! However, what I can say is that we—a group of surveyors and public interest organizations concerned with sustainable development—are working on having the law clarified to make it easier for local authorities to sell at a price that reflects the uses they want to see on the land.

DAVE SMITH: The question of who the community might be is far easier to answer in more rural areas, isn't it?

STEPHEN HILL: It is. Communities of place in villages and small towns are more readily identifiable, and the places provide a focus for community organizing. But, as you were able to show in the workings of London CLT, you could tap into the social structures of the member organizations of London Citizens, faith institutions, schools, trade unions, and so on. They provided a good way into the social anthropology of the city, you could say. Also, having worked on many large-scale urban revitalization projects, I can say there are strong communities of place with their own identity and history. This is a phenomenon that local authorities mostly ignore or imagine to be of no consequence when they embark on those projects.

Lifting Up Community-Led Housing

DAVE SMITH: I want to move on to the more recent national picture. Now, for me, your defining contribution has been to pull together— at times, kicking and screaming, but very successfully—very distinct strands of people who now think of themselves as the "community-led housing sector." That wasn't a phrase before. That wasn't a thing. They were co-ops. They were CLTs. They were the self-builders. They were people in between.

We each thought that we should plow our own field. We had unique and compelling stories. But you were of the opinion that it was actually far better for us to work together as a sector. Perhaps you could tell us the story of that.

STEPHEN HILL: Well, I suppose, that idea became very concrete in my mind when I did some research for the Joseph Rowntree Foundation in 1999–2000, on the current state and potential future of community self-build housing. This was social housing for rent funded by the then Housing Corporation, the government's main funder of social housing. It drew on some particularly strong traditions and projects of collective community self-built housing for rent, promoted particularly by London local authorities like Lewisham. They supported people using the Walter Segal method of construction: a simple timber post-and-beam structure that didn't require specialist building skills or heavy machinery. It was particularly well-suited to small sites with difficult ground conditions, sites that no one else wanted. So, it was just right for smaller communities! The report was jointly commissioned with a number of organizations that had grown up to promote the idea of community self-build. In England and Scotland, there were four different organizations, each with its own particular take on self-build. They were all bashing away at government for financial and policy support, quite independently of each other. I would have to say that they pissed off government officials mightily, because they all seemed to be asking for the same thing. Yet, each one would defiantly claim, "Oh no, we're quite different from the others. We've got something special." As one government official told me, "They need to get out of the small and special box!"

To cut a long story short, I was able to talk to people both in England and in Scotland, in government, community groups, professional enablers, and housing associations to get a picture of how self-build had been working and how it could be made to work better in the future. I was able to make a number of recommendations for practical changes to policy and practice, but the big issue was this cultural impasse of each organization thinking they were special and needing special treatment that would be unique to them. And, on that issue, the report foundered! The organizations couldn't agree on the recommendations and Rowntree drew the project to a halt, whilst inviting me to publish my findings independently in whatever way I thought might be most helpful to policymakers and community self-builders, which I did.

The point of telling you this is to draw attention to what happened to those four organizations. Today, you'd do well to find any trace of them, either online or in real life. It was a tragedy that could have been avoided, and I was determined that community-led housing did not end up the same way.

The other point I want to make is that many of the interview transcripts were unpublishable, because the responses to my questions were shot through with that contempt for citizens and communities that I mentioned earlier, at least in England. Scotland was a very different place in which sturdy community self-reliance was part of the political tradition.

DAVE SMITH: I went through a similar process as you, where I learned that there are commonalities that stretch just beyond the concept of a community land trust. "Community-led housing" is now a thing because of you. Do you believe, in essence, that these things share a commonality?

STEPHEN HILL: Yes. I go back to William Beveridge, a Liberal politician and the architect of the post-war settlement of the Welfare State. But almost immediately, he was concerned that there were too many officials and professional people involved in trying to control what he had proposed. He complained at the absence of voluntary efforts and what he called "private action for social advance . . . on the road to reconstruction." He believed that the spirit and activity of voluntary action was at the heart of what it meant to be free. He was convinced that ordinary people had to be involved directly in the delivery of services, since this was the most effective way to "personalize and humanize" the Welfare State.

The commonality comes from the freedom of people to make choices about their own destiny. Where you are housed, how well you are housed, and how much you have to pay for your housing is absolutely core to that. It affects everything you do, and the community that you live in. These are such fundamental issues for the quality of our daily lives. CLTs, co-ops, cohousing communities—they're all trying to do the same thing, trying to help make the best choices for themselves and their communities. We shouldn't be denying citizens the opportunity to do that. Surely, an intelligent state should be encouraging and supporting voluntary action by its citizens to do the things that it doesn't do very well, or can't do at all. But government never talks with the demand side in housing. It talks only to the supply side and about how to serve their interests.

DAVE SMITH: I want to move on and discuss what is arguably the apex of your work, your Churchill Fellowship, which included a trip across the United States. As a segue into that topic, however, I would note that combining national advocacy groups into a single sector voice is not what groups in America have done. They're still very distinct. Would you say there's some lessons from the UK experience in teaming up?

STEPHEN HILL: Yeah. It's certainly been my experience in supporting community groups, whether they're doing co-ops, CLTs, self-build or cohousing, that, in essence, they're all coming from a very similar place; they're all driven to answer the ultimate question, "How do we want to live?"

It's such a strong idea. There are different dimensions, obviously, to actually finding more environmentally and socially sound ways of living. But, in the end, it's the same question: "How shall we live?"

They have an extraordinary amount in common.

The warning from the Rowntree work was that if you don't find ways of having a good story to tell the people who hold the money or who shape the policies, they're not going to listen to you. They're just going to trade one group off against the other. Or they will just ignore you and hope you'll go away.

So, it's absolutely essential in political terms for the four strands of community-led housing to work together, particularly in the UK where we have such a centralized system of government. It's very difficult for mainland European countries and certainly the United States to imagine the extent to which the state is so centralized here. It's a political necessity for the housing advocacy groups to work together. And they're doing it reasonably well. There's a long way to go; it's early days. We've only had the Community Housing Fund since 2016. That ran out in 2020, but the groups are working reasonably well together to try and get it reinstated.

In the United States, by contrast, the diversity of political administrations right across the country makes that kind of national cohesion of different community-led housing strands less of a necessity. You have to work much more with the grain and within the historical traditions of each place. Vermont is clearly a very good example of that, with its own very particular political history, going back to the 18th Century. CLTs just fit in with that. Bernie Sanders, when he was Mayor of Burlington, was just working with the grain of that political context in supporting their growth.

The Churchill Fellowship:
Property, Justice, and Reason

DAVE SMITH: I want to ask you to opine on the United States because you, more than most, have spent a fair bit of time there. In 2014, you were awarded a traveling fellowship by the Winston Churchill Memorial Trust to go to both the US and Canada. That trip resulted in your paper "Property, Justice, and Reason: Reconnecting the Citizen and the State through Community Land Trusts and Land Reform in Nine Narratives." It was hugely influential to my own thinking, when I read it. Could you start by telling the story of it. Where did you go on that tour?

STEPHEN HILL: It's almost, where *didn't* I go? I think that 13 cities in seven weeks was mad. But it was bloody good fun. The reason why I went to those places, and why I went to so many, was simply to try and get a view of the diversity of different stories in different places about why communities and the local state were collaborating.

At one end of the spectrum, there was the example of Vermont where CLTs sit comfortably in its liberal history going back to the 18th Century. At the other end, there was a place like North Carolina, which was then a Tea Party state, where the people in power had absolutely no empathy with Black Americans.

But in a city like Durham, North Carolina, where they'd lost their dominant tobacco-related employment, politicians and public officials were trying to reinvent their downtown area. They were realizing that, if they didn't do something about this inner suburban ring of poor housing around the downtown with a predominantly Black American population, then all the investment that they were trying to attract into their city center would disappear—say, if you had a riot or civil unrest there. So, they had a mutual self-interest, which made them necessary to each other.

To the politicians, CLTs seemed to be a good vehicle for what was federal money through the Community Development Block Grant program. The state wasn't putting in any of its own money, so federal money was free money to them. If they gave it to the CLT, they could help to secure both that part of the city and the city center. There was a pragmatic relationship.

I described the places I visited as "principled" versus "pragmatic." The important message was that both the community groups and the politicians needed to have a story about why they were working with the other, even if they weren't the same story.

There's a lesson to community groups here. If you need political support, which you nearly always do, even if it's only for planning, there has to be a good story about why the politicians should support you. But you have to recognize that they have a story too. You have to try and help them to understand what your story is, without them having to endorse it as theirs.

I started off in the Northeast and migrated down to the Southwest and then up to Toronto. In every place, there was a well-developed and sophisticated process of storytelling between a community and the politicians about why they were collaborating in this particular case.

That was really an important lesson. I tried to bring home to the UK some of these ideas—"nine narratives"—so that politicians, if they heard some of these stories, could see, "Oh yeah, that's similar to the situation we're in." They could then recognize that as a valid reason to support CLTs.

DAVE SMITH: The racial justice aspect of a CLT's work is far more pronounced in the places you went in the US, but it is increasingly an aspect of our work here in the UK as well. I know that interests you, so I wanted to give you the opportunity to talk about that.

STEPHEN HILL: Yeah. Well, as you say, there isn't quite the racial dimension in the UK. But I think, in both America and here, there is an increasing awareness that, if people are not sufficiently well-off to afford the housing that's available, it's a situation that has been constructed through policy. It really hasn't happened accidentally. It's the way it is because somebody made those policy decisions. People live in bad and unaffordable housing because of explicit political choices that that are deemed by policymakers to be okay and tolerable. It's not. It's totally unjust.

A key objective of the CLT mechanism is to reverse that situation, with the CLT as a real driver of political justice. It may not be only racial injustice the CLT is tackling, but also economic and social injustice. Absolutely.

DAVE SMITH: What would you say were the ultimate takeaways that you brought back to the UK from your travels in the US?

STEPHEN HILL: Well, I suppose optimism. You have to remain optimistic, and you have to recognize that it's a long haul.

Looking at the roots of the CLT movement in the States, you go back to the Sixties and the Civil Rights Movement, and CLTs are still going. In the case of New Communities Inc., there were years and years of being dispossessed of their assets, and then eventually winning them back through the courts.

Communities don't give up. They don't go away.

That is also true of the experience here of doing individual projects. You can say to local authorities, "If you engage with this community group, they're not going to walk away when it's suddenly economically inconvenient." They are not like private developers who will just walk away if the market turns, and then do something somewhere else. A community group will just stick it out because there's so much more at stake for them.

I think it's in the mindset of the country now. There's a recognition that once you've got a CLT in your community, it's not going away. It is in it for the long haul.

You look at Dudley and its CLT in Boston. They started in the Eighties. They operate at the scale of an entire neighborhood. You could say their work will never be done. It is the on-going process of making the city work.

There aren't any CLTs in England yet with that scale of ambition, although I know there are people in the fledgling Norwich CLT who are looking at that broader city-wide perspective, and thinking how they can frame their work in that context.

So, optimism was a takeaway from my time in the US—and accepting that it's a long-term task. And hoping that politicians here will gradually warm to the CLT and see how it can help them. The fact that there are now political leaders who are speaking out for it has been really important.

There were just three big recommendations in the paper I wrote afterwards. **One** was that the different strands of community-led housing have to organize together and represent themselves as the voice of the demand side in the housing market. If anybody in power ever bothers to ask us, this is what we want; this is the kind of housing we want to live in; and this is how much we would want to pay for it. As I've already mentioned, it has never occurred to national or local government to find a way to work with the demand side.

The *second* was that there needs to be a different understanding about the role of land, especially public land, in the way that all public policy is made, and for which we need both a national (English) and local land commissions. We don't have the same understanding that Scotland has, where political and practical choices about potentially competing land uses are moderated by the Scottish Land Commission. It functions as a source of evidence and information, providing independent advice to government and supporting practical innovations. Transfers of land into community ownership has been an important development. In the United States, some of these functions are carried out by conservation land trusts, like the one in Vermont.

There is now much greater awareness in England of the centrality of land to almost every area of public policy, particularly regarding climate change and environmental sustainability.

You know, we're a small country. Events like those in Ukraine and Brexit show that food and energy markets are much less secure than ever before. If we're going to become more self-sufficient, how do we manage those priorities in relation to the demand for new housing and infrastructure? We currently have no government machinery to align and to manage all these competing interests.

The House of Lords produced a report last December about land use in England. It talked about the need for a new national land-use management framework. It begged the question, however, of whether we need an English Land Commission to advise government and landowners and communities about how to achieve some of these objectives. You feel that events are now moving in that direction. There are already one or two local land commissions in Liverpool and now one in the London Borough of Southwark.

Although the land commission idea is cottoning on, there is a gap in thought leadership and professional practice on the subject from the professional bodies concerned with the land, especially my own, the Royal Institution of Chartered Surveyors. So my **third** recommendation was addressed to my own professional institution and other built environment professional bodies, about playing an important role in making this land commission idea a reality.

Going back to my potted guide to surveying and the role of the planning and development surveyor, a land commission would be a fine opportunity for providing disinterested professional advice in the public interest, which chartered institutions are obliged to provide under the terms of their Charters. But as a professional body, the RICS had rather lost its way in articulating the public interest, even though it talked a lot about it. So, I recommended that it should set up a Public Interest Sounding Board alongside, but independent of, its formal governance. Its function would be to raise awareness of public interest issues in the institution and its members and to advise and challenge its governing body on responding to the interests of the public.

That recommendation was made in 2014. Then the RICS was rocked by a governance scandal in 2020, followed by an organizational and cultural meltdown. As a result, it was necessary to bring in independent figures to carry out a review of both the governance and the future of the profession.

To encourage the process of remaking the profession and giving it a forward-looking vision, I got together a number of fellow surveyors and a few civil society organizations. We proposed that they needed to set up, yes, a Public Interest Sounding Board. We made that submission to the Future of the Profession review team without much hope, I would have to say, of being taken seriously. When the review report was issued in June of last year, we went along to the RICS' building to hear it launched. And, lo, one of its main recommendations was the establishment of what Lord Bichard, who led the review, called a "public interest panel." He also proposed a "sustainability panel" to raise awareness of the critical role that the land and surveyors have in meeting the challenges of climate change. The Governing Council had adopted our proposal lock, stock, and barrel! That was quite, quite, quite pleasing! But there's a long way to go before it actually works.

DAVE SMITH: It was a hugely successful trip. Your paper is frequently cited in the UK.

CLTs Amidst the Left-Right Political Divide

DAVE SMITH: One of the interesting things for me about your work, one of its most seminal contributions, is your criticism not just of the market, but of the state as well. You are saying that neither of these two is providing a suitable solution in isolation.

If you look at the housing context today, it's very easy to think, "Well, the lack of resident voice is just an outcome of the market, which has got no time for it. If the market is serving low-income families, why would it waste time and effort and money on that?"

Effectively, what you're saying is, even when the state was the biggest client and you were working for local councils who were commissioning housing at scale, there still wasn't a conversation with their residents across the rent desk. You clearly had this frustration with **both** the market and the state from an early point.

STEPHEN HILL: Oh, completely. Ironically, I think the market could potentially be much more responsive to this. For example, cohousing groups have worked with housing associations, but they've mostly found the relationship to be quite uncomfortable. Housing associations have become more like local authorities. They don't really treat their residents with great respect.

I've often said to cohousing groups, "You might do much better working with a private developer because at least they know who the client is. If you're the person that's going to pay them the money, they've gotta work with you." The experience of working in the very successful and now much-visited Marmalade Lane cohousing project in Cambridge was that the cohousers worked with a developer who really understood that.

Just going back to the point you were making before, the short-comings of the state, as I found it in Islington, and later elsewhere. Contempt for communities and their residents was very much a function of the whole post-war reconstruction period; what Beveridge was concerned about. You know, the big state had to take on responsibilities for doing a hell of a lot of work very quickly at a very large scale. Nobody else but the state could do that, so the state would always know best. On housing, it still thinks it does. We haven't lost that centrality of the state deciding for everybody what's good for them. Most of the post-war period has also seen a diminution in civil society and a great suspicion by the state of certain charitable organizations when trying to remedy some of the shortcomings of the state. We don't really have a strong civil society to efficiently balance or complement what the state does.

What I was experiencing, particularly during the Nineties when I had started my own business working on large-scale regeneration schemes, was that there was no expectation that the community would play any active role in determining the future of this new place once it was remade. That seemed to be a really big gap.

DAVE SMITH: What's interesting about the CLT in the British context is it just doesn't map neatly onto the political Left-Right divide of the parties, which we've had in the UK. One of our shared experiences in working on the London CLT was that it didn't sit naturally with either party. From my perspective, I had presumed it would sit more naturally with the Labour Party. At the beginning of London

CLT, I think they might still have been in power at the Greater London Authority (GLA), under Mayor Ken Livingston. But the CLT was total anathema to a governmental organization that just wanted to build council housing, which they believed that people should just be grateful for.

Boris Johnson's administration had, shall we say, a more lackadaisical, non-doctrinaire approach, which created more space for us to do what we were interested in doing.

STEPHEN HILL: Yeah, I think that's absolutely fair. I won't say what I usually say about the Labour Party because they might decide to sue me, as it's not very complimentary. But it is very disappointing, because we both favour the idea of progressive political parties. But I think you're right. The CLT ought to be something that appeals to any political party. All political parties, at their heart, should have something about helping their citizens feel free to do the actions that are important for them.

Certainly, in the current Labour Party, people like Lisa Nandy (now Shadow Secretary of State for Levelling Up, Housing and Communities) do talk the language of community empowerment and the necessity for communities to play a role in deciding their own futures. She is sounding really encouraging about all communities under a new Labour government having the resources to develop their own assets and to give themselves a degree of autonomy with less of a reliance on the state for money.

That's all good. When I started doing my Churchill Fellowship in 2014, Nandy's views on the Left were mirrored by Rory Stewart in the Conservative Party, who was a great supporter of CLTs in his rural constituency in the Lake District in Cumbria.

But equally, he was asking, "Where does power lie in modern Britain?" He was saying it doesn't really lie anywhere. It's not with the press. It's not with industry. It's not with government. He said that we almost have to reinvent democracy from the ground up. And you have to start in the places where people have a sense of responsibility for their place.

So, in a way, it was obvious that he would support CLTs. They had been legally defined by then, and that's exactly how they were set up, on the understanding that center-Left and center-Right would be pretty close together in recognizing the value of CLTs.

The further you get from the center, it's harder to see how the CLT would appeal to those political ideologies. At the extreme Right, you could see people objecting to the identity of a particular group of people trying to do something to benefit their community of interest or place. And the further Left you go, there's less regard for identity, while saying we have to do the right thing for everybody. Of course, there are the Lib-Dems who sit nicely in the middle. They have also been good supporters of CLTs, particularly in rural areas.

Recognition Across the Pond

DAVE SMITH: Part of the story which isn't told over here, however, is that your work has been quite influential in the United States as well. I know, for instance, that in 2017 you were at the conference of the Grounded Solutions Network in the US, where you were nominated for an award in a letter written by John Davis. He wrote, "Stephen Hill is a rare combination of practitioner, mentor, teacher, and scholar who has used his professional and intellectual standing to champion the cause of community land trusts in his native country. His nurturing hand has helped to seed and till the soil for the United Kingdom's flourishing CLT movement and helped it to grow."

I was at that conference as well. I wanted to ask you what it felt like when you received that award. Perhaps you could also tell us that it wasn't just a nice certificate that you received. There was another bit of wizardry, shall we say, that went along with it.

STEPHEN HILL: There was, yes. It's the Wizard's Hat that was first given to John Davis, after whom the award is named. Unfortunately, I can't rush to show it to you. It's all packed away, because we're moving house. It's packed safely in a box, so that it will ultimately get passed to its new wearer.

I have to say that John and others were really sneaky. In the lead-up to that conference, we'd all been working together to nominate Catherine Harrington, who was then the director of the National Community Land Trust Network, for the other big award given out by Grounded Solutions, the Swann-Matthei Award. There were quite elaborate preparations put in place. She had to be told in advance, so she knew that it was coming. I had been called up onto the stage as part of the presentation. Brenda Torpy, as Chair of Grounded Solutions, was on the platform too. Just I was about to go back into the audience, she said, "Could you just help me? Just sit to the background, because I want you to help me with something else." Then she launched into this second award and, of course, it was for me.

It was a very, very sweet nomination and award. Very kind. I really appreciated it. Recognition from all those wonderful people in the US was a wonderful and heartwarming experience.

DAVE SMITH: Well, I think I speak for everybody when I say it was one of the most well-deserved awards that Grounded Solutions has given out. It's a huge, huge congratulations, Stephen.

Keeping Eyes on the Prize:
Putting Democracy Into Development

DAVE SMITH: You were an active participant in SHICC, "Sustainable Housing for Inclusive and Cohesive Communities." This was an EU-funded initiative to increase the size and number of CLTs in Europe and England. What role did you personally play in SHICC and what success did SHICC have in accomplishing what it set out to do?

STEPHEN HILL: In the days before Brexit—ah, happy days!—it seemed quite natural to work in partnership with others on the European mainland who were struggling with similar challenges of affordability, to share experiences and ideas and, particularly, to help give CLT's greater credibility at home. If everyone was doing it, it would be harder for the sceptics and opponents to ignore.

The decision to participate in SHICC was a tricky one for the trustees of the CLT Network. There were anxieties that the focus on the UK would be diluted, and momentum could be lost. As a natural fan of the power of joining things up, I was a supporter of the European project. In the end, we all agreed that it was the right thing to do.

I was asked to be the lead trustee for the project. It was a role that I undertook just for the early stages of the project, before I started to wind down my trustee responsibilities at the CLT Network in the UK. I particularly remember an early meeting of all the project partners in Lille, in northern France, where we were exposed to the whirlwind energy of Geert DePauw from CLT Brussels. It was a great encouragement to others in the UK, who were also working in contested urban settings, to see what CLTB had achieved as a campaigning organization, engaging directly with government and enabling the most marginalized of citizens to be properly housed.What does success look like? This month, the European CLT Network has been established. It was quite inspirational seeing the many (mostly young) people from the whole community-led housing world at the International Social Housing Festival in Barcelona, all working together, whether CLTs, co-ops, or cohousing communities. It was inspirational seeing their enthusiasm, commitment, and determination to make sure that community-led housing was never put back into the "small and special box."

I wasn't even there! That just came from reading the blog posts during and after the event. Barcelona was probably the perfect setting for such an event. I visited the city in 1974 when I was still at architecture school, and I still remember going round a housing cooperative project, developed and owned by a trade union, with a canteen and childcare facilities built in, and with rents related to actual earnings. That project embodied all the most important elements of CLTs, co-ops and cohousing communities.

DAVE SMITH: Stephen, you've been promoting community-led housing for a long time. You've been a major advocate for CLTs. Neither of these measures are in the mainstream of the strategies preferred by either public officials or private, market-oriented developers. You've confronted passive inertia or active resistance throughout your career. Why and how have you kept you going? What has motivated you and grounded you in helping you to "keep your eyes on the prize," to use a familiar phrase from the American Civil Rights Movement?

STEPHEN HILL: Everyone deserves to be treated with respect. CLTs, as legally defined, give agency to citizens and communities, with enough democratic legitimacy to ensure that respect cannot be withheld. That's about it! But it is also more complicated. Yes, civil rights, that's absolutely the heart of it. That early experience in Islington when the council treated its residents with such contempt and disrespect, that was the moment that crystallized my feelings from two earlier experiences.

The first of those was going to South Africa in 1966 in my gap year between school and university and observing first-hand what prejudice looks and feels like. It was the self-serving narrative of educated middle class English-speaking White people that chilled the soul. They found a way to justify racial segregation and the politics of apartheid and make it sound normal.

The second experience was a few years later in 1969. Going back to those moments of indecision about career prospects that I was speaking about earlier, and despite what I initially said about not going into the army, I did think about doing a three-year Short Service Commission. Through the university's Officer Cadet Corps, I was sent to join the regiment that I would have signed up for.

That took me to Northern Ireland, just as "The Troubles" were beginning. British troops had been sent to restore calm in the country. Roman Catholics in Northern Ireland were treated in a very similar way to Black South Africans, so the situation felt disturbingly familiar. It would not be overstating the situation to say that Northern Ireland operated as an apartheid state. My great good fortune was to meet Austin Currie, a Stormont MP and a leader of the civil rights movement. He used to come regularly to the police station in Dungannon where we were stationed to complain about harassment of the Catholic community at the hands of the Protestant B Special Constabulary, a state-sponsored but unregulated militia. After a while, I was deputed to be the person to respond to his complaints. After we had logged the "complaint of the day," he would tell me about the denial of civil rights and how Catholics were denied access to decent housing and council-built homes. So, apart from deciding not to join the army, I was shocked to find such prejudice and injustice so close to home. I then found it again when I started to work in housing myself.

DAVE SMITH: I'm surprised that you didn't decide to go into politics, then, rather than become a professional.

STEPHEN HILL: Yes, I did think about it. But having worked for a local authority, I could also see the limitations of what politicians can achieve. I felt that a professional could achieve just as much, albeit in different ways.

Of course, it is one of the accepted nostrums of professional life that professionals have to maintain an objective position in their advice and work; i.e., we don't do politics.

I've often been chided for taking positions that are too political, though not a party position. I've always thought that's a naive cop-out. Politics is about the allocation of resources—and land is one of the most critical and finite resources for human existence. How then can the choices we make or the choices we advise others to make not be political?

CLTs, for me, are as much about enabling citizen participation in choices about their homes and their way of life, as a particular way of providing those homes. When I've been writing on this subject, therefore, I've sometimes used the idea of "putting politics into" whatever the topic might be.

My riposte to the chiders, mostly other surveyors, is that our primary duty is to the public interest. That's what our 1881 Royal Charter says. That usually shuts them up!

But it has meant developing my own narrative about what I think the public interest *is*, in order to be able to justify my advice and actions. My preoccupation has become the underdeveloped state of our democratic life in the UK. Citizens get to vote once every few years, but they are otherwise excluded from the political choices that impact on their everyday lives. Indeed, they are treated pretty contemptuously and shabbily if they presume to "interfere" and take it on themselves to act in their own interest and the public interest.

Over the course of my professional lifetime, no government has had the courage to design and implement housing policies that would ensure all its citizens are housed safely, healthily, and affordably. That doesn't sound too much to ask, but nationally we have failed on all three counts.

Against all the odds, CLTs manage to do exactly what governments can't. So, perhaps, government should listen to its citizens for a change?

The wording of the CLT definition which I drafted with the late

Catherine Hand and Dave Rodgers, when he was the CEO of CDS Cooperatives, was a quite explicit attempt to "put democracy into housing."

DAVE SMITH: That seems an appropriate point on which to end this interview. I want to extend my thanks for your support and tutelage over the years. I have no doubt that, if they ever come to write a definitive history of the community land trust movement, not only in England but across the world, there will be vast waves of chapters devoted to Stephen Hill. Thank you very much for your time today.

7.

María E. Hernández Torrales

The Attorney Who Guided the Adaptation
of Community Land Trusts in
Informal Settlements

Interviewed by Line Algoed
April 7, 2023

María E. Hernández Torrales has devoted nearly 20 years to assisting the Proyecto ENLACE del Caño Martín Peña and the Fideicomiso de la Tierra del Caño Martín Peña, the first CLT in Puerto Rico. She has advised on the formation of two other CLTs in Puerto Rico as well. Drawing on this experience, she has written a number of articles focused on community-owned land as a strategy for the regularization of land tenure in informal settlements. Since 2008, María has worked as an attorney and clinical professor at the University of Puerto Rico School of Law. She is a co-founder of the Center for CLT Innovation and has served on the board's executive committee since 2018.

LINE ALGOED: Hola, María. It's very nice to see you. I am going to ask you a few questions for the new book being published by the

Center for CLT Innovation. The whole book is about thought leaders in the CLT movement, so of course you had to be included in that. I've been wanting to sit down with you and ask you about your work for quite a while.

MARÍA HERNÁNDEZ: It's nice to do this. Thank you for having me, Line. It's an honor to be here. It's an honor to be included in the book.

LINE ALGOED: It's an honor for *me* to be talking with you. I want to start by asking about your background. Where did you grow up? How did you decide to become a lawyer? What sort of work did you do prior to joining the Legal Assistance Clinic at the University of Puerto Rico?"

MARÍA HERNÁNDEZ: I was born and grew up in Santurce, which is part of the Municipality of San Juan, the Capital City of Puerto Rico. My family then moved to Río Piedras, and I lived there until I was an adult. Then I moved back to Santurce. Right when I graduated from high school, I received a job offer, a very good one from the electric power company in Puerto Rico. I wanted to go to the University, but the job offer was good. So, I decided to accept the job and give myself some time to get used to being a full-time worker. Two years later, I was admitted to the University and started studying during the evening. When I finished the Bachelor's degree, I earned a Master's in Higher Education from New York University. Shortly after finishing the Master's degree, some friends invited me to join them in pursuing a law degree and I accepted. After four years of studies, I became a licensed lawyer. I got a promotion at the electric power company as a labor lawyer and then as head of the Personnel Division. By the time that it was my time to retire, I was promoted to Human Resources Director for the company. After retiring, I studied for a Master's degree in environmental law at the Vermont Law School. When I came back to Puerto Rico, the University of Puerto Rico Law School was looking for a professor to teach the Community Economic Development Clinic and I was chosen as an adjunct professor. I've now been practicing law for 25 years and, for the last 18 years, I've been teaching at the Clinic, combining law and education.

LINE ALGOED: Throughout your career, you've worked very closely with several different communities in Puerto Rico. The common thread running through your work is helping these communities to address land tenure issues and helping them, in particular, to address those issues collectively. Right? Can you say a bit about that work?

MARÍA HERNÁNDEZ: Here in Puerto Rico we have a long history of informal settlements or non-planned communities. Those communities' residents have difficulties when they are asked to show valid legal documents that support that they have the right to live where they live, even though they may have spent many years in their community. I can recall this was the situation since 1989 when Puerto Rico was hit by an extreme weather event, Hurricane Hugo. When the federal government agency, the Federal Emergency Management Administration, arrived to help, they conditioned that help to the proof of a title to the land in order for the residents to be able to receive the support from the federal government. People in informal settlements started having trouble with that. As the time passed by, these extreme weather events have become more regular and the situation of not having a written title has become a problem for a lot of families in Puerto Rico.

Many of them have turned to the Legal Assistance Clinic for help, trying to regularize their relationship with the land where their houses are. Not all of them are squatters. A lot of them are people whose land was inherited from past relatives. They are family of the people who first owned the land. But when they inherited the land, there was no paper for showing a valid title. It turned out to be a problem. So, a lot of communities came to the Clinic and asked us for help in how to deal with the situation.

LINE ALGOED: Many readers of this book will be unfamiliar with the unique problem of land tenure in informal settlements. They may not understand what you meant, therefore, when you said that people living in such settlements are "trying to regularize their relationship with the land where their houses are." Could you say more about this tenure problem and what you mean by "regularization"?

MARÍA HERNÁNDEZ: In Puerto Rico, the cost of living is disproportionate with wages. The minimum wage is $8.50/hour, and many households have to work two or three jobs to cope with the family's expenses. In terms of housing, the median price of a house in San Juan, where most of the jobs are to be found, fluctuates around $300,000. On the other hand, public housing, social housing and subsidized rental housing have become extremely difficult to access. Most of the time families must wait for years to get access to a house or apartment.

But life doesn't wait. People form families and want to have a place for their own. Informal settlements or unplanned communities start that way. People find abandoned, vacant land and build their houses there. First, they build shanties and are followed by others with the same need. As time goes by, they start building permanent housing on land with no infrastructure, risking their health and safety. But they have a necessity that overcomes those risks. In the 1970s, the squatters—or "land rescuers" as they called themselves—were very common in Puerto Rico. We still see some undeveloped land being "rescued" and occupied today.

But mostly there are older, unplanned communities like the ones in the Caño Martín Peña area that are called "slums." They were caused and enticed by the total irresponsibility of the government, both the state and the municipality, during the first half of the 20th Century. Instead of dealing with poverty and providing poor families with a decent place to live, government officials simply ignored them. The people had to provide for themselves and their families with the scarce resources they had. Shanty towns were formed all over San Juan to the point that there were shacks not only on land that was then considered the outskirts of San Juan, but also on the water in houses raised on stilts. This is one of the reasons why the Caño Martín Peña water is so polluted.

By the time those weak houses were rebuilt, the government provided basic infrastructure and some families got a land title from the government. Nevertheless, for a number of reasons, many families didn't get the land title. Whenever there is an extreme weather event, and some help from the federal government is offered, federal officials always ask for a land title to make the family eligible for the benefits. In the absence of one, the family never gets the help they desperately need. The act of helping those families to get a written, valid, and recordable land title is what I call "regularizing their relationship with the land."

LINE ALGOED: When residents of informal settlements come to the Legal Assistance Clinic, what sort of help do you provide?

MARÍA HERNÁNDEZ: We do civil law to help people. We also offer notary services. We ask them what they really want and how they envision the regularization of their relationship with the land. Drawing from the experience of the Caño communities, we help them to know that there are good alternatives to holding land as individual property. They have learned about different ways of owning the land collectively, like a co-op or a community land trust.

This has proved to be a long process. Some of the people have decided, after a full knowledge of the alternatives, that what they really wanted is individual ownership of the land under their houses. Others have decided that what they want is some form of collective ownership.

LINE ALGOED: When did your work start with the Caño communities?

MARÍA HERNÁNDEZ: Well, I recall that in 2003 a professional planner called Lucilla Fuller Marvel looked for me to give the people from the Caño communities some sort of talk about what a community land trust was. What was the model about? How does it function? I was invited to participate in a conference at the Universidad del Sagrado Corazón near the Caño Martín Peña. There was not only me, but also other professors from the University of Puerto Rico. One was talking about individual property. I talked about the community land trust. There was another one who talked about housing co-ops. So, the residents of the communities had the basic information that they would need to decide the sort of landownership that was most convenient for them according to the rehabilitation process that the communities were planning.

They wanted to make their project serve the communities as long as possible. By "project" I mean the rehabilitation of the seven communities included in the Special Planning District surrounding the Martín Peña Canal. They wanted to see the ecological restoration of the Caño Martín Peña, but without displacement of the people living along the Canal. The model of land tenure they chose would have to comply with those two characteristics.

Okay. So, they were in the process of evaluating which of the models presented at the conference would support the ecological restoration of the Canal and the rehabilitation of the whole area with new infrastructure, while also ensuring their community would not be displaced, not be uprooted. The whole process of planning the project started in 2002. A year later, residents of the Caño communities were deciding what model of land tenure to use. That's when I went to that conference. Then I started getting involved with the Caño communities again in 2005.

LINE ALGOED: The story of the Caño CLT's formation has already been told in articles written by you and me and others, some of them published by Terra Nostra Press. But your own part in this story is not well known. I'd like to ask, therefore, how exactly were you involved with the Caño from 2005 onward? What roles did you personally play in supporting and guiding the Caño CLT?

MARÍA HERNÁNDEZ: In 2005 a good friend of mine who was a consultant to the Enlace Project asked me to meet the recently appointed executive director for the *Corporación del Proyecto ENLACE* (ENLACE Project Corporation) to help her in organizing the board of directors. They needed help on how to draft regulations, documenting board's decisions, keeping records of the board's meetings and so on. I started to get more involved, learned about the Enlace Project, got to know the community leaders, attended community meetings, and helped with interpreting and clarifying legal terms and legal information.

In 2006 I left for the Vermont Law School to study for a Master's degree in environmental law, but I continued to be in contact with the executive director and helped by answering questions over the phone. Back in Puerto Rico in 2007, I continued helping, but it was now the time to start working with the *Fideicomiso de la Tierra* (Caño CLT), identifying the land that was transferred by law to the communities. It was a hard task, because the government transferred the land with no information at all about the registration. It was a task that the *Fideicomiso* had to perform to have a clear understanding of the land received and to start recording it under its name at the Real Property Registry. Since the *Fideicomiso* didn't have any staff, I offered to do the job. Finding the records took a while, but most of the land was identified.

Then it was the time to draft the general regulations of the *Fide-icomiso*. We looked for some lawyers who could do the job, but no one offered to do the job pro bono and the quote that we received to draft the general regulations was extremely high. The *Fideicomiso* didn't have resources to pay for that.

I recalled that, when I was at the Vermont Law School, I had attended a housing conference held at the Law School and had kept information about the Burlington Community Land Trust, which was then merging with another nonprofit to become the Champlain Housing Trust. By that time, I had also acquired a copy of the *Community Land Trust Legal Manual*, published by the Institute for Community Economics. I reviewed that literature and felt confident that, with the level of detail that I had about the Enlace Project and about what the communities envisioned for the Caño CLT, I could do the job of drafting the general regulations. I volunteered to do the job pro bono and hired a friend of mine to help, paying her professional fees with fresh fruit shakes that I prepared during the long working days.

In drafting the general regulations, we used every legal reference we had at hand and the papers that I had brought from that conference at the Vermont Law School. One of the most useful reference documents was the one prepared by the *Fideicomiso* community committee. In this document they specified the needs that they expected the *Fideicomiso* to fulfill and their vision for the future as residents in the *Fideicomiso*.

When the regulations were approved, it was then time to select members for the board of trustees. There were two seats for people from outside the communities who would be selected with the advice of the G-8, the communities leaders' group. I was honored to be asked to be one of those two people. Then, during the first meeting of the board of trustees, I was elected President of the board. I continued to be the board's President for 10 years, which is the maximum length allowed by the regulations. As a trustee, I served 12 years, the maximum term allowed by the regulations. After that, I became a volunteer and part of the advisory board.

Communities of the Caño
Form a New Kind of CLT

LINE ALGOED: How did the Caño communities come across the idea of a CLT for the first time?

MARÍA HERNÁNDEZ: Well, it was Lucilla Fuller Marvel who introduced them to the community land trust. She shared with them that it was an interesting model that could make possible the rehabilitation of the communities surrounding the Caño without displacing people. There was also a visit that Lucilla did to Boston. I think that she knew people from Dudley Neighbors Incorporated, the CLT in Boston, or at least she had heard about this CLT. A person from this CLT was then invited to come to Puerto Rico.

In this way, what the communities' residents heard about the community land trust in 2003 was combined later with more information about the nitty gritty of the everyday life and administration of a community land trust. How does it work? How do you organize it? How do you manage it? This practical information they got from Julio Henriquez, the person who came from the Dudley Street Neighborhood Initiative. Julio was both President of the board of directors of Dudley Neighbors, the CLT, and a resident of the CLT. That gave the communities' residents the opportunity to understand better what a community land trust was.

LINE ALGOED: What was there about the community land trust that made people in the Caño think—and, of course, made the professionals supporting them think—that something similar to the CLT in Boston could be done in Puerto Rico? What do you think those key elements were?

María Hernández: Well, the residents had a matrix they had previously designed to evaluate any form of land ownership. They wanted to stay rooted in their houses and in their community. They wanted their rights to the land to be inheritable. They wanted to keep the community's housing affordable, so that young people from the Caño communities could have the opportunity to live in a physical space completely rehabilitated and healthy, with water in the Canal that was as clean as their ancestors found it when they settled there almost a hundred years ago.

I always enjoy it when the oldest residents from the community talk about when they swam in the Canal. They recall learning to swim in the Canal. They are very romantic thinking about it. They want their children to have the same opportunity to enjoy a clean canal and enjoy a very rehabilitated physical environment. So, probably, that's the main reason why they chose the CLT model; that's the main characteristic of the CLT they really liked. They wanted the benefits of rehabilitated communities to go further and last longer so the younger generation could enjoy them.

Line Algoed: Many people in the Caño prefer not to speak of the "community land trust" as it's called in English. They see it as something slightly different. Can you say a little bit about that?

María Hernández: Well, you know a lot of people in the Caño settled there during the migration of the 1940s and 1950s. They migrated from the inner country to the city, looking for jobs. At the same time as these people were coming to the Caño, in Puerto Rico there was an unwritten policy of the government stimulating people to move to the United States. So, for a lot of people who live in the Caño communities, most of their family probably lives in New York City, Rhode Island, Boston, or Chicago. There's a saying, which is true, that there are more Puerto Ricans outside of the island, most of them living in the United States, than on the Island itself.

Many of the Caño's residents are very familiar with the English language and they themselves understand and manage to speak English fairly well.

When people from the Caño learned about the community land trust, therefore, they adopted the Spanish term for "trust" which is *fideicomiso*, and they kept "community" because it emerged from the community. It was the community's decision to adapt the community land trust to meet their necessities. So the name that they chose was the *Fideicomiso de la Tierra del Caño Martín Peña* (Caño Martín Peña Community Land Trust), a tool that will serve their communities well, dubbed in the language next to their heart.

LINE ALGOED: What is different about this CLT in the Caño than, for example, the CLT in Boston or the CLT in London or Brussels? What would you say are the key differences?

MARÍA HERNÁNDEZ: Well, the first and foremost purpose of the Caño Community Land Trust is to avoid displacement because of a major environmental justice project: the dredging of the Martín Peña channel.

The purpose of most CLTs in the United States and Europe is to develop affordable housing for low-income families. I think about the one in Albuquerque, New Mexico. They got a large piece of land from the city government, and they built affordable houses. But in this community land trust in Puerto Rico, the people already had their houses. They just wanted to keep them. They wanted to stay on the land and not be uprooted. So they adopted and adapted the community land trust. Their main intention was not to build homes. Their intention was to regularize the ownership of the land on which they already live, provide land for the new infrastructure, and secure the land for the next generation.

LINE ALGOED: I believe that the third big difference, compared to most CLTs in the United States, is the Caño CLT's use of a surface rights deed to give people security of tenure for the land beneath their houses. Right? Could you explain that particular approach to land tenure and what role you played in adapting the surface rights deed for the CLT in Puerto Rico? I'm also interested in why you chose that legal instrument instead of a ground lease to regularize tenure for people living on lands along the Caño.

María Hernández: I must say that the law that created the *Fideicomiso de la Tierra* enabled the CLT to choose to convey to the occupants the right to use the land either by means of a land lease agreement or by a surface rights deed. The *Fideicomiso* chose to use a surface rights deed because of a very important fact. This fact is that the people living on the CLT's land do not have their houses registered at the Puerto Rico Real Property Registry due to the origins of the settlement. The authorization of a surface rights deed will make it possible for the recording of houses as a separate property from the land. This is very important for the residents, since the legal effect is more beneficial for them. The property of their housing structure will be recognized. They will also be the owner of the surface of the land under the structure, which is a real right.

Seeding Other CLT Efforts in Puerto Rico

Line Algoed: You've played a key role in making connections with other communities in Puerto Rico that have expressed an interest in possibly forming a CLT. Could you say something about that?

María Hernández: As part of my legal work at the Law School Clinic, I'm in contact with many communities. There's one very special community in the Municipality of Loíza. It's located on the northern part of Puerto Rico. This community faces the Atlantic Ocean. The residents are very poor in terms of economic resources, but they are very rich in the sense that they have the privilege of this spectacular ocean view in their lives every day. They enjoy a beautiful life there. I think that your days have a different perspective when you have the immensity of the ocean in front of you every single day. Money can't pay for such a feeling.

But after Hurricane María in 2017, many of those residents suffered a lot of damages. As expected, wealthy people seized that opportunity to try to grab land for the development of resorts and short-term rental housing. These wealthy people, who seek economic opportunities everywhere, are trying to displace these communities that don't have a written legal title to that precious land.

One of the residents of these communities in Loíza heard about the community land trust model. He started to think about how the community land trust might help them to get a legal title for the land, not an individual land title, but a collective one. So, he came to the Clinic looking for more information and legal advice.

We began working with them, doing a lot of research about their land back to the 1790s, over two centuries ago. We had a meeting with a group of residents to start educating the communities about collective land titles so the people can ponder and decide. It's not for the Clinic to decide, and it's not for the community leader who invited us to be there, either. This is the community residents' decision collectively. By now, we are in the process of providing them with the best information at hand so they can make a wise decision.

LINE ALGOED: That's great. I understand there are other communities, like the one in Loíza, that have learned about the Caño CLT and have thought, "Maybe this is something that we can do." And you've played a role in supporting them.

MARÍA HERNÁNDEZ: Well, yes. There is this community leader, for example, just one person who is doing all the work, looking for information because his community is in jeopardy of being displaced with the aggravating factor that they don't have title to the land where their houses are built. He learned about the community land trust happening at the Caño while he was outside of Puerto Rico. Then he came back to Puerto Rico and looked for the Caño's leaders. He has attended a number of meetings at the Caño and has shared his questions and concerns. Then he shared with his community what he learned about the CLTs. A while ago, he invited the president of the G-8, Ms. Lucy M. Cruz, to talk to his neighbors at the Medianía Alta Community. Lucy shared with them about the Caño communities' decision-making process when they were considering the CLT as a form of land ownership. There were around 30 people from the community at this meeting. They attended and listened very attentively to the account that Lucy was sharing with them.

As a result of this meeting, the attendees are starting to think about the community land trust as a possible solution to their titling problem. They also wanted us to have more community meetings, so a larger group of residents can learn what they just learned and can join the conversation and contribute to the analysis. It is not an easy decision, but they feel the pressure due to the speculators that prowl the community and the rumors of involuntary displacement.

LINE ALGOED: Have there been other communities in Puerto Rico that were inspired by the Caño and assisted by you? Can you say something about that?

MARÍA HERNÁNDEZ: Yes. We also have the *Fideicomiso para el Desarrollo de Río Piedras* (Río Piedras Development Trust). This is another CLT created after a thorough community participation process.

Río Piedras used to be a progressive urban center. It is the home of the biggest campus of the best public university on the Island, the University of Puerto Rico. It is part of San Juan and is well located. Two train stations and many public transportation buses make a stop there. Nevertheless, with the construction of big shopping malls around the metropolitan area of San Juan, this urban center started to decay and now it is very, very depressed. Both stores and people have fled. Even government offices have left. But there are people who decided to stay and to fight for their communities. They started to discuss the future of Río Piedras and paid attention to what the Caño was doing with the *Fideicomiso de la Tierra*.

There are eight communities that comprise this urban center. Title to the land is not a problem in these communities. Nevertheless, there are a lot of vacant, privately-owned buildings that need to be rehabilitated. In 1995, a law was enacted to provide for the drafting of a rehabilitation plan for Río Piedras and the designation of a planning district. The plan was approved, but not much happened after that, except that Río Piedras continued to decay and the owners of the vacant buildings wanted to speculate with them. In 2016, community leaders embarked in a comprehensive process of drafting amendments to the Río Piedras's law. Knowing about the *Fideicomiso de la Tierra del Caño Martín Peña*, they first met with each community individually, and later with all of them together. They discussed how the CLT instrument would help them to provide and maintain affordable housing in Río Piedras and how the CLT could help them to revitalize the economic activity in the urban center.

After several meetings, and with the legal advice of the Community Economic Development Clinic of the University of Puerto Rico School of Law and with the help of law students of the Pro Bono Program, both of which I'm very proud to lead, they were convinced that a CLT was the right thing to do. They drafted amendments to the above-mentioned law that, among other provisions, included the creation of a CLT in Río Piedras.

The law was approved and the CLT was created with the responsibility of providing affordable housing and promoting economic growth of the urban center. On the board of trustees of this CLT not only are community residents represented; there is also the clergy sector, the professional sector, the business sector, and higher education professors and students who are represented.

The Municipality of San Juan agreed to fund the *Fideicomiso para el Desarrollo de Río Piedras* with seed money for operations and for buying buildings. Also, this *Fideicomiso* has received three buildings at no cost from the municipality and from the state government. One of these buildings used to be a theater and has a lot of meaning for the communities. They are in the process of rehabilitating it and have celebrated with some gatherings to keep the community involved. Also, a cultural center with a lot of meaning for the communities was transferred to the *Fideicomiso*. The *Fideicomiso* signed an agreement with the community leaders for them to administer the center and use it as the place for their community meetings. Also, an abandoned school was transferred at no cost to the *Fideicomiso* and they are rehabilitating it to provide affordable housing.

We have another CLT that is focused on agriculture.

LINE ALGOED: I was just going to ask you about that.

MARÍA HERNÁNDEZ: Yes, we have another one. This is a group of professional young people who heard about the *Fideicomiso de la Tierra del Caño Martín Peña*. They thought about using the CLT, not for the provision of housing as the main purpose, but for providing land for agriculture. Collectively-owned land for producing local good food. This CLT focuses on people who are farmers that lack the money to buy farmland. This group of young professionals went to the Community Economic Development Clinic looking for information about the CLT. After learning about its elements and how the CLT has been used in other places, they said, "This is it."

At the Clinic we have advised and guided them toward the creation of the community land trust according to their specific purposes. Different from the other two CLTs that were created by virtue of law or directed by a law, this CLT was created by means of a deed of trust. It is probable that, in the coming weeks, this CLT will be receiving the first donation of a piece of farmland at the center of the island, 30 acres approximately. A couple donated their land to the community land trust to make it available in smaller plots for landless farmers. We will be very, very pleased to see that happening.

LINE ALGOED: Fantastic. That's such good news.

Communal Land Tenure in the Caribbean

LINE ALGOED: I was wondering whether you see connections between the CLT in Puerto Rico, which is a newer idea, and the many other forms, often much older forms, of communal land ownership and customary tenures that are found in different islands in the Caribbean.

MARÍA HERNÁNDEZ: Well, we are part of the Caribbean, but we have been a colony since our first days. The native people didn't have any land titles. The people who came from Spain started thinking about owning and grabbing land for themselves. After that, we went into the arms of the United States in 1898 which wasn't different.

I don't know, sometimes it is confusing. We have different views about owning land. We, as a country, are used to seeing the land as an individual property. This is the law of the land, you know, individual land property. But as communities, we are very used to seeing groups of people occupying vacant land. We don't have any fear of living together as a group with common needs, especially the need of having a place to establish our homes. If there's a piece of vacant land, and there are people who lack a place to live individually or with his or her family, there is a great probability that the land will be occupied. The titling issues will be resolved later, but the most important need will be met. There's no need to segregate the land.

Two examples of the early 1980s. There were several families—I think it was fifty or seventy families—who moved onto a vacant lot in Río Grande, Puerto Rico. They settled there and they started to grow food. But it was public land and the government displaced them. It was a very violent displacement.

When they got displaced, the government offered to help them to look for housing. They told the government that they wanted to stay together as a community. So, after two or three years, they were able to buy a piece of land in the Canóvanas Municipality. Some of them are still living there on collective land. The land is owned by the community organization which is *Villa Sin Miedo, Incorporado.*

As the old residents died, some heirs got legal advice and started to segregate the land. All of them knew that they collectively had a right to use the land, but they heard the legal advice that it would be better if they segregated the land into parcels and have individual land titles.

Well, some of them started to segregate, but there are families that still are collective owners of the land. One or two years back, one of the community leaders came to the Clinic and asked me how, for the rest of the land that hasn't been segregated yet, they could keep it together as a community land trust. It would not be for the purpose of building houses or keeping housing affordable, because they already have their houses there. It would be for the purpose of keeping the land for future generations as a community.

Another good example is a piece of land in the municipality of Toa Alta at the northern part of the Island. These are people who do have a need for housing. They are families that used to live all crowded in houses of relatives. There was a piece of land that was vacant, and they gathered, and they went onto the land and cleaned it from all kinds of rubble. Then they started living there and built their houses. It was a young community, one or two years old when I met them. The government tried to evict them from the land because it was public land, and the people didn't have any kind of title to the land.

The community called the Clinic for help. Together with my law students, I went there and we managed, as transactional lawyers that we are at the clinic, to negotiate with the Land Authority so the people could stay there as long they rent the land collectively. It's the first time ever in Puerto Rico that a community has had a negotiation with the Land Authority in order to lease the land where they built their houses. This lease contract was a lease-to-own. So all the money that they would pay on that lease would be credited to the price of land at the end of the term of the lease.

But with this community, we went a step further because we thought that it was unfair and onerous for the poor families to pay almost a million dollars for 29 acres of land with no infrastructure at all. It was too much. So, we went to the legislature of Puerto Rico, and we lobbied for the transfer of the 29 acres to the Housing Authority. After it was transferred, the Housing Authority started to do the arrangements to be able to give the land titles to the families. Those arrangements included the provision of the infrastructure for potable water and electric power. But the point is that they were not afraid of occupying the land together and of leasing the land collectively. It is fascinating to see that people who barely knew each other embarked in situations that since the very beginning required a lot of trust in each other.

Global Influence of
the Caño Martín Peña CLT

LINE ALGOED: Great to hear about that. Now I want to move on and talk about the global influence and example of the Caño. Ever since the Caño CLT won the 2016 World Habitat Award, there's been so much interest from other places around the globe to know what the communities of the Caño are doing. Can you say a little bit about what's been happening since they won that Award?

MARÍA HERNÁNDEZ: How we started communicating with the international community was the result of the need for support in times when the *Fideicomiso* needed it the most. Back in 2009, immediately after the Caño Community Land Trust had been established, we had a setback with the land. By way of an amendment to the law that created the *Fideicomiso*, the government took back the land we'd been given. That was the flashpoint, when we said, "We need to go abroad for help because this kind of collective land tenure is unknown in Puerto Rico."

We were aware that our support would come from outside the Island where the CLT model was well known. At that time, we thought that nobody in Puerto Rico could understood why the Caño communities had made this decision to have collective title to the land. The residents of the Caño communities frequently were asked why, if they owned the houses, they didn't want to own the land. It's a simple question that cannot be responded to with a simple answer, but this collective land tenure under the CLT would mean so much for the future of the Caño communities. They were willing to defend it and keep it.

You know, when the Caño residents were dispossessed of their land, it was very painful for all. We felt like the rug was pulled from under our feet. Of all that I can recall, this was the time when we felt that we needed all the support of the people in our country, not only from San Juan, but from all over the Island, because this project not only benefited the Caño communities. It would benefit the entire Island. Even if they didn't fully understand the decisions made about the land by the Caño residents, we appealed for their support.

The government, on its part, especially the municipal administration, was demonstrating complete disdain for the Caño communities. It was like saying, "Here are these very, very poor communities, full of crime, mired in the deepest poverty, responsible for the pollution of the Canal. How could they even think that they deserve to live in such a 'delicious' part of the Island? Do they really think that they can own this land?"

The acts of the government were shouting that land with so much potential should not be in the hands of such poor people. One of the then-legislators said in a news interview that the reason why they took the land back was because "progress could not be stopped." Remember, these communities are situated in the heart of San Juan in a very convenient location.

When we had that setback, we felt that we needed not only the support of other Puerto Ricans, but that we also needed to go outside of Puerto Rico to look for support. I asked one of my students to Google the term "community land trust" and we found the National CLT Network. We wrote an email asking for help. I had a response from the then-executive director, and he provided me with very useful information. We asked him to write a letter about the success of the CLTs in the United States. He sent it to the Puerto Rico legislature and to the Governor of Puerto Rico. Also, the Dudley Street Neighborhood Initiative wrote a letter to the legislature of Puerto Rico in support of the Caño CLT.

This is how we started to get acquainted with people involved in the CLT movement in the US and we wanted to cultivate that relationship. Then we started to attend the National CLT Network annual conferences. We learned how important it was to participate and be part of the Network. We had the opportunity to present the case of the Caño communities and we received their support.

This is how we met John Davis. We were lucky to have John and Connie Chavez from Albuquerque, who was President of the National CLT Network at the time, come to Puerto Rico in 2010. During their visit, we organized meetings with the communities' residents

María Hernández, Judith Berkan, Connie Chavez, and John Davis, San Juan, Puerto Rico, 2010.

and shared more in depth the way we had forged this CLT. We also convened meetings with consultants and professionals to hear a presentation from John about community land trusts.

Five years later, John Davis encouraged us to present the work of our CLT to the BSHF (now World Habitat), an organization in charge of evaluating programs and projects worthy of being presented as examples of good practice, which we did. John wrote a recommendation for us. There were two winners of the World Habitat Award for 2015-2016 and the *Fideicomiso* was one of them.

Winning that Award and the peer exchange arranged by the BSHF, which followed the announcement of the Award, launched to another level what we had started in terms of letting the world know that the *Fideicomiso* exists and all the good it was doing for Puerto Rico. The peer exchange brought to the Caño people from

Latin America, Europe, the US, and the African continent. It was an honor for us to receive them and to share what we had achieved so far.

After that, Line, you facilitated an interchange with *favelas* in Brazil and with Catalytic Communities (CatComm), an organization based in Rio de Janeiro. It opened the doors for a long-term relationship with CatComm and residents of some favelas.

LINE ALGOED: Why do you believe you won that prize? What was there about the Caño's story that World Habitat found compelling— and that people around the globe continue to find compelling when they hear about it?

MARÍA HERNÁNDEZ: Something about this project that attracts the attention of people and other organizations is the community participation. The communities, through their community leadership, take an important role on every action that implies the betterment of the Special Planning District. Marginalized communities are the ones that spearhead this whole project. This project is one that exemplifies what a bottom-up rehabilitation should be. It attracts the attention of a lot of people because poverty is found around the world and because people living in informal settlements are also found around the world. The Caño communities are a great example of what these communities can collectively achieve. Even if informal settlements and extreme poverty are not so evident in the Global North, there are people suffering from scarcity of the most basic needs just like in the Global South. And there are people who need affordable housing all over the world. The fact that common people can arise with solutions to these basic problems is good news that everyone wants to hear.

I think that's the key point. Poor people around the world can accomplish a lot if they unite and if they do it together. That's why the story of the Caño communities is very inspiring.

LINE ALGOED: Do you think that CLTs can work in other communities in Latin America? Similar to what the Caño has done, can CLTs work in other areas facing similar challenges of poverty, informality, land insecurity, and climate change?

MARÍA HERNÁNDEZ: Yes, I believe that community land trust organizations like the one in the Caño communities can be established in countries in Latin America and in other developing countries. But, just as the Caño communities did, interested communities in other countries must envision the community land trust within their own needs and characteristics. The *Fideicomiso del Caño* never has pretended to be a blueprint for every community to follow. Those three key elements that define a CLT must be adapted to the necessities of the interested communities, to the resources they have, and to what they really want to do.

The first word in this system of land tenure is "community." There are a lot of land trusts around the world, but "community" is what made the Caño CLT, and many other CLTs around the world, different. It's the community working together for the common good and creating knowledge for other communities to use and to put into work if they would want to create a CLT.

If their endeavor is the common good, the community land trust is a very, very useful paradigm to look at. The elements of the CLT's structure are very important, and communities who would want to create one can adapt its characteristics to meet their own needs.

Center for Community Land Trust Innovation

LINE ALGOED: I have a question for you about the Center for CLT Innovation, since you were a founding member of the board and have helped to guide the growth of that organization for several years. What do you think the role of the Center should be in helping other communities to learn about CLTs and in helping them to implement CLTs?

MARÍA HERNÁNDEZ: Well, the Center has a key role to play in sharing existing information, producing new information, and then sharing again the information that's been produced. "Education" is the first thing it says in the Center's statement of purpose, if I'm not mistaken. Its purpose, among others, is to educate about the community land trust classic model and core characteristics. This is something that the Center does well.

It's not enough for this information to just be "available," however. The Center needs to actively let people know that it's there. And the Center needs to make sure that the information is written and shared in a way that people can understand it and use it. This information must be made available and understandable to them in their own language.

Here's an example. We often say that a community land trust is a viable 501(c)(3) organization that holds land in perpetuity and provides housing that remains affordable. I understand what that means. I know what a 501(c)(3) is. But most people from the Global South probably don't.

If the Center wants to support the growth of CLTs in the Global South, it has this huge responsibility of producing information and sharing information so that people can understand the meaning of its content. We have to always be looking to find new ways to communicate what a community land trust can do for low-income communities and unplanned communities.

The Center can also help communities to look at different land tenure models and decide for themselves which one might fit their needs. That's what the Caño communities did. Prior to adopting the community land trust, they studied different forms of land tenures. They knew what they had and what they wanted to keep. They then chose the model that would help them to accomplish what they really needed.

LINE ALGOED: I'd like to end on a personal note. What motivates you to continue fighting the good fight for social justice in general and for CLTs in particular? Rowing against the current of mainstream interests of property and power can be exhausting. How do you keep going? How do you "keep your eyes on the prize" as an earlier generation of activists in the Civil Rights Movement would have said?

MARÍA HERNÁNDEZ: That's a great question and a tough one to answer. Working as a transactional lawyer for 18 years with low-income communities and their leadership, I have had the opportunity to see for myself how difficult it is for these folks to have access to opportunities, not to mention access to justice. Sadly, we're not all equal under the law. This lack of access doesn't have anything to do with the capabilities of the person or the community, but because of their socio-economic background and, often, the color of their skin or how they dress or their lack of formal education. There is a lot of prejudice and inequity.

The Legal Assistance Clinic at the University of Puerto Rico School of Law gives me the opportunity to provide them with information that helps them to comprehend the complicated tapestry that the laws represent. What I love the most is when the community leaders have this "aha moment" and realize that they are perfectly capable to understand whatever law they need to apply. It is not rocket science. It just requires dedication and courage, of which they have a lot.

The process of creating a CLT involves a lot of decisions. The process itself is very rich; it involves a bundle of information and learnings. By the time the CLT is created, the community and its leadership have been through an array of experiences that got them ready to take any wise and sound decision in whatever project they must undertake. I won't say that it empowers them, because they are powerful people since the beginning. The knowledge and compre-hension of the processes give them the confidence they need.

The community land trust is about people caring for people. It is also about caring for the land and introducing practices that make us better and more participative citizens. We need more of that in this world in which we live. It is also a way of providing access to satisfy the most basic need that an individual has, which is a home. Once you feel the safety and the comfort that an adequate home provides, then you're able to give to whatever dreams you have, the opportu-nity to grow and thrive. Just imagine this happening all around the world.

LINE ALGOED: That's excellent. Thank you so much, María. Those were all the questions I wanted to ask.

MARÍA HERNÁNDEZ: Okay. Thank you so much, Line.

María Hernández with Shirley Sherrod, Athens, Georgia, 2009

8.

Yves Cabannes

The Troubadour Who Travelled
the World Sharing Powerful Stories
of Community-Owned Land

Interviewed by John Emmeus Davis
January 10 & 19, 2022

Yves Cabannes is an urban planner, ac-
tivist, and scholar. For over forty years,
he has been involved in research and de-
velopment on community-led initiatives
and local democracy with NGOs and
local governments in Asia, Latin Amer-
ica, Africa, and the Middle East. Since
the early 1990s, his teaching and pub-
lications have focused on participatory
budgeting, urban agriculture, community
land trusts, and housing rights in many regions of the world. In 2014,
he and the former mayor of Letchworth, Philip Ross, published a "man-
ifesto," proposing Garden Cities for the 21st Century. *He is Emeritus*
Professor of Development Planning at the University College London.

JOHN EMMEUS DAVIS: There are people who will be reading this interview who may not know you, so I'll start by saying that issues of

257

land tenure and land insecurity have been at the center of your career—as a teacher, as a writer, and as a consultant doing international development. You have also been a tireless champion for community land trusts, a global ambassador who has helped to spread the word about CLTs to countries where the model has not yet taken root.

We're going to cover all of those topics, but let's begin with where *you* started. Could you talk a bit about where you were raised, where you were born, and your family?

Family Background

YVES CABANNES: Well, I was born in the south of France in a deprived area called Landes, not far from Spain. My grandparents and the generations before them were farmers. More exactly, they were sharecroppers. This regime comes from feudal times. You do not own the land, but have to divide up the crops or animals you raise by half. I remember my father telling us that once the crop was harvested, they were dividing it into two heaps. The owner of the land would come and take the one he preferred.

JOHN EMMEUS DAVIS: That was also the sharecropping system in the southern United States. You were living and farming on somebody else's land and the landowner got a percentage of what you produced, whether it was cotton, cattle, tobacco or whatever.

YVES CABANNES: This was exactly the case. Giving away 50% of the total produced was hard, especially on farms where the soil was poor and required lots of tilling.

JOHN EMMEUS DAVIS: Was French or Spanish your first language?

YVES CABANNES: French. My parents still spoke a Latin Occitan language called Gascon before they moved to the city, a vernacular related to Catalan, Galician, Spanish, and Portuguese. This probably explains why refugees from the Spanish Republic who fled the fascist regime, and poor Italian workers who had migrated, and Portuguese who were coming to work in the pine tree forests of Landes, settled so easily. I was raised in that multi-Latin community where solidarity and fun were part of the day-to-day struggling for life. This is the culture I'm from and that I still strongly feel as mine.

JOHN EMMEUS DAVIS: Did your parents ever reach a point in their lives where they were no longer leasing the land?

YVES CABANNES: Absolutely. They were not accepting the difficult conditions of sharecroppers and, anyway, the land was not producing enough. After World War II my parents migrated to a small city one hour away, Aire sur Adour, where my dad became an electric worker. This is where I was raised in quite a happy family, never feeling poor.

One of their first efforts was to largely self-build a house and to get a large garden around it to feed our family of five. After the War, the self-help housing movement was called Castor (*beaver* in English, animals well-known for their capacity to build dams and lodges). In the case of my parents, they had help from masons and builders, notably Italians. Mutual aid was still a common practice among workers.

The piece of land around the house was essential. When I was a kid I admired how my parents gradually reclaimed and enriched the soil, using domestic waste that was transformed into compost. I was exposed every day to the beauty of not being landless and was regularly taught about the difficult conditions my parents and grandparents had faced when being landless. That was a key element of awareness and reflection.

JOHN EMMEUS DAVIS: So you became aware of issues of land tenure, landlessness, and land insecurity from a very early age?

YVES CABANNES: Yes! On the one hand, I was seeing how the garden was becoming more and more productive and beautiful through the seasons. Nearly every day I would help out with intensive gardening to feed the family: watering the plants, pulling out weeds, picking up vegetables and fruits, feeding the chickens, rabbits, or ducks, collecting eggs, et cetera.

At the same time, I was regaled with endless stories about our family before we had land. Without this lived experience, I would never have been so aware about landownership, and the necessity for land to be under the control of those who till it.

Reflective Practice & Engaged Scholarship

JOHN EMMEUS DAVIS: How did you go from a small town in southern France to becoming a college professor and an international development consultant? What was your path?

YVES CABANNES: I studied until high school in my home town, then a couple of years in Bordeaux, and then in Paris where I started to engage in various movements. Post-1968 was a time when Marxism, anti-imperialism, and anti-colonialism were very strong. My PhD at Sorbonne University was on understanding the drivers of the urban-rural contradiction in Iraq and how it had evolved since the first cities emerged in Mesopotamia and ancient Iraq around the Tigris and Euphrates, about 5000 years ago. I had worked a couple of years in Iraq in urban planning. This PhD provided me a unique exposure and some theoretical understanding on the status and importance of space and land throughout history.

Then I started working with NGOs. That gave me an opportunity to work in the field. I believed at that time that a professional who was committed to social causes and, in my case, committed to affordable housing for all, should link up a political vision of the world and a day-to-day grounded practice. I still believe so.

At that time, my objective was to have a practice based on four pillars: One was to be involved in transformative projects. A second pillar was teaching, constantly transforming acquired practice in the field—hopefully innovative practice—into knowledge and then let it be criticized by students. A third pillar was applied and participatory research. A fourth pillar was policy advocacy for the causes you believed in—in my case, appropriate technologies and local building materials for self-help housing and mutual aid, cooperatives, and housing rights.

After navigating among these four pillars in various countries—Latin America in particular—I became a lecturer at the Harvard University Graduate School of Design, teaching participatory planning and design. I also served as vice director of the Center for Urban Studies until it was closed. After two years there, I went to being Chair of the Development Planning Unit at the University College London.

However, I never left the world of practice and the link with transformative actions. I always tried to keep my cocktail with its four ingredients, sometimes more research, sometimes more teaching, sometimes more advocacy, sometimes more projects. But, most of the time, everything all together.

JOHN EMMEUS DAVIS: Most people choose a career that goes in the direction of being *either* an activist, organizer, and community developer in the field *or* being a researcher, teacher, and scholar at a university. You've gone back and forth between the two worlds throughout your career. How has one informed the other?

YVES CABANNES: Without my engagement as an activist and advocate, and without my involvement in projects with local government and with social movements like in Brazil, I would never have been able to engage with students and to share with them an inductive approach, anchored in my decades of lived practice in the field and, from there, connecting practice with theories.

If you have not lived positive experiences in the field, you tend to focus more on problems than on solutions and your capacity to inspire students is reduced; you might fall into merely transferring scholastic knowledge. When I visited the Burlington CLT in 2008, for example, I was so inspired by you and other colleagues. This inspiration gave me the energy, continuing until today, to study and to deepen my knowledge and practice about CLTs.

JOHN EMMEUS DAVIS: I believe that it engages students when they know that you have been a practitioner; you have not just been an academic. That inspires them and also gives them a vision of another possible path in their careers.

YVES CABANNES: This is absolutely the case. I have tried to show how people are reacting to adversity and how they are building their own resilience. My stories and narratives focus on positive cases and why they succeeded, how barriers were overcome or by-passed. It plants a seed of what is possible and gives people confidence. It plants a seed that says it *is* possible and another seed saying *how* it's possible. That goes beyond inspiration.

JOHN EMMEUS DAVIS: Particularly for graduate students who are going into planning or geography or development or affordable housing, I think they want a path of being a "reflective practitioner." That was the term that a professor at MIT used to write about, Don Schon. He said, "We need more reflective practitioners."

YVES CABANNES: I believe totally in the centrality of supporting students and people engaged in the field to become reflective practitioners. It's what I'm fully convinced of and trying to promote.

Part of my work during my ten years in Brazil, or in Ecuador with the Urban Management Program, was to push practitioners to produce knowledge. You need to understand that production of knowledge cannot be only the privilege of those who have studied at university; it also needs to be coming from practice.

JOHN EMMEUS DAVIS: Yes. I find that so much research is completely irrelevant to practice in the field. On the other side, practitioners are so overwhelmed by their day-to-day challenges that they don't often have the opportunity to step back and read, reflect, and interact with other people in the field. Any time you can be that bridge, I think it creates both good scholarship and good practice.

YVES CABANNES: Agreed! In addition, you learn much, much more. What I've continued to learn from reflective practitioners is absolutely impressive, and it makes you more humble intellectually.

In addition, when practitioners do a Masters or a PhD with their practice as a case study, the results can lead to a huge leap forward for the city and for their own development. I think of the case of two agronomist colleagues from Rosario in Argentina who, after decades of practice in urban agriculture, decided to go back to their studies. One of them deepened his research on organic urban farming; and the other one explored the importance of greenbelts and green corridors for peri-urban areas. Their work contributed to transforming Rosario into a world-leading city in organic farming. Today, 800 hectares have become protected for urban farming, supporting the transitioning of conventional agriculture to organic farming. It is truly impressive.

Garden Cities, Past and Present

JOHN EMMEUS DAVIS: That sounds like a modern-day version of the Garden City, combining housing and agriculture; combining urban growth with protecting the greenbelt. It's a verification of the vision that you and Philip Ross were laying out in your manifesto for *Garden Cities of the 21st Century*.

YVES CABANNES: Yes! We were arguing that we need to transform *existing* cities into Garden Cities, in addition to building new ones. Rosario is a good example with its greenbelt and the expansion of multiple spaces and practices for urban agriculture in the more densely urbanized areas.

JOHN EMMEUS DAVIS: How did you and Philip meet? How did you begin working together?

YVES CABANNES: It was just by chance. I was teaching with my colleague Robert Biel a course on food and urban agriculture in cities at the Development Planning Unit at UCL. We decided to take the students to Letchworth to expose them to a city that was envisioned and planned with quite a different perspective about food, which had been integrated into its planning since Letchworth was quite close to London. We also wanted them to appreciate the benefits of common ownership of land which was part of the course.

Students were from different parts of the world. When we got to Letchworth, everything was closed; winter was still there. Suddenly, we saw a small office saying "City Hall," a simple one-room office. I knocked at the door and, by chance, I found Philip. I said, "We are from University College London." I remember him putting a big golden chain over his shoulders and saying, "I'm the Mayor." He then started to explain this beautiful story of Letchworth, the first-ever Garden City.

JOHN EMMEUS DAVIS: I've been impressed that you and Philip Ross have taken an idea that is 120 years old and said, in effect, "This is not some historical artifact. This is an aspirational, practical program for the future." What you were saying about Rosario kind of confirms that possibility.

YVES CABANNES: It truly does. In Rosario a broad alliance of actors, with a leading role played by those involved with the urban agriculture movement, were able to transform an industrial, port city into a greener one, with more jobs all along the local food chain. That included, for instance, agro-industries to transform local products and regular fairs in different parts of the city where producers could directly sell their products.

It works! And it demonstrates on the ground that alternatives are possible. This is a far cry from Thatcher's motto of TINA [*There Is No Alternative*]. CLTs, too, are a way to defeat TINA!

What remains amazing about Letchworth Garden City is that, despite being located half-an-hour by train from London and despite skyrocketing land prices, more than 50% of Letchworth's land is still cultivated through farms, allotments, and backyard and front-yard gardening. There is also a vast educational farm that is largely subsidized by the Heritage Foundation, the community-based owner and developer of the land.

JOHN EMMEUS DAVIS: Part of what you and Philip have been emphasizing in your work and in your speeches is that the Garden City was not just about housing. It was a complete urban economy, integrating agriculture and housing, combining an urban settlement with orchards and small businesses.

YVES CABANNES: And small industries as well. I'm glad that you are raising that, John. It is one of the first planned cities that considered the generation of wealth and income for the common good, where workers and farmers were at the center, along with the city's residents.

Unfortunately, this part of the narrative and these original ideas very quickly became an untold narrative. Garden Cities are mostly remembered, first, for their excellent planning and design, adapting the city to the contour lines, to the existing natural watercourses and water drains, and being quite respectful of nature and the environment.

They are remembered, as well, for their chocolate-box small houses with a strong Arts and Crafts Movement influence. A unique aspect of Letchworth was an open national competition in the early 20th Century, challenging architects to design workers' and farmers' homes that were dignified and healthy, but small in size. Letchworth became a vivid catalogue of early social housing solutions, including the first light prefab housing that was built there, close to the Arts and Crafts houses.

The untold part of the story is why the city has **kept** its high quality of life and why "the garden" is still cultivated 120 years down the line. Through a close examination of the evolution of the Garden City, Philip and I identified some crucial reasons. Number **one** was collective ownership of the land. That allowed Letchworth to maintain rural land-use zoning and helped in resisting the transformation of Letchworth's land for speculative housing and dormitories.

JOHN EMMEUS DAVIS: Collective ownership of the underlying land was crucial?

YVES CABANNES: That was the case, collective ownership. Letchworth's pioneers and the new settlers were never the owners of the land; instead, they enjoyed 120-year leaseholds. These leaseholds were not limited to housing, but were also used for farms, services, or industries. We can say that Letchworth was a community land trust in its own right—the only one I know of encompassing an entire city.

What I learned in Burlington, with you and other colleagues, is the importance of having a steward and a manager for the land. In Letchworth this is the Heritage Foundation, where there are 145 people working to manage all sorts of lands and to manage the income resulting from the leases. We highlighted this as the *second* reason behind Letchworth's resilience.

The *third* reason is the strength of the grassroots organizations that have been able to influence the transformation of the land according to new necessities. One of these organizations is the Society of Horticulture, which evolved into the Letchworth Allotments and Horticultural Association. It is still going strong, counting over 800 members today. Through all these years, and despite two World Wars, they have been holding annual fairs where farmers can show their best produce, while keeping traditional and forgotten and delicious species like English apples, for instance.

A *fourth* element we identified in explaining the resilience of Letchworth are partnerships, gathering together national or local authorities and programs with social enterprises and communities.

The *fifth* and last reason behind Letchworth's success are entrepreneurs and small-scale enterprises committed to building a local social economy, rather than realizing a short-term profit. Remember when I mentioned cultivating old and forgotten species of apples? Well, an entrepreneur is now transforming part of these apples into a cider consumed locally. But to do so he had to have access to land! This is what Letchworth still offers through its Heritage Foundation, which is the owner and developer of most of the land.

JOHN EMMEUS DAVIS: What most city planners know about the Garden Cities is that they're well-designed. But more radical elements like community-owned land were stripped away. The whole model was kind of domesticated, yes? The more radical elements of the Garden City were lopped off and pushed to the side.

YVES CABANNES: You are absolutely right. City planners and the Town and Country Act played an unfortunate role in this domestication. (My colleague planners at UCL will probably disagree!)

The New Town Movement that followed the construction of the first Garden City in the early 20th Century retained the heritage of design and planning. This was positive, but what was left behind and abandoned were the pre-Garden City ideals resulting from the bubbling socialist ideas that were under debate in late 19th Century London. The planners that designed Letchworth were permeated with these ideas about the importance of land.

The people behind the creation of Letchworth were often vilified as "utopian Marxists" by the Marxist-Leninists. Community-based cities were regarded as too dangerous a model. The Bolsheviks were not for that.

All these ideas of commonly-owned land and of a community-based approach to development were disregarded in Welwyn Garden City, the second one built. It had a more interesting design and retained the idea of having some cooperative housing, but the land was kept in public ownership. It was built primarily for survivors of the First World War who had been fighting against Germany in Belgium and in other places in Europe. Welwyn became something totally different than Letchworth.

JOHN EMMEUS DAVIS: It's interesting to me that you have the Letchworth experiment pulled in a *conservative* direction by a planning profession that wanted to emphasize only design. And you have it pulled in a *statist* direction because of the Bolsheviks' opposition to the community ownership of land. They preferred to have public ownership.

YVES CABANNES: My view, on the other hand, is that the main influence on the Letchworth experiment came from a communitarian vision and pre-enclosure references. Philip explained to me once that some colors and symbols in Letchworth relate to the Diggers Movement and Gerrard Winstanley. During the English Civil War in the mid-17th Century, they had resisted the enclosure movement and promoted the common ownership of land.

When Philip Ross became the Mayor of Letchworth, he was absolutely essential to challenging what the Heritage Foundation had become during Thatcher's wave of privatization. The Heritage Foundation, which managed and developed Letchworth's land, was turning into a real estate company, one that was more interested in transforming the land into projects such as golf courses for the benefit of a few.

Philip and a couple of others were bold enough to take the Heritage Foundation to court, arguing that the Garden City's income resulting from the leasing of the land had to remain for the benefit of the *whole* population, not only the few. Such a position was completely in line with Ebenezer Howard's thinking.

And they eventually won in 2009 at the House of Commons! I was amazed by this small group of people. It still continues, you know.

Philip has played a major role in keeping Letchworth faithful to its original ideals.

The Challenge of Scale in Garden Cities

JOHN EMMEUS DAVIS: You and Philip Ross have developed a nice partnership, writing and teaching about the Garden City.

YVES CABANNES: We became friends and started to learn one from each other. We later traveled together to China, because some Chinese cities were interested in Garden Cities. They had requested the Institute of Garden Cities to come, and the Institute took Philip and me along on the trip.

We eventually reached Chengdu, the capital of Sichuan Province. The various people we met liked our stories and conversations, but they were not impressed at all by the *scale* of the UK's Garden Cities. One of the top authorities told us seriously, "We would like to build a Garden City in Sichuan. How many people live in Letchworth?" We said, "30,000." "Oh," he said, "We are planning a Garden City for

Philip Ross (4th from left) and Yves in China, 2012.

900,000 people. Would you be interested in being our planners and advisors?"

I remember that night in the hotel wondering what can we do? We are full of ideas, but we have no capacity to say yes to such an incredible invitation. We just had to say we cannot take that on. And that was the end of the story.

On the aftermath of this visit, one year later, colleagues from the Chinese Academy of Sciences led a delegation to visit Letchworth. I organized the visit and the exchange around how the Chinese communes at the periphery of large cities could benefit from the Letchworth model. The story continues, but it was unfortunately stopped by COVID restrictions and the situation in China.

I see opportunities to be doing Garden Cities, but they need to change scale and be updated to Twentieth-first Century constraints. And this is what, in essence, gave birth to our manifesto in *Garden Cities for the 21st Century*.

JOHN EMMEUS DAVIS: Well, that's certainly a different concept of scale than what we talk about in the United States. When we talk about "going to scale" in building the community land trust movement and getting more housing units built for more people, a community land trust serving 900,000 people is far beyond the vision we've had in the United States.

YVES CABANNES: Let's keep this big scale in our rainbow horizon! Transformations are unpredictable. What is little-known about the Garden Cities is that each one of them was a Garden City in its own right but, at the same time, they were clustered into what Howard was naming the "Social City." If you look at his famous round chart, you will notice how multiple small Garden Cities, each counting about 30,000 inhabitants, were connected among themselves and connected with a central one of about 55,000 inhabitants. In total, the Social City was planned for 250,000 people.

Unfortunately, this Social City perspective was erased from the narrative on Garden Cities, which was narrowed down to physical planning and leaving the perspective of a social city buried in the Garden City cemetery—or in the cemetery of utopian ideas.

A scale of 250,000 people is a middle-scale in relation to 900,000. But one could multiply the clusters. The main idea was a decentralized perspective, already announcing "Small is Beautiful."

Another interesting aspect was that all of these Garden Cities were separated by buffers of rural agricultural or forest land, but were extremely well-connected by public transport and canals. In fact, the idea of public transport connecting Garden Cities was quite advanced for urban planning, but quite in line with 19th Century industrial England. I think this more regional planning scale has been forgotten and also lies in the Garden Cities cemetery. Sometimes when I give lectures with architect colleagues, they have a great difficulty with the idea of Garden Cities because of scale, which is a small one. We need to remember Howard's clustering and decentralized, self-sustained concepts of the Social City.

JOHN EMMEUS DAVIS: Within Howard's vision, it seems to me, he was always combining ownership and citizenship. When he envisioned the Garden City, he was thinking not only about a scale that could be *managed economically*, but one that could also be *governed democratically*. Each Garden City could be separate with a certain amount of self-governance, but you could cluster them. You could connect them on a regional basis.

YVES CABANNES: Very important to remember! As a matter of fact, various so-called utopian communities were built during the 19th Century, primarily in the USA, that designed and tested various ways to combine ownership and citizenship. They developed economic models that were combined with forms of direct democracy and self-government. There is still a lot to learn from them, including what should ***not*** be done. Howard learned a lot from failures in the USA before writing his own manifesto.

I would also like to come back to the redistribution of wealth that was part of the original Garden City proposal. I once made an exercise of totaling the income collected from the lease fees by Letchworth's Heritage Foundation, divided by the number of its residents. The figures are striking. The budget per inhabitant is higher than the funds transferred to the city by the central government, per inhabitant! And the Heritage Foundation's budget is largely used for multiple actions and programs benefitting directly Letchworth's inhabitants and users of the city.

This explains in part why the model is quite appealing. We have not learned enough about these economic models for the capture of value and redistribution that has been made possible because of the community's ownership of land.

JOHN EMMEUS DAVIS: Historically, there's been a separation of economics and politics. What we're talking about here, however, is ***political economy*** where ownership and citizenship are integrated.

YVES CABANNES: Absolutely. We need to think seriously about what can be decentralized and remain in the hands of the community—a community that has collective ownership, for example—and what should remain in the hands of national, regional, or district governments.

JOHN EMMEUS DAVIS: One of the things I found most appealing about the chapter that you and Philip contributed to *On Common Ground*, the book we published in 2020, was your argument that you don't have to wait until you have 500 acres of land to create a Garden City. You don't have to wait until you're going to have a planned city of 30,000 people before you can create a Garden City. You can start small. You can build incrementally.

I think that's part of the overlap between your vision of the Garden City and the community land trust. You can get started now. You can buy parcels of land. You can build new housing or rehabilitate existing housing. Instead of starting big, you can start small and build incrementally. You can also build your base of social and political support at the same time as you're buying parcels of land. I found that part of the argument which you and Philip were laying out to be very compelling.

YVES CABANNES: In fact, what you are mentioning now creates a bridge between what you gradually built in Burlington and what was built in Letchworth. In both cases, the process was quite evolutionary. Since the mid-1980s in Burlington, you have been acquiring quite different kinds of housing and buildings: derelict homes, rented apartments, condos, a bus station that was closed, and at the same time building up a unique CLT model.

Coming from many years living in Latin America and other Global South countries, I was always struck by how innovative solutions were often quite evolutionary and could take years to consolidate as a viable and robust solution. You can begin with housing and then start connecting the dots, with allotments, industrial areas, transport, etc. Or you can start with renewable, decentralized energy and then move into creating decent jobs. There are multiple avenues, depending on local realities, but you need an entry door. It can take 50 years or 100 years; it doesn't matter. What is important is the direction, not forgetting that you need to generate a city of rights for all that builds and defends the "Right to the City," as dreamt by Henri Lefebvre in 1968. This principle is one of the twelve entry doors that Philip and I envisioned in *Garden Cities for the 21st Century*.

These aspects illustrate how Philip and I worked together in a complementary fashion. He brought to our collaboration his UK perspective on the City of Rights for All. I brought my French perspective on the Right to the City, post 1968. We explored how best to link both parts.

Community Ownership of Land

JOHN EMMEUS DAVIS: Your vision of the Garden City and your concept of the community land trust are very expansive. At the Center for CLT Innovation, we are committed to encouraging the global growth of community land trusts. But we also recognize that CLTs are different from country to country. So we've adopted a more expansive focus, supporting and encouraging all forms of community-led development on community-owned land.

It seems to me that you got there before us. That's *always* been your focus. Your concept of the community land trust has been not just the "classic" CLT from the USA, but this more expansive, inclusive idea of community-led development on community-owned land. Is that correct?

YVES CABANNES: Yes. That's true with respect to community-led development, but it's also related to a communal, collective, or cooperative use and ownership of land.

What is surprising, for instance, according to my Mexican sources, are the 28,000 to 39,000 *ejidos* in Mexico, born on the aftermath of the 1917 Revolution. They are another true form of community ownership and use. At the end of the century, a constitutional amendment opened the possibility to turn them into individual property and to sell them, but over 100 million hectares of *ejidos* still exist. So that's a very interesting model.

There are many more, such as what are called *baldios* in Portugal. These are common lands with free pasture, use of natural water, and collection of wood. The most recent assessments indicate there are half-a-million hectares under this regime, a significant number for a small country such as Portugal. These lands are a huge opportunity and a source of knowledge for future actions.

The famous Chinese communes that were consolidated after 1949, when the Maoists took power, are still there by the thousands. They contain an immense amount of collective and indivisible right of use, considering that all land was nationalized in China and belongs to the State.

I could go on and on, highlighting customary land regimes, essentially of a communal nature. They are being absorbed in numerous countries by the expansion of cities. Interestingly, these "urban customary lands" have generated innovative hybrid land-use and ownership regimes, which are largely under-studied and little-understood. The consideration of such a broad array of collective practices and land regimes could cross-fertilize in order to make them stronger. Such cross-fertilization seems to me a powerful way to scale them up globally and to make them more visible. Taken as a whole, they are a real and robust alternative to private ownership and use.

JOHN EMMEUS DAVIS: At the center of both the Garden Cities and community land trusts is land, community ownership of land. That's the platform on which everything else is raised. That used to be at the center of political economy and political thinking, as well. Land was central. But land has been pushed to the side. Capital, labor, technology, information—all of that is raised up. Land is put on the periphery. But it seems to me that, in your thinking about Garden Cities and community land trusts, land becomes the center of the proposition once again.

YVES CABANNES: Yes! And here is the cause of my love at first sight with the US model of CLTs. It was an eye-opener for me. I was coming from mutual aid and housing co-ops and especially the

Uruguayan model of collective ownership. This model has had significant success in Uruguay and has now spread throughout fifteen
Latin American countries. I was also involved for a couple of decades
in strengthening and adapting the Uruguayan model in northeast
Brazil in particular.

The big innovation of CLTs, for me, is that they are not limited to
housing. This is exactly the leap forward we struggled to achieve in
Brazil through the *Mutirão 50 Project* and later on with the *Comuni-
dade Program* in the Fortaleza Metropolitan Area. In the aftermath
of the dark dictatorial times, from 1988 on, we were trying to produce "pieces of city" under a communal regime, largely according
to the values and solutions of Garden Cities. You might imagine my
joy in 2008 when I discovered you in Burlington sharing the same
vision: communal land at the center of urban development and not
limited only to housing.

Unfortunately, community-owned land beyond housing is
something of limited consideration in Europe. I hear colleagues,
mostly coming from housing movements, singing the praises of

Porto Alegre, Brazil, 2008

landownership and land use in collective terms, but essentially limited to housing only; not to housing plus farming, plus industrial zones, plus places for enjoyment such as parks. There is a big risk, I think, to limiting the CLT to being a tool for affordable housing only, rather than a tool for producing neighborhoods in cities at scale. This is going backward.

The Meaning & Vitality of "Community"

JOHN EMMEUS DAVIS: At the Center for CLT Innovation, we talk about "community-led development on community-owned land." The key word, of course, is "community." How do *you* talk about the role of "community" in Garden Cities, CLTs, and related forms of tenure?

YVES CABANNES: We first need to unpack what we mean by "community." When I was teaching at Harvard, I started to realize that the notion of "community" bears many different edges. There is an Anglo-Saxon perspective of "community" as being inward-looking and exclusionary, sometimes tightly united to conservative values. In Europe, "community" is often seen—and criticized—as being the same as "communitarism." Then, you have an embracing and inclusionary notion of "community" as used by many CLTs, one that is broader and more transformative. When I translate the "community" of a CLT into French, I often use "collectivité" in order to capture the more inclusive meaning of "community."

This being said, it's hard to keep "community" a vital part of land and housing movements. To go from a movement approach to an institutionalization of what's been won is difficult. Do you get my point here?

JOHN EMMEUS DAVIS: I do. That's always a bit of a challenge, right? You want to institutionalize the gains of struggle, but as soon as you formalize and institutionalize them you start to lose some of the energy and radical edge of the politics that you started with.

YVES CABANNES: It is a problem. I can go back to my years in Brazil. I started working with the urban landless movement. I saw the energy of being a movement. Then, after we started to have institutionalization of the land and of the housing units, most of the chosen few who got a home were closing their doors, but they were only ten percent of families in need of a home. Through institutionalization, there was a sort of losing the energy and inclusiveness that had been a big part of the movement.

Recognition of CLTs by World Habitat

JOHN EMMEUS DAVIS: The Building and Social Housing Foundation, now called World Habitat, has been reviewing applications for its World Habitat Award for 30 years or so. This Award, sponsored by UN Habitat, highlights innovative housing strategies from around the world. Community land trusts have done very well in this international competition, haven't they?

YVES CABANNES: Yes. I recently made a review of the World Habitat Awards, looking for all projects related to CLTs or collective forms of land tenure.

JOHN EMMEUS DAVIS: These were both the applications and the winners of the World Habitat Award?

YVES CABANNES: More exactly, I reviewed the finalists that we recommended each year as the Technical Committee. During my 14 years serving on the Committee, ten CLTs and similar forms of collective land tenure made it into the final round. Three CLTs were eventually chosen as winners.

JOHN EMMEUS DAVIS: The three CLTs that won a World Habitat Award were the Champlain Housing Trust in Burlington, Vermont; then the Caño Martín Peña CLT in Puerto Rico; and, this year, the Brussels CLT in Belgium. Are you saying there have been seven other organizations that are similar to CLTs which made it into the final round?

YVES CABANNES: Yes. The number of entries is about 100 to 120 each year. To have ten forms of collective land tenure make it to the final round over the years has been very good.

JOHN EMMEUS DAVIS: Shall we go through the list together?

YVES CABANNES: We have the Champlain Housing Trust as a winner in 2008, which opened the door. The peer-to-peer visit that occurred as a result of the World Habitat Award became a milestone in generating an active international network of activists working with these models. Then in 2013 you have Milton Park.

JOHN EMMEUS DAVIS: The housing cooperative in Montreal?

YVES CABANNES: In Montreal, yes, 22 cooperatives sharing a piece of indivisible land. I had visited Milton Park a couple of years before. I was impressed and convinced their experience deserved recognition. During a conversation with one of Milton Park's historical leaders, Dimitri Roussopoulos, I remember telling him, "Dimitri, you need to have more impact internationally. Why don't you come to the World Urban Forum? I'll propose to organize a session to put in perspective Letchworth Garden City and Milton Park." This happened.

Then came a further conversation with Dimitri Roussopoulos following the World Urban Forum when I suggested, "Why don't you spend time applying for the UN World Award? Milton Park could be a finalist or a winner." Milton Park became a finalist in 2013. They deserved it!

Then, you have another one which relates to a review of collective forms of tenure that I made for Raquel Rolnik, the United Nations Special Rapporteur for Adequate Housing. In Brazil, the Statute of the City law introduced an innovative form of collective use of land in 2001, called *Usucapião Coletivo*. It corresponds to a form of adverse possession, where a property can be obtained after years of uncontested occupancy of a piece of land. One of the first experiences of *Usucapião Coletivo* emerged in Santos, Brazil. The *Coletivo* in Santos made it into the World Habitat finals.

JOHN EMMEUS DAVIS: What next? Weren't there also a couple of World Habitat notables from the UK?

YVES CABANNES: Right. In 2015, LILAC Community Led Homes in Leeds became a finalist. LILAC is a mutual homeownership society. The residents, as in a CLT, have a say. Their decision-making power is not limited to their own housing project but is extended to the whole site development. What LILAC did was amazing in terms of low-carbon-footprint energy solutions and tackling climate change challenges.

Then in 2016, one year later, Granby Four Street CLT in Liverpool was another UN Habitat Award finalist.

JOHN EMMEUS DAVIS: What do they do?

YVES CABANNES: They do home improvement of derelict buildings for the poorest of the poor. They've been able to reach far below what you do at the Champlain Housing Trust, at least when I was there in Burlington in 2008.

JOHN EMMEUS DAVIS: The Champlain Housing Trust has, in fact, been able to go further down the economic ladder over time. We started higher up, but we've gradually moved lower, serving people who are poorer. We still offer single-family houses and condominiums for sale to households earning between 70% and 120% of the Area Median Income, but CHT has also been developing co-ops and rental housing for people who earn less. Most recently, CLT has been buying old motels, rehabilitating them, and making them available to people who were formally homeless.

YVES CABANNES: Wow. But the nice thing about Granby Four Street is that they began at that level. They started with the poorest of the poor.

In 2017, another finalist I knew was Düzce Hope Homes, located in Turkey. It was a post-disaster, earthquake rebuilding project. People who were not eligible for aid were able to mobilize resources to buy a piece of land and to start a form of cooperative. One of their advisers and supporters was an ex-student of mine. On various occasions, while in Turkey, I spoke a number of times about CLTs and collective forms of ownership.

I encouraged them to submit something for a World Habitat Award, even if they had only the land and had not built the homes yet. To my great satisfaction they were finalists. That shows that we need to continue spreading the word about CLTs and introducing many people to CLTs and other forms of collective tenure, so the soil is prepared and will one day become fertile and bear fruit. It is only a matter of time.

Also, in 2017 there was the Caño Martín Peña CLT, which was a winner.

JOHN EMMEUS DAVIS: We'll talk more about the Caño CLT in a moment, but let's finish your list of World Habitat finalists and winners.

YVES CABANNES: In 2019, La Borda Housing Cooperative in Barcelona was a finalist. They presented a collective ownership solution that was very interesting and the quality of the architecture is amazingly good. They did not win the World Habitat Award, however, probably because they were seen as too middle-class and not very multicultural.

Then, in 2021, you have CLT Brussels as a World Habitat winner. That same year there was also a community-driven recovery, reconstruction, and relocation process in Palu Bay, Indonesia, following a tsunami. A community of fisherman looked eagerly for a piece of land close to the shore and refused to be displaced. They got resources from an airline company's foundation that allowed them to buy the piece of land they had identified. That was bought in collective ownership through an international NGO.

When I look back over 14 years, that's not a bad record for CLTs and other forms of collective tenure.

JOHN EMMEUS DAVIS: There's enormous variety among the many organizations you just talked about, a lot of variety in who they serve and the kind of housing they do. Some of them don't even do housing as their primary activity. Why do you look at them and say, "They're part of the family of community land trusts?" What do they have in common?

YVES CABANNES: One thing is very clear. All these projects use collective land tenure as a way to prevent displacement, to promote security, and to root people in place.

The other similarity is they all are helping people to build community, to be part of a collective. Either they were an existing community, say the villagers in Palu Bay; or they are building community through the process of commoning, like communities in CLT Brussels or in Turkey. In the case of Turkey, most of the people didn't know each other. What they had in common was that they wouldn't accept what the Turkish government was offering. It was a rejection of a state solution. They became a cohesive community— with conviviality, with things which are not housing-related or simply economy-connected.

JOHN EMMEUS DAVIS: What role does land and land tenure have across all of these models?

YVES CABANNES: The feeling of people living on community-owned land is that they are stronger together in front of market forces or in front of public evictions.

I feel close to these kinds of initiatives. They are emerging out of civic and social movements. They are not only involved in one issue, say affordable and secure housing, but in larger and deeper transformations. They have broader views on society. Many are more politicized or more conscious of what CLTs and other forms of cooperative and communal forms of land tenure can do to generate not only a new model of urban development or a new model of affordable housing, but a pathway to building an alternative society.

JOHN EMMEUS DAVIS: It's land reform as a platform for social transformation.

YVES CABANNES: Yes. Exactly.

Caño Martín Peña CLT & Informal Settlements

JOHN EMMEUS DAVIS: Earlier, you mentioned the Caño Martín Peña CLT in Puerto Rico. Why did you support their application for a World Habitat Award?

YVES CABANNES: One role I want to insist upon is that you need to be proactive and support organizations and communities. You must encourage them to apply for this Award.

JOHN EMMEUS DAVIS: That was certainly my role in the case of the Caño Martín Peña CLT. I encouraged them to apply. Then I wrote a letter formally nominating them.

You happened to be on the World Habitat jury, so we found ourselves on opposite sides of that process. So, you received their application and you read my nomination. What was it about the Caño CLT that appealed to you?

YVES CABANNES: Let me start saying that your letter was very good. I'm one of the guys on the jury who's very careful about the content of a letter and who writes it. Your letter was extremely important. I could refer to it and say, "This is somebody who knows what he speaks about and look at what he says." It adds an external view which is very, very good.

JOHN EMMEUS DAVIS: But why did they win? What was it about the Caño CLT that had power and appeal for the World Habitat jury?

YVES CABANNES: Number one, what was appealing and what was decisive was the scale.

JOHN EMMEUS DAVIS: The number of people, the number of hectares, the number of houses that were being benefited?

YVES CABANNES: Yes. Hectares, parcels, et cetera. The main point was to say, "See, it is possible not to have only small CLTs, as in the UK and the US." So, the scale was essential.

And the variety in the use of land was essential too. They were moving from an exclusively housing approach to something broader. You cannot solve the issue of floods, for example, if you do not have a proper piece of land that you can control. The Caño CLT was connected to housing, but it was also part of a more urban perspective. I insisted on arguing, "They connect to the rest of the city: transport, water, you name it." That was the second important element.

The third one was the link to climate change and to environmental issues. You can, at the same time, address the problem of low-income housing and also be able to face environmental issues. That was extremely important.

Another factor, which I think was decisive too, was that the Caño CLT was not so much an Anglo-Saxon case. Even if Puerto Rico is part of the United States, the *fideicomiso* is based on a different legal framework. I defended that aspect of their application, saying, "Look, this is something which is exportable to a good portion of Spanish-speaking Latin America."

JOHN EMMEUS DAVIS: After winning the World Habitat Award, there was a peer-to-peer exchange between the Caño Martín Peña CLT and the *favela* network in Rio de Janeiro that Catalytic Communities has been supporting.

YVES CABANNES: You see, right away you had an application to another set of informal settlements, even if the legal and historical background in Brazil is quite different from the rest of Latin America.

I saw this as a big opportunity to say, "It's scale, it's a kind of *favela*, and it can be transferred; you can transfer CLTs to the Global South." Remember, one of the three pillars of the Award is to make the case for transferability. Are you able to transfer it to other cultures and legal systems? This was the potential I saw with the Caño CLT.

JOHN EMMEUS DAVIS: I believe that the United Nations estimates there are something like one billion people living in informal settlements around the world. This would seem to provide a very rich opportunity for applying a strategy of community-owned land to the precarious situation of these populations. Yes?

YVES CABANNES: Yes, and for showing it could work in a *favela* kind of approach, improving the housing in existing *favelas* and to maintaining the people there. I've thought for years, "Let's find ways in the World Habitat Award for local improvement without displacement." We don't have so many cases. This was an important issue, being able to say, "Hey, we have here a tool and an approach which allows people to stay in place."

JOHN EMMEUS DAVIS: Most community land trusts in the United States have found an empty piece of land and built something new on the land, whereas in many informal settlements, like the *favelas* in Brazil and the Caño Martín Peña in Puerto Rico, you have existing structures on land where the people in those homes have insecure tenure. The challenge then becomes, how do you get control of the land under their feet so that they're not displaced from buildings they and their families have been occupying, sometimes for several generations?

YVES CABANNES: This looks essential to me. For the first time with the Caño CLT you had a solution at scale where you could have neighborhood improvement without displacement. It was about the entire neighborhood. They demonstrated that you can use the CLT, the *fideicomiso*, to help people stay in place and to improve their environment, despite huge challenges of water, flooding, exposure to hurricanes, et cetera.

Looking to the Future: Opportunities for Growth

JOHN EMMEUS DAVIS: Why don't we continue in this vein, thinking about cutting-edge areas that community land trusts and other forms of community-owned land ought to be moving into. Let's look ten years down the road. We've already talked about potential applications of CLTs in informal settlements. What are some other opportunities, other innovative, cutting-edge applications for community land trusts?

YVES CABANNES: One is very much related to the impact of climate change. What I discovered, for instance, with participatory budgeting is when you have a sort of climate change overcoat you are boosting your agenda. There is so much interest in finding ways to face the dramatic impacts of climate change. Anything related to adaptation and mitigation is good, so you are listened to.

JOHN EMMEUS DAVIS: You are saying that climate-change-induced displacement can be addressed by CLTs to allow people to stay put, to stay in place?

YVES CABANNES: Exactly. That's why Palu Bay in Indonesia that I was mentioning is so crucial. That's why Düzce Hope Homes in Turkey is so crucial. Related to that, I can make a bridge to another sector. Remember the request for information that the Center for CLT Innovation had from Somalia? Those refugee camps are climate-induced, conflict-induced. When you look at the number of displaced people, it is in the range of at least 30-50 million, and the number will increase in the future to unsuspectedly massive numbers. Everything is pointing to the possibility that we're going to have 100 million very soon.

I'm thinking too of the new camps in Bangladesh of the Rohingya, the people from Burma. There are 900,000 people in one camp alone. The opportunity, if we want to solve the problem, is to get collective ownership and collective land use. If not, it won't go anywhere.

JOHN EMMEUS DAVIS: You mentioned *ejidos* earlier. How do they fit into your thinking about opportunities for the growth of community land trusts?

YVES CABANNES: Recently Claire Simonneau wrote to me from France. She said, "Yves, I'm sending you two documents, and you were the inspiration for them. You are the one who told me about *ejidos* in Mexico as one of these collective forms of tenure. I thank you for that."

She told me that somebody had written his PhD on *ejidos*. Here is this publication on how much area is still in social ownership, despite privatization. He brought unique data on urban *ejidos* that corresponded to those agricultural lands that have been absorbed by the expansion of cities over the last 100 years. I asked him, "How much of all this land is still in social ownership?" According to the information he gathered, only 14% of *ejido* land is no longer in social ownership and under a process of individual titling. That means that 86% of *ejido* land has not been privatized. Additional data indicates this process might take a lot of time and that currently less than 1% of all *ejido* lands have been effectively registered as private. It shows the resistance to privatization.

JOHN EMMEUS DAVIS: Following the Mexican Revolution, creation of the *ejido* system expanded access to land and housing for lower-income people. Am I correct?

YVES CABANNES: Yes. But it was primarily for people in the country, the peasants outside of cities. Now, with the expansion of cities, this land sometimes became incredibly well-located. These *ejidos* were no longer agrarian. The government had neither the willingness nor the money to invest, so the people on *ejidos* were persuaded to privatize. This has been a windfall for private investors and for-profit developers.

So there was dismantling of the *ejidos*. Huge pieces of land were sold for private development at a very low price, with a bit of corruption between investors and the local government. The intention was to develop these lands for housing a suburban middle class, not for housing the poor.

JOHN EMMEUS DAVIS: Do you see a role for community land trusts to play—or, perhaps, for the Center for CLT Innovation to play—in supporting people who are trying to defend the *ejidos*?

YVES CABANNES: Yes. Obviously I'm thinking of that. And we need help and guidance from researchers and various persons we have come across through time, including Mexicans. Maybe ex-Mexican students. I want to identify one good *ejido* in which collective owners, called *ejidatarios*, have not been accepting the privatization. One way to act could be to identify some good *ejidos* which have symbolic value from the Mexican Revolution, and help to transform them into *fideicomiso*, improving poor rural housing and presenting another way of producing cities and neighborhoods.

JOHN EMMEUS DAVIS: Just like your family, part of my wife's family is Mexican. Bonnie's cousins all live in Mexico. I would have a great interest in making connections to the *ejidos*.

YVES CABANNES: Super! I have an excellent ex-student of mine in Santiago de Queretaro. We have been looking for years for good *ejidos* which have been resisting privatization. She has identified a couple. What I hope is to have a more systematic and strategic approach to supporting some of these *ejidos*.

I'm also interested in continuing to make the case for collective ownership of land within the General Assembly of the United Nations, as we did already for community land trusts. *Ejidos* are part of that broad family of non-individual tenure systems. You should not privatize this land for the benefit of private investors.

JOHN EMMEUS DAVIS: This sort of privatization of traditional, customary tenures is happening all over the world, isn't it?

YVES CABANNES: Indeed! All over the world.

JOHN EMMEUS DAVIS: You come from an agricultural background and you've always had an interest in food and agriculture. How does food security fit into the community land trust movement?

YVES CABANNES: I think this is a major cutting-edge issue. I have tried to push that issue through with my links with the United Nations and working regularly for the UN. Even when I was working for Raquel Rolnik, I tried to get food security and land for food as part of the right to housing. But you have the Special Rapporteur for Housing, on the one hand, and the Special Rapporteur for Food, on the other. Okay? Two different persons, two different fields. And when you look at their mandate, urban land for food falls into the cracks. It is nowhere.

That's precisely why I invited Greg Rosenberg to be part of the Expert Group Meeting for the formulation of the New Urban Agenda at the UN Headquarters in New York in 2016. We were successful in inserting the CLT into it. It was a strategic move to get collective ownership, CLTs, and collective uses of land into the New Urban Agenda, which included land for food. The New Urban Agenda has been approved by all governments and constitutes a UN roadmap for cities in the years to come.

You know, we need to rethink the planning of cities. This is another area where I think we should work much better to include land for food, with different regimes, within the planning of cities. I'm a planner by training. You don't have a single manual which exists for planning cities and integrating food into the planning of modern cities. The one exception is the Garden City.

I think, as well, that the Troy Gardens CLT in Madison, Wisconsin is a guide to how you combine co-housing, farm allotments, and a natural reserve. Troy Gardens would deserve a World Habitat Award! This is planning at its best. We don't have many cases like that. I have been using Troy Gardens a lot in my lectures. This is a major field of innovation that is largely underrated. I think that we should put aside housing as the main entry point for CLTs. We should have land for food as a key entry point and, connected to that, providing housing for the people who are producing the food. We should turn the tables. If you want my opinion, we should concentrate more on land for food security or food sovereignty, then see how housing fits into it.

Looking to the Past:
A Visit with Vinoba Bhave

JOHN EMMEUS DAVIS: We've been talking about the future, but I also have a personal interest in the past. You are someone who is very much aware of that history, the origins of the modern community land trust model. You know that it's rooted in the Gramdan Movement in India. Not only that, you are one of the only people I know who had a personal encounter with Vinoba Bhave. I wonder if you would speak about that experience. How is it that you happened to meet Vinoba Bhave?

YVES CABANNES: That happened in 1980 or 1981. It was just after my long years in Mexico, where I was very much inspired by the *ejidos* and by the Mexican Revolution that we spoke about. In the nonprofit association I was working with, we were working on alternative technologies and transferring technologies from one place another, empowering people to control local development.

That was very much in the spirit of the of the Gandhian Movement. The Center of Sciences for Villages was the organization at the service of the 60,000-plus Gramdan Villages that were existing at that time. My small group was invited to go to India.

I went there by myself, and I remember having a Samsonite luggage that soon became an odd object. I appeared in Wardha and a leper who was part of the Gandhian organization was waiting for me with his rickshaw. I remember that my luggage was a problem for him because he was a leper without fingers and driving a rickshaw.

And I looked so big and heavy. I was totally ashamed. He later spread one sheet on a couch, with a wonderfully gentle smile. I couldn't sleep because I thought that I was going to be contaminated. I still feel quite ridiculous about all this, despite decades that have elapsed. Such ignorance!

Staying with lepers was a unique introduction to Gandhian realties and philosophy, you know, an approach to understanding the situation of the most excluded. I was sharing the collective's food with them. We were not using plates but banana leaves instead, a much healthier and low-cost artifact. We were combining lives and sharing food in a convivial way. I remember being the only non-leper, along with the doctor.

I stayed there a couple of days, studying texts about Gandhian philosophy and actions, feeling restless most of the time. Then the head of the Center of Science for Villages was starting to communicate with me, and maybe feeling like I was the right kind of person. To my surprise, he said one day, "We're going to visit somebody in the Gandhi Ashram and introduce you." I said, "All right." I didn't know I was going to meet Vinoba Bhave himself, who I knew was considered the spiritual successor of Mahatma Gandhi. He had led the Bhoodan Movement in the 1950s. His nonviolent 50,000-miles-long march over the years, influenced by Gram Swarajya and the Sarvodaya Society, resulted in millions of hectares of land donations from landlords to landless. It was probably unique in history. That later allowed for the Gramdan Villages to expand.

After a one-hour drive we eventually reached the Ashram. Devendra Kumar simply said, "Okay, sit down." I sat there for a couple of hours, among many people who were there. Nobody was speaking. They like you to observe and respect what's happening. Your capacity to listen and see in silence was important.

After a couple of hours, I entered into a medium-sized, empty room, dimly lighted. Vinoba Bhave was sitting there. He had made a vow of silence and only communicated through small papers he wrote upon. We sat down in the Indian way. Devendra Kumar, the CSV Director, approached him and said a few words in his ears. Then he started looking at me.

He kept silent for a couple of minutes. Then he looked very warmly to me and wrote on a piece of paper something that he gave to a village girl of 12 years old by his side. She was, according to what I learned later, believed to be the proper reincarnation of the Mahatma. Vinoba Bhave was looking at how awkward I was sitting. I'm nearly two meters high, you know. He was not laughing, but he wrote in his nice way, "Hey, he is very tall." Meaning, "He can't sit down properly." I didn't get that when he said it. What was written on the paper given to Devendra said, "Yes, you can work with these guys. They are fine."

That was important. They were accepting to work with Europeans for the first time, at least this is what I understood. It was a great, great honor for me to work with them and exchange ideas and work together. I took it as a big responsibility that Vinoba Bhave was putting his trust in my hands. You must not fail, you see.

During another visit, sometime in 1983 or 1984, I inquired about Vinoba Bhave. My CSV colleagues told me that, after a short break of his vow of silence, he decided to go mute again, to stop eating and drinking, and to let his corporal envelope die, freeing his soul for reincarnation. His legacy on sharing land and promoting Gramdan Villages never disappeared from my soul. That Indian legacy merged with the revolutionary Mexican legacy of *ejidos* and my own origins. It might explain why I was immediately tuned in, politically and emotionally, with each one of you and what you called CLTs. Do you see what I mean?

JOHN EMMEUS DAVIS: Yes.

YVES CABANNES: Land was obviously crucial in these Villages. Supporting the movement and the philosophy meant that local technologies should be maintained for building their homes. That was part of my job.

JOHN EMMEUS DAVIS: Here's an interesting circle. I think that you helped to open the door to allowing Europeans and Americans from outside of India to come and meet with Vinoba Bhave. Shortly after you were there, Bob Swann and Marjorie Swann from the United States came to visit. Vinoba Bhave was still observing his vow of silence. They sat down and they exchanged notes in which Bob and Marj Swann tried to explain to Vinoba Bhave what a community land trust is—and the debt of gratitude that the CLT Movement owed to the Gramdan Movement. What Marj Swann later said to me, when I interviewed her a number of years ago, was that his face lit up. He seemed to be very pleased at that connection between the Gramdan Movement and the community land trust movement.

YVES CABANNES: Wow. How impressive! In my case, I never felt in a position to send messages back to Bhave, feeling too respectful and shy to do so—something not too much in my nature, I must add.

JOHN EMMEUS DAVIS: All of this was an exchange with little pieces of paper being passed to you?

YVES CABANNES: Yes, this is how he communicated. You know, after the piece of paper exchanging with Bhave, he wrote another one. After this silence, he looks at you and transfers this responsibility and gives empowerment in his best tradition. And then, you know, nonviolence is then ingrained as another part of you.

JOHN EMMEUS DAVIS: Thank you for that story. I believe that it's important for us always to recognize the pioneers, the philosophies, the roots of the CLT.

YVES CABANNES: John, can you imagine, that was more than 40 years ago when I lived in the hut of Vinoba Bhave. It was a poor man's hut. I was there with a friend of mine who later became a Jesuit. We were staying there among the poorest of the poor, which was what you had to understand—not to understand only, but to feel. Despite the dire and extremely simple living conditions, I had the privilege to sleep in the same hut and on the mat that Vinoba was occupying at a time. On my later visit, I was with a young engineer colleague of mine. We lived in the palmleaf-covered hut where Vinoba Bhave used to stay in absolutely simple and dire conditions. The very idea was that only by sharing such a life can you work with people who might push the world into the right direction of emancipation.

JOHN EMMEUS DAVIS: Well, we've come to the end of our scheduled time. It's been an honor for me to have these conversations with you.

YVES CABANNES: It's been a pleasure. At our age, this dreaming about the future, about new horizons, must be for the next generation. Unfortunately, we are not going see it. But fortunately, others will continue.

JOHN EMMEUS DAVIS: There is a Greek proverb that says, "A society grows great when old men plant trees in whose shade they know they shall never sit."

YVES CABANNES: Wow! That's beautiful. Let's stay with that beautiful image. I will sit under this tree, dreaming about the future.

JOHN EMMEUS DAVIS: I will sit there as well. Thank you, Yves.

YVES CABANNES: John, once again, a wonderful talk. And we have Mexico to look forward to as our next potential connection.

JOHN EMMEUS DAVIS: Oh yes. And we'll have Bonnie join us.

YVES CABANNES: Wow. And making her fantastic drawings. That would be super.

Conference and Expo on Garden Cities & Community Land Trusts, Bangkok, Thailand, 2019

Afterword:
Questions for the Editor from
Contributors & Reviewers

QUESTION: Let's start with the title. Your last book focused on community engagement, the challenge of keeping the "C" in CLT. The central concern of the present publication is the CLT's distinctive treatment of land, the "L" in CLT. How did community ownership of land become the book's main theme?

JOHN EMMEUS DAVIS: The decision to focus on tenure, specifically the growth of community-owned land, was somewhat serendipitous. Some of the leading lights in the current, younger generation of CLT organizers and practitioners had starred in *Community Matters*, the previous book published by Terra Nostra Press. I had always planned on featuring "elders" of the CLT movement in the next one.

These were individuals with a lengthy history of working with the CLT model who had been personally involved with multiple CLTs in multiple locations. More significantly, they had played pivotal roles in laying the foundation for the global growth of CLTs.

I was attracted to that combination of longevity, variety, and groundwork. These folks were still with us, but they wouldn't be here forever. I wanted to capture their insider's knowledge of how the community land trust had evolved and to gather any insights they might offer as to where CLTs might be headed.

Over the years, I had "banked" oral histories with several of them. I had transcripts in hand from interviews that Helen Cohen had recorded with Shirley Sherrod and Mtamanika Youngblood in 2011 and 2012 when we were working on a couple of films, *Arc of Justice* and *Streets of Dreams*. I had recorded three interviews with Kirby White back in 2015, not really knowing what I'd do with them. I just wanted to preserve the wit and wisdom of my slow-talking, deep-thinking friend who had done so much in the formative decades of the 1980s and 1990s to lift up this odd little model of ours. I had recorded the first of two interviews with Gus Newport back in 2020.

It was only later, when reviewing the transcripts from these older interviews and while editing the transcripts from the newer interviews being recorded by myself and others, that I realized how central the land question was to the thought and practice of these eight individuals. They all made the case for giving place-based communities control of the land beneath their feet and giving those same communities a collective voice in how their land would be used. To my ear, these elders seemed to be saying that community ownership of land was the model's defining feature and guiding mission. Tenure mattered. Indeed, it was the foundation on which community engagement and permanent affordability were built. "Reweaving the tapestry of tenure" seemed like an appropriate title.

QUESTION: How about the subtitle?

JOHN EMMEUS DAVIS: I had a much harder time with that one. I first had to check with several of the people we had interviewed to make sure that "elder" would be viewed as a term of respect. I worried that it might be seen a way of subtly dismissing people whose time is past. You know, "Let's give 'em a gold watch and hustle them off the stage." But most of them are still active. They are still making "good trouble," as John Lewis famously said.

I especially wanted to hear from María Hernández, the youngest member of this Gang of Eight, gauging whether she was okay being considered an "elder." When she gave me a thumbs-up, I decided we were good to go.

My biggest problem was choosing an active verb for the subtitle. I went round and round on that one. I couldn't say these eight individuals had "invented" community-owned land or had single-handedly "caused" the growth of it. That seemed too strong. I couldn't say "nourished" or "encouraged." That seemed too weak.

My Goldilocks compromise was "championed." Its appeal lay in combining a sense of something being **enabled** and something being **promoted**. Also, champions aren't afraid of sticking their necks out on behalf of unconventional ideas, which definitely described the eight people we had interviewed. So "championed" became my verb of choice.

QUESTION: But isn't every CLT practitioner a "champion" for community ownership of land? How can you have a CLT without community-owned land and long-term ground leasing?

JOHN EMMEUS DAVIS: I remember asking Mtamanika a similar question during my interview with her. I wanted her response to the notion that common ownership of land might have been the cornerstone of New Communities, but perhaps it didn't matter as much in the inner-city neighborhoods in which she had worked. We were on a zoom call together, so I could see her perplexed reaction as she raised her eyebrows and shook her head and said something like, "That's a confounding question. How do you even **do** a community land trust without the land?"

She's correct, of course; how do you presume to be a CLT if you are NOT removing land from the speculative market and holding it in trust for present and future generations of low-income and moderate-income people? Even so, I think that Kirby White is right when he says in his interview that the importance of land has diminished over the past 50 years in the priorities and pronouncements of many CLTs—especially *urban* CLTs that focus most of their attention on housing.

That's regrettable, because I still believe "common ground" to be an unusually effective way of engaging members of a place-based community and preserving the affordability, quality, and security of affordable housing. It makes stewardship more effective and enforceable. It is an expansive, durable platform for equitable and sustainable development, encompassing both affordable housing and non-residential land uses. My own belief, therefore, is that CLT practitioners need to be clearer and louder in trumpeting the benefits of community ownership. Maybe this book will embolden them to do so.

On the other hand, I would readily admit that CLTs are not the only way of decommodifying land and using it for the common good. Several of the "elders" we interviewed would agree. They talk with respect about cooperatives and other forms of customary and communal ownership.

QUESTION: In selecting these eight individuals, you necessarily ignored many others. Are there additional "elders" of the CLT movement who you might have included?

JOHN EMMEUS DAVIS: Yes, of course. Lots of people played significant roles in the early days of the CLT. Part of my motivation for producing *Roots of the CLT*—a narrated slideshow that I've revised again and again since 2006—has been to identify and to honor the extraordinary people who brought the CLT into being. Most of them, unfortunately, are no longer with us. If I'd had the foresight to record oral histories with them, they would certainly have been included in this book.

There are two people, in particular, who I've long regretted not having interviewed: Fay Bennett and Albert J. McKnight. Both of them served on the founding board of New Communities, in addition to being involved in the start-up of numerous cooperatives and training programs for Black farmers, sharecroppers, and migrants in the rural South. When we inducted them into the "CLT Hall of Fame," I wrote short bios for each of them. I've also included them in *Roots*. But there is much more that needs to be written (probably not by me) about these remarkable people who led such meaningful, impactful lives. I wish I could have met them. Both had died by the time I began telling the story of the CLT's origins.

QUESTION: We lost another "elder" of the CLT movement in the middle of producing this book. Could you say something about Gus Newport?

JOHN EMMEUS DAVIS: He was one of three major CLT figures who died in the past year. First there was Charles Sherrod. Then John Whitfield. And now Gus. I had lunch with him in Berkeley a few months before his death. Despite losing a leg to diabetes and being confined to a wheelchair, he was the same buoyant, feisty guy I had known for more than 40 years. He was looking forward to publication of the interviews we had done together. He had reviewed and approved the edited transcript, of course, but that's different than holding the book in your hands and seeing your words in print. I'm sad he didn't have that opportunity.

There is so much I could say about my affection and admiration for Brother Gus, sentiments that I believe are apparent in the conversation that appears in Chapter Five. I don't want to say anything that overshadows his own words in those interviews. I *will* tell one anecdote, however, which is revealing of Gus' expansive humanity.

He served as co-chair of the Diversity, Equity, and Inclusion committee of the Center for CLT Innovation. In an early meeting of that committee, we were debating the content of a proposed DEI policy. Most of that draft had focused on racial equity, speaking specifically to the inclusion of persons of African descent. Gus objected, pointing out that Asians, Jews, and various immigrant groups in his own city were being targeted for discrimination and vilification as well. Here was a life-long African American activist who been fighting for racial justice since his youthful days in Rochester, telling us that any DEI policy had to look beyond skin color. Remember that old union motto, "An injury to one is an injury to all"? Gus embodied that ethos of solidarity. He's going to be greatly missed.

QUESTION: Why aren't you in the book? Aren't you being unduly modest in featuring others, but not yourself?

JOHN EMMEUS DAVIS: Well, I'm certainly old enough to qualify as an "elder," although I'm a tad younger than my buddy Gus, who often claimed to be "older than baseball."

I chose not to be one of the people featured in this book mainly because I'm included in many other ways. I didn't want to turn it into a vanity project. I'm the book's editor, as well as the person who conducted several of the book's interviews. I wrote the Introduction and now I'm answering questions in this Afterword. That's plenty of me for any publication.

You'll notice, too, that my name keeps popping up in the stories told by several of the people who *are* included in the book. As I reviewed the transcripts and edited the interviews, the manuscript started to feel like we were doing a remake of that popular children's book, *Where's Waldo?* You know, the book where the title character keeps appearing in one unexpected place after another? You have to hunt for him amidst the clutter. Having unintentionally produced a book that my dear daughter might have dubbed *Where's Papa?* I couldn't bear to add a chapter applauding my own contributions.

Our publisher at Terra Nostra Press, Greg Rosenberg, is not going to let me get away with that deflection, however, so let me offer a more serious answer. I came of age at a time when my friends and I were totally in thrall of the mystique of the "community organizer." Our role models were not the big-name leaders of the Civil Rights Movement like Martin Luther King or Roy Wilkins, but the quiet, behind-the-scenes agitators, educators, and creators of campaigns and organizations bigger than themselves. The mark of their success was to work themselves out of a job, once people had started seeing things and doing things for themselves. They were teachers rather than preachers.

Bob Moses was one of my heroes. He had done voter registration and grassroots organizing in the most hostile territory imaginable: "Mississippi Goddamn," as Nina Simone had described that benighted place. I also admired Ella Baker, who had been a mentor for the young people of SNCC. Indeed, she had called the meeting at Shaw University in 1960 out of which SNCC emerged. She once said something like, you'll never see me on TV or in the news because I'm too busy assembling the pieces of organizations. Long ago, I jotted down an exact quote from her in a notebook that I've carried around for a long time: "What is needed is the development of people who are interested *not* in being leaders as much as in developing leadership in others."

I took that to heart when I naively signed on to be a community organizer in the Appalachian region in my early 20s. I was also captivated by the work of the Brazilian educator, Paulo Freire. *Pedagogy of the Oppressed* appeared in English the year I arrived in Appalachia. The examples and ideas of Moses, Baker, and Freire were a pretty heady brew for a wobbly young fellow trying to find his sea legs, working among the poor for the very first time. I internalized their perspectives on leadership development and critical consciousness and never outgrew them.

Look, in essence, I'm a roadie, not a rock star. I'm better at setting the stage than appearing on stage. I enjoy helping to prepare the next generation of CLT organizers and staffers, as we did during the bygone days of the National CLT Academy. I enjoy shining the spotlight on people who have done exemplary work, like the eight "elders" who are featured here.

QUESTION: You edited *On Common Ground* back in 2020, along with Line Algoed and María Hernández. That book was a collection of essays and case studies. You've now published two books of interviews. Why have you switched to this conversational format in your latest publications?

JOHN EMMEUS DAVIS: Few practitioners have the time to write—or, if they do, they fill their pages extolling the origins and accomplishments of their organizations. Getting them to talk about themselves or persuading them to type out critical perspectives on CLTs and related topics is like pulling teeth. It's a slow, painful process that most practitioners prefer to avoid.

But even busy people are willing (on occasion) to sit down in front of a digital recorder or a computer screen to answer questions. As long as they are later given an opportunity to correct and to supplement their comments before the transcripts are shared with the larger world, they are even willing to allow such interviews to be published.

I've lately gravitated to interviews instead of essays not only for the sake of convenience, however. I find that people being interviewed by a peer (not by a journalist) are more likely to be candid about the difficulties of doing community development, the doubts and setbacks that inevitably occur in doing this work, and the adjustments that go into navigating around them. Learning how practitioners deal with obstacles and losses is informative and inspirational in ways that carefully considered essays and case studies seldom are. The latter tell us what's been accomplished. The former tell us how people got there—and how in the heck they kept going.

In most of the interviews we conducted, we made a special point of asking, "What motivates you? How do you keep your eyes on the prize? How do you keep doing this slow, frustrating work, day to day?" I'm deeply interested in the answers to those questions. I believe that other readers are too, especially young people who may be encountering the first frustrations of a career they have chosen in community development and may be wondering whether they've made a terrible mistake. Interviews don't provide a roadmap for how to hang in there for the long haul, but they do show that it's possible and rewarding and—if the *joie de vie* of the elders we interviewed is any indication—this difficult work is actually a lot of fun.

QUESTION: Were there any surprises? You've known most of these "elders" for a long time. Were there things that you learned about your colleagues that you didn't know before?

JOHN EMMEUS DAVIS: Oh yeah. There were lots things I didn't know about their backgrounds and careers, as they zig-zagged their way toward the CLT. None of them followed a straight and narrow path, which is part of what makes them such interesting people; it is also part of what has made their contributions to the growth of CLTs so varied, pivotal, and complementary.

Some of their anecdotes were both surprising and amusing. I loved hearing that Mtamanika once got a "D" in Black history, that Kirby was called "The Codine" by his students in Wyoming, and that Gus as a young activist was once chided by Malcom X for being too hot-headed, too militant. Kirby also shared the story of how Rodale Press, a publisher of books and magazines about organic farming, accidentally published *The Community Land Trust Handbook* in 1982, a book about social justice. It was a funny tale that I had forgotten.

I liked learning about people who had an early influence on the thinking and attitudes of these eight individuals. Shirley talking about the bravery and leadership style of Charles Sherrod.

Mtamanika talking with affection about Shirley and Charles as her mentors. Kirby talking about his association with Chuck Matthei. Susan talking about Bob Swann and E.F. Schumacher. Gus talking about his grandmother.

I was intrigued to discover that María had first learned about CLTs while studying at Vermont Law School. She had also snagged a copy of *The CLT Legal Manual*, which Kirby had edited for ICE. Speaking of Kirby, I had no idea that he held the National CLT Academy in such high esteem. I was a bit taken aback, but my heart was warmed, when he called the Academy the "pinnacle" of the CLT movement in the United States.

I also enjoyed listening to Stephen and Yves as they recounted formative experiences that had shaped their attitudes and politics. In Stephen's case, I had previously heard him talk about his distress at seeing the low-income residents of council housing being treated with contempt, an experience that had nudged him toward community-led housing and the CLT. Before doing this book, however, I had not known of his earlier exposure to racial and religious prejudice when visiting South Africa during apartheid and visiting Northern Ireland during "The Troubles."

As for Yves, there are surprises every time I talk with him. His travels are so extensive and his stories are so vivid. It's hard to pick one over the other. But I live in Vermont, so I'll say that I had not realized the degree to which Yves had been impressed by his exposure to the Champlain Housing Trust when he visited Burlington back in 2008, after CHT won the World Habitat Award. More than that, however, I was moved by his narrative of meeting Vinoba Bhave and the inspiration that Yves took away from that encounter. It seemed particularly fitting to end a book about community ownership of land with Yves' story of meeting the man behind the Gramdan Movement, a precursor to the modern-day CLT.

QUESTION: How about historical information. Did you learn anything new about the early days of the CLT movement? Were there any discoveries in these interviews that might cause you to revise your current rendition of "Roots of the CLT"?

JOHN EMMEUS DAVIS: There were no major revelations, just a few nuggets of historical significance scattered here and there.

I hadn't known, for example, how little connection and communication occurred between New Communities and the Institute for Community Economics once New Communities was up and running. Mtamanika had moved to Albany in 1971, one year *after* the land had been purchased and one year *before* publication of the first book about CLTs. She was intimately involved with New Communities throughout the Seventies. But she never met Bob Swann, Shimon Gottshalk, or anyone else associated with ICE. Nor, apparently, did she or anybody else at New Communities read or discuss the 1972 CLT book, which held up New Communities as a "prototype" for what a CLT could be. In the interview we did together, Mtamanika surprised me by admitting she had not even known how important New Communities had been to the birth and growth of the larger CLT movement until she saw a slideshow I presented in 2008, when we were working together on the Atlanta Land Trust Collaborative.

If ICE played a *lesser* role in the later development of New Communities than I had originally supposed, the Dudley Street Neighborhood Initiative has played a *larger* role in the global spread of CLTs than I have given them credit for. María Hernández, in her interview, talks about the influence of DSNI in helping to inspire and to inform residents of the Caño as they were thinking of forming the Caño Martín Peña CLT. Stephen Hill talks about the influence of DSNI in his own thinking about community-led development. And, of course, there is Gus talking about the people from other countries who visited DSNI while he was there. I would mention, too, the wide exposure given to DSNI by the two films made by Mark Lipman and Leah Mahan, one of which captured a stellar performance by Gus rapping with a bunch of kids.

More significant for me than these two minor corrections in the historical record, however, was the stark reminder of just how dangerous southwest Georgia was in the 1970s for African American activists who were simultaneously fighting Jim Crow, doing voter registration, AND laboring to keep New Communities alive. When we were making *Arc of Justice*, Helen, Mark, and I did our best to portray the seedbed of struggle out of which New Communities sprang and to document the resistance from White neighbors and politicians to everything that New Communities tried to do. But a 20-minute film gives only a glimpse of how bad things really were. The longer interviews that Helen Cohen recorded with Shirley Sherrod and Mtamanika Youngblood provide a fuller, bleaker picture of the hostile environment in which they lived and worked. It was a terribly oppressive world of White supremacy, voter suppression, and socially acceptable violence against anyone who dared to object, especially those with darker skins.

Re-reading those interviews, I was inspired anew by the courage and tenacity of the people who created New Communities. I was depressed anew by the realization that **this** is the world the MAGA crowd longs for. When they say they want to make things great "again," they are talking about times and places like southwest Georgia in the days before a bunch of "uppity" Black folks demanded their rights and had the temerity to get their hands on 6000 acres of land.

QUESTION: On the flip side, were there unpleasant surprises? Were there distortions in the historical record you were tempted to correct?

JOHN EMMEUS DAVIS: I will confess to being dismayed at times by who was being given credit for what or by how an event was said to have happened. But people have different interpretations of the same reality. I wanted to respect each speaker's words and views. It wasn't proper for me or for any of the other interviewers to be censoring them, even when it sounded like they might be misrepresenting something.

There were only two times in any of the interviews when someone's point of view was challenged. In the conversation between Kirby and me, he objected to my characterization of New Communities as having been the "first CLT." I pushed back, asserting that NCI may not have fulfilled its original purpose or displayed every feature of what later became known as the "classic CLT," but it still deserved to be seen as patient zero in tracing the viral spread of CLTs.

The second objection can be found in the interview between Susan Witt and Lisa Byers. When Susan talks about CLTs being "lured" into a focus on affordable housing, becoming overly dependent on public funds, and unwisely taking on responsibilities best handled by a separate community development corporation, Lisa calmly notes that many CLTs have become CDCs in order to further the CLT's main purpose of being the keeper and steward of land. Indeed, the success of Lisa's own community land trust, OPAL, for which Susan expresses admiration, is due in large part to its focus on affordable housing, its ability to secure public funding, and its expertise as a developer of permanently affordable housing on community-owned land.

Both of these mild objections to an interviewee's point of view were left on the page, letting readers form their own opinion. There were assertions in other interviews which I considered somewhat questionable as well, but my red pen was kept in the drawer. I resisted scratching out material that wasn't to my liking. Transcripts were edited for clarity and length, not for content.

QUESTION: The book is premised on the notion that that CLT movement is growing, that more CLTs are starting up and more land is coming under their control. Despite such growth, you have to admit that the holdings of most CLTs are relatively small. In particular, the number of housing units produced by CLTs around the world remains rather modest, compared to the production of affordable housing by for-profit builders, social housing providers, and government agencies. The lack of "scale" is, in fact, a common complaint of CLT critics. Is there an answer to their criticism?

JOHN EMMEUS DAVIS: The "elders" who are featured in the present volume provide a variety of answers. I'll get to them in a moment. But I want to chime in as well, because I believe this criticism misses the mark in two fundamental ways. First, a CLT's success should be measured by its impact, not by its scale. Second, putting numbers on the board is not what a CLT is "really about." Its forte is stewardship, not production.

That's not to say that scale is unimportant. If land reform and permanent affordability are priority aspirations of the CLT movement, then every CLT should try to bring into its portfolio as much land and as many units of housing as possible. I probably wouldn't go as far as Stephen, therefore, when he says that delivering large numbers of housing is a "false ambition." I think that CLTs *ought* to be as ambitious and accumulative as possible.

Even modest portfolios can have a major impact, however. That's where Stephen's concept of "massive small" comes in. By multiplying the number of CLTs, by connecting them with each other and with allied organizations, and by working together to promote a common message of community-led development on community-owned land of homes that remain permanently affordable, small CLTs can make a big difference.

Stephen shows, in fact, that CLTs have impacted the affordable housing field in the UK in significant ways. He points to their ability at the local level to remove resistance to new housebuilding—what we'd call "NIMBYism" over here—by the commitment of CLTs to build a base of support within their communities and to involve that community in guiding and governing the CLT itself. That helps CLTs to enlist the support of local and national politicians of different political persuasions, cutting across the left-right divide.

I also like what Stephen has to say about providing people with more choices as to where they are housed and how they are housed. My favorite affordable housing advocate of yesteryear, Catherine Bauer, once bemoaned the "dreary deadlock" of public housing by pointing to its cookie-cutter approach to tenure and design. What is needed, she said, by the poor and the middle-class alike, is more choice in the type and location of affordably priced housing.

That's where CLTs make a major contribution, I believe. They can never come close to meeting the enormous need for affordably-priced housing in this country or in any other, but they can add new rungs to the housing tenure ladder and provide more choices for families being poorly served by both the market and the state.

The place where scale and impact overlap, however, is in informal settlements. María's work in Puerto Rico, adapting the CLT to fit the special circumstances of people living on land to which they didn't formerly hold title, may have wide applicability. The UN estimates there are more than a billion people worldwide who are living on customary lands or in dwellings with insecure control over the land beneath their homes.

Finally, I would question whether it makes sense to continue beating CLTs over the head with the stick of scale when stewardship, not development, is the main purpose and function of a CLT. To be criticized for a game that few CLTs will ever play nearly as well as their biggest, richest competitors is to ignore the fact that CLTs are skilled at a different game with a different set of rules.

Stewardship is what a CLT does best, preserving forever the affordability, quality, and security of lands and buildings entrusted into its care. Most of that happens after lands are acquired and after structures are built, but there is also a virtuous feedback loop here.

The back-end commitment to watching over whatever is built on a CLT's land tends to shape the front-end decisions that go into designing those buildings, tilting development toward materials that last longer and toward systems that are more efficient, affordable, and green.

Even so, it is stewardship that adds value, more than the number of units produced. That prompts me to say that, in a perfect world, it would be better if the production of housing and other buildings were left in the hands of entities other than a CLT—community development corporations, Habitat for Humanity affiliates, or for-profit developers subject to inclusionary zoning. Title to the land and responsibility for stewardship could then be conveyed to a CLT. Let a CLT do what it does best, not forcing it to be both developer and steward. Susan Witt, echoing Bob Swann, wasn't completely wrong in proposing such a scenario.

The problem with that rosy picture, of course, is that every jurisdiction doesn't have a high-performing nonprofit developer that is willing to partner with a CLT; nor does every jurisdiction have inclusionary zoning. (And many cities that do have IZ are not interested in long-term affordability.) Lisa Byers is certainly correct in pointing out that many CLTs have become developers out of necessity.

Despite their numbers and holdings, it must also be said that the CLTs' advocacy for stewardship has had a major effect on housing policy in the United States. As Mtamanika, Kirby, and Gus noted in their interviews, there was a time not too long ago when CLTs were a voice crying in the wilderness. Governments, nonprofits, academics, and even residents of low-income neighborhoods were nearly unanimous in rejecting the whole idea of permanently affordable housing, especially in the case of owner-occupied homes. That isn't true today. There's been a seismic shift in public policy and nonprofit practice. Hence Kirby's observation that, "I haven't heard a CDC person in a long time say that people in subsidized homes ought to be able to pocket the subsidy."

CLT practitioners have not been alone in causing that change, of course, but they have pushed for it longer and louder than most of their peers. They have had an outsized impact on making permanent affordability acceptable and active stewardship advisable.

QUESTION: Before we leave the topic of scale and impact, what about opportunities for future growth of the CLT movement?

JOHN EMMEUS DAVIS: Among the people we interviewed, I was struck by how often something other than housing was mentioned as the best way for CLTs to increase their holdings and to widen their appeal. Nobody said that CLTs should cease their commitment to affordable housing, but they wanted CLTs to consider diversifying their programs and portfolios. They believed the potential for future growth lay in looking "beyond housing."

Gus talked about CLTs serving "the total needs of the community," not just housing. Kirby said something similar, suggesting that the most "exciting CLTs" will be those that are open to doing whatever it takes for a community to develop a "stronger sense of place," including things like planting an orchard or promoting commercial activity. Susan talks about community land trusts and conservation land trusts working together. Gus wanted CLTs to get involved in the national conversation about racial reparations, which Susan mentioned as well. María is working with an urban CLT in Puerto Rico that is focused on the revitalization of a commercial district and a rural CLT that is focused on agriculture. Yves goes the furthest of all in arguing that CLTs should concentrate in the future on using food security and food sovereignty as their main "entry point," instead of housing.

QUESTION: Speaking of Yves, in the subtitle for the book's final chapter, you refer to him as a "troubadour." Why did that image come to mind?

JOHN EMMEUS DAVIS: Go back to the interview with Kirby. Quoting Julie Eades, he talks about a technical assistance provider being "nothing more than a troubadour," carrying stories from one place to another. He was referring to Chuck Matthei, but the same could be said of every person in this book. That's why I opened the Introduction with stories of Johnny Appleseed and the Lupine Lady. The global spread of CLTs happened, in part, because our eight "elders" spent many years scattering seeds and carrying stories hither, thither, and yon.

Yves is a special case, however. His singular contribution as a teacher, consultant, writer, and world traveler has been to collect exemplary tales of community-led development on community-owned land and to sing their praises wherever he goes. Listening to Yves, you get caught up in the powerful, inspirational spirit of people and places at the hot edges of the CLT movement.

Here's a funny twist. When I asked Yves whether the subtitle I was proposing for his chapter was acceptable, he responded with enthusiasm. It turns out that "troubadour," as a word and role, originated in the region of southern France where Yves grew up. His parents spoke a Latin Occitan language called Gascon. "Troubadour" is an Old Occitan word meaning "to compose," from which the wandering minstrels took their name. Yves was quite pleased to be called a troubadour.

QUESTION: It's customary in an Afterword to acknowledge key people who contributed to the book's production. Who deserves credit for making it possible for Terra Nostra Press to publish *Reweaving the Tapestry of Tenure*?

JOHN EMMEUS DAVIS: I am grateful, first of all, to my four talented colleagues who conducted several of the interviews. I predict that the next generation will look up to them as having been CLT "elders" in their own right: Line Algoed, Lisa Byers, Helen Cohen, and Dave Smith.

There is our talented book designer, Sara DeHaan, who deserves recognition for her fine work on this publication and the ones preceding it. She makes us look good, while coaching us on creative ways for a small Press to produce and to distribute books as economically as possible.

Terra Nostra Press is committed to making its publications widely available and highly affordable for readers around the world. That was made possible in the present case by the generous financial support of two philanthropies, Porticus and WEND.

Greg Rosenberg gets a shout-out for being the hidden hand behind most of the recordings and all of the transcripts. He also deals day-to-day with the tedious and often thankless tasks of being the publisher for Terra Nostra Press. He manages the money and the contracts and the distribution of our books, while giving unstinting encouragement and support to the book's editor.

I should acknowledge, too, the multi-colored contributions of Bonnie Acker. Not only did she create the artwork that is found on the cover; she also lent her eagle eye to proofreading every chapter. The entire publication is more attractive and more accurate because of her. Any mistakes that remain are mine, not hers.

Finally—and most importantly—I must express my sincere thanks to the eight individuals who agreed to be interviewed for this book. Their participation didn't end when the interview was over. They later reviewed the edited transcripts, making corrections where needed. Several of them even took the time to add important information that had been overlooked in the original interview. It was an honor being entrusted with their stories. I am grateful to all of them.

Interviewers

LINE ALGOED is a PhD Researcher and Teaching Assistant at Cosmopolis, Center for Urban Research at the Vrije Universiteit in Brussels, where she is working on a PhD about collective land tenure as a climate change adaptation strategy. She has worked closely with the Caño Martín Peña Community Land Trust in Puerto Rico on international exchanges among communities involved in land struggles. She is a founding board member of the Center for CLT Innovation and serves on the Center's executive committee. Previously, Line was a World Habitat Awards Program Manager at World Habitat, and a Director at the International Urban Development Association (INTA). She interviewed María E. Hernández Torrales for the present volume in 2023.

LISA BYERS has been the Executive Director of OPAL Community Land Trust since January 1996. She was a co-founder of the Northwest Community Land Trust Coalition and the National Community Land Trust (CLT) Network, serving as founding President of the Network's board. A throughline of her work—first in historic preservation, then land conservation and ultimately community land trusts—has been to help people live on the land in a manner that assures access for future generations. She and her wife live in a community land trust home where, among other things, they enjoy visits from their children and grandchildren. She interviewed Susan Witt for the present volume in 2022.

HELEN S. COHEN is an award-winning documentary filmmaker with a history of activism and professional work with cultural, educational, and community development organizations. She is a long-standing member of New Day Films, a national cooperative of independent filmmakers. Among her many film credits, Helen has produced and directed a series of short documentaries showcasing CLTs in diverse communities throughout the United States. With her husband and filmmaking partner, Mark Lipman, she also produced and directed *Arc of Justice: The Rise, Fall, and Rebirth of a Beloved Community*, the powerful story of the civil rights activists who created the first modern-day CLT. She conducted interviews with Shirley Sherrod in 2012 and with Mtamanika Youngblood in 2011 and 2012. These interviews were lightly edited for the present volume.

JOHN EMMEUS DAVIS is President of the Center for CLT Innovation and Editor-in-Chief of Terra Nostra Press. He is a founding partner of Burlington Associates in Community Development, a consulting cooperative that has assisted over 120 CLTs throughout the United States since its founding in 1993. He was the city's Housing Director in Burlington, Vermont, under Mayors Bernie Sanders and Peter Clavelle and was previously employed by the Institute for Community Economics. He conducted three interviews with Kirby White in 2015, two interviews with Gus Newport in 2020 and 2022, and two interviews with Yves Cabannes in 2022. He interviewed Mtamanika Youngblood in 2023, supplementing the earlier interviews conducted by Helen Cohen.

DAVE SMITH is a community organizer and affordable housing practitioner. He served for several years as Chair of the London Community Land Trust and was the organization's founding Executive Director from 2008 to 2014. He previously worked for the

British Council and on Barack Obama's 2008 primary and presidential campaigns. More recently, he has worked at the National Housing Foundation. He is currently Head of Communities at Eastlight Community Homes, a nonprofit housing provider based in Essex and Suffolk. He interviewed Stephen Hill for the present volume in 2023.

Index

Photo Credits

Page 1: Screen shot from *Arc of Justice* (2016), a film by Helen Cohen and Mark Lipman.

Pages 13, 19: Photos contributed by Charles and Shirley Sherrod, included in *Arc of Justice* (2016).

Page 36: Photo by J.E. Davis.

Page 43: Screen shot from *Arc of Justice* (2016), a film by Helen Cohen and Mark Lipman.

Page 49: Photo contributed by Charles and Shirley Sherrod, included in *Arc of Justice* (2016).

Page 69: Production photo from the filming of Arc of Justice. Photographer unknown.

Page 97: Photographer unknown.

Pages 101, 114, 138: Photos contributed by family of Kirby White. Photographer unknown.Page 139: Photo by Christina Lane.

Page 150: Photo provided by Susan Witt.

Page 153: Photographer unknown.

Page 158: Photo contributed by family of Gus Newport. Photographer unknown.

Page 164: Photo by Kathy Orlando.

Page 168: Screen shot from *Holding Ground* (1996 & 2006), a film by Mark Lipman and Leah Mahan.

Page 184: Photo by Leah Mahan.

Page 185: Photo contributed by Stephen Hill. Photographer unknown.

Pages 229, 250: Photos contributed by María E. Hernández Torrales. Photographer unknown.

Page 255: Photo by J.E. Davis.

Pages 257, 260, 270, 278, 297: Photos contributed by Yves Cabannes. Photographer unknown.